INTERESTING STORIES ABOUT CURIOUS WORDS

INTERESTING STORIES ABOUT CURIOUS WORDS

SUSIE DENT

JOHN MURRAY

First published in Great Britain in 2023 by John Murray (Publishers)

4

Copyright © Susie Dent 2023

A CIP catalogue record for this title
is available from the British Library

Hardback ISBN 978 1 399 81167 5
ebook ISBN 978 1 399 81169 9
Exclusive edition 978 1 399 81483 6

Typeset in Plantin Light by
Palimpsest Book Production Ltd, Falkirk, Stirlingshire

Printed and bound in Great Britain by Clays Ltd, Elcograf S.p.A.

John Murray policy is to use papers that are natural, renewable and
recyclable products and made from wood grown in sustainable forests.
The logging and manufacturing processes are expected to conform
to the environmental regulations of the country of origin.

Carmelite House
50 Victoria Embankment
London EC4Y 0DZ

www.johnmurraypress.co.uk

John Murray Press, part of Hodder & Stoughton Limited
An Hachette UK company

To my parents,
whose quiet pride and support
have never gone unnoticed.

CONTENTS

INTRODUCTION

It felt like we were always on our way to some freezing destination on the south coast. I would be sitting in the back of my parents' car, wrapped in a blanket to ward off the winter chill and only vaguely aware of my sister alongside me, as she experimented with her new eyelash curlers or lost herself in the pages of a Nancy Drew Mystery. My own focus was on a different world, one as exciting to me as any tales of Crocodile Island or cities buried beneath the desert. It was as simple as it was seductive, and the gateway was always a French or German vocabulary book. Ever the reluctant conversationalist on these endless journeys, I would pretend to guess at 'I spy' whilst silently mouthing the German for 'dragonfly' (*Libelle*) or the French for 'grapefruit' (*pamplemousse*). I will never know quite why I wanted to learn these words – certainly it wasn't for any homework or impending test. I just know I *needed* them. It was the start of a lifelong passion; some children collected stamps, others fossils or soft toys, and I collected words. The more I knew, the more I wanted to know.

At my convent school, I continued to indulge the habit of eavesdropping that I'd developed as a small child, tuning in to the conversations of nuns and fellow pupils as we approached the confessional or chalked out our hopscotch patterns in the playground. And, like everyone, I occasionally got things very wrong. I spent years singing a hymn called 'I am the Lord of the Dance Settee', fondly imagining Jesus clapping along from his comfy sofa.

At university, I began to notice the invisible threads that join our languages – the family trees that reveal that not only are a mortgage and a mortuary linked, but that the word for a muscle in many languages involves a tiny mouse – because a flexed muscle looks so much like a mouse scurrying beneath the skin. But it was German that had me wrapped around its finger, a language so intensely lyrical and – yes – playful, that I felt chagrined on its behalf for its reputation of cold gutturalness. Who could resist such beauties as *Fernweh*, the longing to be far away? Or admire the usefulness of *Verschlimmbesserung*, an attempted improvement that ends up making things worse? As the jottings in my notebooks proliferated, I had little sense where they would take me, but I did know I would always want to live amongst words.

And that indeed is how it panned out. Years later, working as a lexicographer, it was during one rainy lunchtime at Oxford University Press that I casually pulled down a book from the shelves in my office. Walter Skeat's *Etymological Dictionary of the English Language*, published in 1882, was to become a source of daily magic in the weeks and months that followed. It was from Skeat that I learned about the 'intrusive *n*' – the letter we added to the French *messager* and *passager* because 'messenger' and 'passenger' roll more easily off the English tongue. He also taught me that there is a 'crypt' within 'apocryphal', and that 'sarcasm' and 'sarcophagus' are brothers in arms. (I'm pretty sure it was within the same pages that I discovered a word I still find highly topical today – 'rodomontade', inflated talk and behaviour.) This was linguistic archaeology: digging up the foundations of words I loved gave them an extra dimension of magic.

A career can feel like a long and slow-moving thing, yet the word itself is rooted in something far more energetic. Beginning with the Romans' *carrus*, 'wheeled vehicle', 'career' is a sibling of 'chariot'. In English, it first described a knight's advance at full gallop in medieval jousting tournaments. In other words, a career is all about proceeding at pace, with perhaps a few unexpected swerves thrown in. My own took a surprising turn when, thanks to my work at OUP, I ended up on Channel 4's wonderful afternoon show *Countdown*. There, in Dictionary Corner, it became my actual job to find long words and to read dictionaries at top speed. I'm also lucky enough to do the same job (of a sort) in the comedy version, *8 Out of 10 Cats Does Countdown*, where I am in a constant struggle with the anarchic forces of Jimmy Carr. Despite Jimmy's best efforts to persuade the nation that my own writing is a form of euthanasia (look out for a sketch featuring him chopping up a copy of this book on air), I feel the pull of the written word just as strongly as I did on those car journeys all those years ago.

Eric Partridge, the 20th-century chronicler of slang who adored the quirks of English and never tired in his quest for enlightenment about them, declared that 'there is far more imagination and enthusiasm in the making of a good dictionary than in the average novel'. Partridge saw himself as an adventurer, and dictionaries as his golden road. He knew the magic he could unfold in their pages – even if others took some convincing. He loved to tell the story of an elderly lady who, after borrowing a dictionary from the public library, returned it with the comment that it was a 'very unusual book indeed – but the stories are extremely short, aren't they?'

Dismiss reference books and you are missing out. The stories behind words may be short, but they are also golden. I have spent years lost in the corners of dictionaries. Ebenezer Cobham Brewer's *Dictionary of Phrase and Fable*, which is the heart and soul of this book, is the sunniest and strangest of them all.

Brewer is the lexicographer's lexicographer. A cleric and a gentleman collector, his spirit of inquiry inspired the writing of a large number of educational books, eagerly consumed by a growing public readership in the 19th century. He had an unrivalled eye for a novel fact or linguistic knick-knack, and his methodology was simple – read, spot a fact, cut it out, and put it in a pigeonhole. Brewer called himself 'a snapper-up of unconsidered trifles', and his *Dictionary*, finally published in

1870 having been pruned down from a manuscript three times the size, was their ultimate repository.

The titles of the Reverend's books reflect his smorgasbord (Swedish for a buffet of tempting hors d'oeuvres) approach to the gathering of knowledge – they include *Things Not Generally Known* and *Curiosities of History*. When it came to his *Dictionary of Phrase and Fable*, it's clear that if he believed that anything was even vaguely worth knowing, it was worth putting in – and unapologetically so. In the words of Craig Brown, 'Brewer's must be the only dictionary in the world that takes such a fierce delight in its own irrationality.'

Over the years since its birth, his original *Dictionary* has been carefully polished and built upon, layer by layer, so that the past meets the present in myriad ways – often surreal, frequently funny, and always surprising. In 2012, I was delighted to come on board as the editor of its 19th Edition, following in the footsteps of heroes such as Philip Pullman and Terry Pratchett. The book has grown substantially over the last century, taking up 1,480 closely typeset pages. Each entry subscribes to Brewer's original recipe of adding anything into the mix that enriches the mind and whets the appetite for more.

This (thankfully much shorter) book was originally devised as 'a best of *Brewer's*', but rereading material became so enjoyable that I couldn't resist joining the hunt myself. I consequently followed all kinds of red herrings and extra wild-goose chases of my own, and have substantially added in my own discoveries and definitions. I like to think Ebenezer Brewer would approve.

He described himself as a 'babbler', spilling over with good stories won by insatiable inquiry. I would never be so immodest as to place myself in his ranks, but I would include myself among the many lexicographers and linguists who are still babbling happily, standing upon the Reverend's shoulders. His magpie-like swooping on any interesting fact has also been the habit of a lifetime for me. Since childhood I have filled hundreds of notebooks with wordy bric-a-brac. In *Interesting Stories about*

Curious Words, I have brought together thousands of my favourite eclectic stories about the language we use every day – the 'Phrase' in Brewer's title. In selecting them I applied just one criterion: that every fact and every tale might elicit an 'ah!', an 'of course!' or maybe even a 'what?!'

To get a flavour of all three, take, for instance, the story behind 'chancing one's arm'. Legend has it that the phrase rests in an attempt by the 15th-century Earl of Kildare to end a long-running and very bloody quarrel between his family and the Ormondes. Taking refuge in St Patrick's Cathedral, Dublin, he is said to have cut a hole in the door and stuck his arm through, offering the Ormondes the chance to take his hand in peace rather than chop it off. In admiration and with not a small degree of relief, this they did, and the feud was ended.

I find it equally fascinating that flipping someone the bird was as well known to the Romans (for whom the middle finger was called the 'indecent' one, or *digitus impudicus*) as it is to us today. To greet someone with 'wotcher', meanwhile, is to pay lip service to a staple hello of the 15th century: 'What cheer?'

And if you like a hot dog, you might place its playful riff on some rather dubious contents in modern mouths, rather than the 19th-century slang of students from Yale (the Victorian equivalent, you can also discover, was 'bags of mystery').

My favourite etymological curiosity, however, involves the thunder-stealing that features in the subtitle of this book. There are many vivid apocryphal stories behind the coining of phrases, but it's a rarity for lexicographers to be able to pinpoint the *exact* moment in which a word or phrase is born. This particular story involves John Dennis, a disgruntled playwright-cum-inventor, who discovered on 5 February 1709 that the sound-effect machine he had perfected in order to reproduce the sound of thunder for his own ill-fated play had been unceremoniously nicked by the production that took over from his. The witches scene in *Macbeth*, with a dramatic storm in the background, was a booming success – quite literally. 'Damn them!' Dennis cried from the audience. 'They will not let *my* play run, but they steal my thunder!'

Brewer's Phrase and Fable is arranged alphabetically. When it comes to your standard reference book, this is useful if you already know what you're looking for; somewhat harder if you don't. Yet this work is different. In his own Editor's Introduction, Terry Pratchett described browsing through Brewer's *Dictionary* as being pulled into pages that say to us on repeat, 'This is, in fact, not what you were looking for, but it's much more interesting.'

In this book, I would like the adventure to come to you. It offers 53 chapters covering everything from Bottoms to Pub Signs to Four-Letter Words, and on to Fighting Talk and being All at Sea. There's a whole chapter dedicated to Insults and another on Ways to Say Yes.

I have read Brewer's entry for 'boredom' many times. It tells us that the emotion was only given this name around the middle of the 18th century. 'No doubt people had been bored before then,' he writes, 'but evidently they couldn't be bothered to think of a word for it.' You can sense his frustration with such a lackadaisical approach: for him, apathy was unthinkable. Curiosity, on the other hand, would get you everywhere.

Curious minds will always need curious words, and for word lovers, boredom never really stands a chance. What's more, with these stories to hand, it's my hope that you'll never be lost for words, however deeply you're lost *within* them.

Susie Dent
Oxford, June 2023

GREETINGS

Ahoy A shout or exclamation used to hail, greet, or attract attention to someone or something, especially from a distance. The greeting was originally used at sea, and is still preserved in the nautical 'Ahoy there'. It is a later version of 'hoy', also used in hailing a ship.

Ciao The familiar salutation is a variation of *schiavo*, '(I am your) slave/servant', which derives from the medieval Latin *sclavus* ('slave') and the later *slavus*.

Hello A common expression of greeting or of surprise, the latter sometimes in expanded form, as: 'Why, hello!' The word itself is a variant of 'hollo', in turn a form of 'holla', a call for attention, from French *holà*, 'ho, there'. There are many alternative spellings, most dating back to the 19th century.

Long time no see A mock traditional greeting to a person one has not seen for a long time. It is a form of Pidgin English based on Chinese *hǎo jiǔ méi jiàn*.

Wotcher A late 19th-century alteration of the greeting 'What cheer?', 'How are you?'

ANIMAL

The entry for 'horse' in the *Oxford English Dictionary* is quite a ride. It records some 34 expressions involving the animal, from flogging a dead one to eating like one and looking a gift one in the mouth. This is even apart from other words and expressions paying invisible homage to a horse, including 'currying favour', 'croupier', and 'hackneyed'. In fact, look up any animal in the *OED*, or in *Brewer's Dictionary of Phrase and Fable*, and you will be spoilt for choice. Perhaps it is fitting that we can always rely on our fellow creatures to lick our language into shape.

Talk to the Birds

Albatross A large oceanic bird, noted for its powerful gliding flight. It was called the Cape Sheep by sailors from its frequenting of the Cape of Good Hope, and it was said to sleep in the air. It takes its name from the Portuguese *alcatraz*, 'pelican', and was also influenced by the Latin *albus*, 'white'. Sailors have long believed that to shoot one brings bad luck.

In modern usage, the word is used to denote a constant burden or handicap. This sense is first recorded in the 1930s, and thought to have come into general use in the 1960s, but the allusion is to Samuel Taylor Coleridge's poem *The Rime of the Ancient Mariner* (1798), in which the Ancient Mariner shoots the albatross, a 'pious bird of good omen'. As a result, the ship is becalmed, all suffer, and his companions hang the bird round his neck as a punishment.

All one's geese are swans To overestimate; to see things in too rosy a light. All one's children are paragons, and whatever one does is, in one's own eyes, superfluous.

As sick as a parrot Very disappointed or glum; terminally dejected. The expression came to prominence in the 1970s, and came to be regarded as the stock response of a footballer or team manager after losing a match. Its origins may lie in the parrot disease psittacosis, but there is also a much older contender:

> JACINTA: Lord, Madam, you are as melancholy as a
> sick Parrot.
> JULIA: And can you blame me, Jacinta? Have I not
> many Reasons to be sad?
> APHRA BEHN: *The False Count* (1682)

As the crow flies As directly as possible; by the shortest route. It is actually the rook that flies straight to its destination, rather than the crow, but the two black birds are often popularly identified with each other.

Barnacle A species of wild goose, *Branta leucopsis*, allied to the brent goose. Also the popular name of the Cirripedia, the marine crustaceans that live attached to rocks, submerged wooden structures, and ship bottoms. In medieval times it was believed that the goose developed from the shellfish as a frog does from a tadpole.

Booby A species of gannet (*Sula piscator*) is called a booby because of its apparent stupidity. The Spanish *bobo* means 'silly'. It was this that gave rise to the idea of a 'booby prize'.

Canard A hoax; an extravagant false report. This comes from a French word meaning 'duck'. The French lexicographer Emile Littré (1801–81) says that the term comes from an old expression, *vendre un canard à moitié*, 'to half-sell a duck'. As this was no sale at all, it came to mean 'to take in', 'to make a fool of'. Another explanation is that a certain Cornelissen, to try the gullibility of the public, reported in the papers that he had 20 ducks, one of which he cut up and threw to the 19, who devoured it greedily. He then cut up another, then a third, and so on until the 19th was gobbled up by the survivor.

Catbird seat, The In American English, this is the most advantageous position. The catbird is a medium-sized bird of the Mimidae family. Its name refers to its mewing call, but it also has the habit of taking up a high, exposed position to deliver its song, reminiscent of a cat looking down on a bird it is about to pounce on.

Cold turkey A way of curing drug addiction by abruptly discontinuing all doses or supplies. The allusion is to the unpleasant after-effects, which usually include cold sweat and 'goose flesh', like the skin of an uncooked turkey.

Crossbill The red plumage and curious crossing of the upper and lower bill-tips of this bird are explained by a medieval fable, which says that these distinctive marks were bestowed on it by Christ at the crucifixion, as a reward for its having attempted to pull the nails from the cross with its beak.

Cuckoo The cuckoo is among a group of birds whose names echo the distinctive sound of their calls. Other members include the curlew, chiffchaff, kookaburra, hoopoe, and peewit.

Jaywalker A person who crosses or walks in a street thoughtlessly, regardless of passing traffic. The word alludes to the bird, which hops about in an erratic fashion, and to a use of the word 'jay' to mean a foolish person.

Kill two birds with one stone, To To accomplish two things with a single action. The Italian equivalent is *Prendere due piccioni con una fava*, 'To catch two pigeons with one bean'; for the Germans it is *Zwei Fliegen mit einer Klappe schlagen*, 'To swat two flies at once'; and for the Russians *Ubit' dvukh zaytsev odnim udarom*, 'To kill two hares with a single blow'.

Liver bird A fanciful bird, pronounced to rhyme with 'fiver', that first appeared on Liverpool's coat of arms around the 13th century, and two of which adorn the twin towers of the Royal Liver Building in that city. Tradition holds that these curious creatures once lived by Liverpool's original pool, but in fact they resulted from an artist's not very skilled attempt to give a rendition of the eagle of St John the Evangelist, the patron saint of the city.

Magpie The bird was formerly known as a 'maggot pie', 'maggot' representing 'Margaret' (compare robin redbreast, Tomtit, and the old Phyllyp-sparrow) and 'pie' being 'pied', in allusion to its white and black plumage. The magpie has generally been regarded as an uncanny bird, and in Sweden is connected with witchcraft. In Devon it was a custom to spit three times to avert ill luck when the bird was sighted, and in Scotland magpies flying near the windows of a house were said to foretell death. Chattering magpies have been said to foretell a quest since at least the 12th century. Traditional ways of greeting a single magpie include taking off one's hat, bowing or addressing it with an expression such as 'Good morning, Mister Magpie'.

Mews Stables, but originally a cage for hawks when moulting (Old French *mue*, from Latin *mutare*, 'to change'). The word acquired its new meaning because the royal stables built in the 17th century occupied the site of the King's Mews, where formerly the king's hawks were kept.

Ostrich At one time the ostrich was fabled, when hunted, to run a certain distance and then thrust its head into the sand, thinking that, because it cannot see, it cannot be seen. Hence the application of 'ostrich-like' and similar terms to various forms of self-delusion. What it actually does is lie flat on the ground and extend its neck to look for danger. Standing up, it would present an easy target. The adjective 'struthious', 'ostrich-like', can also describe someone who refuses to acknowledge the truth in front of them.

Penguin A rare example of a Welsh word that has become naturalized in English. It is based on *pen gwyn*, meaning 'white head', and was first given to the great auk, another large and flightless seabird with black and white plumage. British sailors may have mistaken penguins for great auks, or simply applied a term they knew to a bird they had never seen before.

Peregrine falcon A falcon (*Falco peregrinus*) of wide distribution, formerly held in great esteem for hawking, and so called (13th century) because it was taken when on passage, or 'peregrination', from the breeding place, instead of straight off the nest, as was the case with most others. The name is based on the Latin *peregrinus*, meaning 'foreigner', which is also at the heart of 'pilgrim'.

Pigeonhole A small compartment for filing papers; hence, a matter that has been put on one side is often said to have been pigeonholed. Today, the most common use of the expression is to assign something to a particular (and often narrow) category.

Popinjay (Spanish *papagayo*, from Arabic *babaghā*) An old word for a parrot, and hence a conceited or empty-headed fop.

Robin Redbreast The popular name for the small songbird *Erithacus rubecula*. It was believed that when Christ was on his way to Calvary, a robin picked a thorn out of his crown, and the blood that issued from the wound fell on the bird and dyed its breast red. Another fable is that the robin covers the dead with leaves. When so covering Christ's body, their white breasts touched his blood and they have ever since been red.

Stool pigeon A police spy or informer; a decoy. The name alludes to the former practice of tying or even nailing a pigeon to a stool to act as a decoy for other pigeons, which were then shot by the waiting hunters.

Stork According to Swedish legend, the stork received its name from flying around the cross of Jesus, crying *Styrka! styrka!* ('Strengthen, strengthen!').

Swallow According to Scandinavian tradition, this bird hovered over the cross of Christ crying *Svala! svala!* ('Console! console!'), whence it was called *svalow* ('bird of consolation').

Swansong In classical times it was believed that swans are born mute, and remain so all their lives until the moment before their death, when they burst into beautiful, elegiac song. A 'swansong' came to mean a final, valedictory performance.

Wild-goose chase, A An impracticable or useless pursuit of something; a hopeless enterprise. The term was first used for a type of horse race in which the lead rider galloped across the open countryside in an erratic pattern. The other riders then followed at different intervals in the exact pattern of the lead rider. The idea is of geese flying in formation, following one leader.

Playing Chicken

As scarce as hen's teeth Very rare. Hens have no teeth.

Cock-a-doodle-doo The traditional English rendering of a cock crowing. In France they go *cocorico*, in Germany *kikeriki*, in Italy *chicchirichì*, in Spain *quiquiriquí* and in Russia *kukareku*. The English word has been influenced by 'cock' itself.

Cock-a-hoop Jubilant, exultant, in high spirits. The expression may derive from the phrase 'to set the cock a hoop', meaning to live luxuriously, from literally putting a 'cock' (the bird) on a 'hoop' or full measure of grain. Equally, the word could derive from the fact that when the spigot or 'cock' is removed from a beer barrel and laid on a hoop of the barrel, the beer flows freely.

Cockalorum A self-important little man, or the boasting ('crowing') of such a man. The word seems to be a combination of 'cock' and the Latin genitive plural ending *-orum*, as if overall meaning 'cock of cocks'.

Crestfallen Dejected or depressed. The allusion is to fighting cocks, whose crests fall in defeat and rise rigid and deep red in victory.

Pecking order A term translating German *Hackliste*, literally 'peck list', applied in the 1920s by animal psychologists to a pattern of behaviour originally observed in hens whereby those of high rank within the group are able to attack (peck) those of lower rank without provoking an attack in return. The phenomenon was later recognized in other groups of social animals. In the 1950s the term was adopted to apply to any form of human hierarchy based on rank or status.

Rule the roast, To To have the main control; to be paramount. The phrase was common in the 16th century, apparently deriving from the master of the household, as head of the table, carving the joint. It has been suggested that the expression is really 'to rule the roost' (now the common form), from the cock deciding which hen is to roost near him, but 'roost' is more likely an alteration of 'roast', the old spelling of which was 'rost' or 'roste'.

Show the white feather, To To show cowardice, a phrase from the cruel sport of cockfighting, a white feather in a gamecock's tail being taken as a sign of degenerate stock, not a true gamebird.

Licking into Shape

As mad as a March hare Hares are unusually shy and wild in March, which is their rutting season.

Bête noire (French, 'black beast') A pet aversion; the thing one dislikes or fears. Black animals are often regarded with ill favour. Black generally is also the colour of the Devil.

Buck the trend, To To oppose or run counter to a general tendency. The reference is to the 'buck' that is a male horned animal such as a deer or (originally) a goat, and probably also to 'butt', the way in which such an animal combats another.

Buff Properly, soft stout leather prepared from the skin of a buffalo, and hence any light-coloured leather or, figuratively, the bare skin. The expert sense of 'buff' began in the US, when volunteer firemen in New York City wore buffalo-skin coats to protect them from the icy winters.

Camelopard (Medieval Latin *camelopardus*, ultimately from Greek *kamēlos*, 'camel', and *pardalis*, 'leopard') The word for a giraffe in the Middle Ages, inspired by its vaguely camel-like shape and its leopard-like markings.

Jumbo The name of an exceptionally large African elephant, which, after giving rides to thousands of children at London Zoo, was sold to Barnum's Greatest Show on Earth in 1882. He weighed 6½ tons and was accidentally killed by a railway engine in 1885. The name may come from Swahili *jambe*, 'chief'.

Leopard The animal is so called because it was thought in medieval times to be a cross between the lion (*leo*) and the 'pard', the name given to a panther that had no white specks on it.

Leopard cannot change its spots, A A person's character never changes fundamentally. The allusion is to Jeremiah 13:23: 'Can the Ethiopian change his skin, or the leopard his spots?'

Lick into shape, To To make presentable; to mould into a satisfactory condition. The expression 'lick into shape' derives from the widespread medieval belief that bear cubs are born shapeless and have to be licked into shape by their mothers. The legend persisted for some time: in Shakespeare's *Henry VI*, Part 3, Gloucester compares his deformed body to 'an unlick'd bear-whelp / That carries no impression like the dam' (III, ii (1592)).

Play possum, To To lie low; to feign quiescence; to dissemble. The phrase comes from the opossum's habitual attempt to avoid capture by feigning death.

Pluck The pluck of an animal is the heart, liver, and lungs, which can be removed by one pull or pluck. It took on the metaphorical meaning of courage, determination, and 'guts'.

Potshot A random shot, or one aimed at an animal within easy reach. The reference is to a shot that lacks any niceties but is simply to 'bag' an animal for the pot.

Teddy bear A child's toy bear, named after Theodore (Teddy) Roosevelt (1858–1919), who was fond of bear-hunting. Roosevelt was shown sparing the life of a bear-cub in a cartoon drawn by C.K. Berryman in 1902 as a spoof on the president's role as an ardent conservationist. In 1906 the *New York Times* published a humorous poem about the adventures of two bears named Teddy B and Teddy G in his honour. These names were then given to two bears newly presented to the Bronx Zoo, and manufacturers seized on the event to put toy bears called teddy bears on the market.

Three Wise Monkeys, The Images of three monkeys carved over the door of the Sacred Stable, Nikko, Japan, in the 17th century. They have their paws respectively over their ears, eyes, and mouth, representing their motto: 'Hear no evil, see no evil, speak no evil.' The monkeys have gained new fame in the form of emojis demonstrating the same gestures.

Wet behind the ears Inexperienced; naive; as innocent as a newborn child. When young animals are born, the last place to become dry after birth is the small depression behind each ear.

White elephant, A A possession that is of little use and that is costly to maintain. The allusion is to the story of a king of Siam who used to make a present of a white elephant to courtiers he wished to ruin.

How Now . . .

Bulldozer The origin of the word is in the verb 'to bulldoze', which originally meant to intimidate by violence, probably from 'bull' (the animal) and an altered form of 'dose'. Coercion by physical means, such as whipping, was meting out a dose of punishment. A bulldozer was an aggressive person who threatened in this way, originally one of various vigilante groups in the US who tried to intimidate African-American voters, and the term then passed to the powerful machine used for levelling.

Earmarked Marked so as to be recognized. Figuratively, allocated or set aside for a special purpose. The allusion is to the owner's marks on the ears of cattle and sheep.

Horns of a dilemma, The A difficult choice in which the alternatives appear equally distasteful or undesirable. Greek *lēmma* means 'assumption', 'proposition', from *lambanein,* 'to grasp'. A dilemma is a double lemma, known by teachers of philosophy as an *argumentum cornutum,* 'horned argument'. The allusion is to a bull that will toss you, whichever horn you grasp.

Maverick An unbranded animal; a stray; a masterless person or rover. Samuel A. Maverick (1803–70), a Texan cattle raiser, did not bother to brand his cattle, hence the practice arose of calling unbranded calves mavericks, and the usage extended to other animals. The name soon took on the sense of someone who did not follow the norm and ploughed their own furrow.

Pecuniary The word is ultimately from Latin *pecus*, denoting cattle, sheep, and so on. These animals were once a medium of barter and standard of value. Ancient coins were commonly marked with the image of an ox or sheep.

Till the cows come home For an indefinitely long time. Dairy herds formerly worked on a more natural cycle than they do today when cows are milked daily, and under normal conditions in a dry spell they would not come in from pasture for some time.

What an Ass!

Donkey An ass. The word is first found in the later 18th century and is perhaps derived from 'dun' with reference to its colour, or else from the personal name 'Duncan'.

Mule The offspring of a female horse and a male donkey, hence a hybrid between other animals (or plants), such as a 'mule canary', a cross between a canary and a goldfinch. The offspring of a stallion and a she-ass is not, properly speaking, a mule, but a hinny. Very stubborn or obstinate people are sometimes called mules, in allusion to the reputed characteristic of the animal. In modern slang, a mule is someone employed exploitatively by a trafficker to smuggle drugs from one country to another, usually concealed in luggage, clothing, or a bodily cavity.

A completely different mule is a women's open-toe and open-heel sandal, in which the upper is a single, wide band of leather or other material over the arch and centre of the foot. In this case the word comes from Latin *mulleus*, short for *mulleus calceus*, 'red shoe', as worn by high-ranking magistrates in Rome.

Talk the hind leg off a donkey, To To talk nonstop; to talk incessantly; less commonly, to wheedle. A donkey's hind legs are its source of strength, so to talk in this way is to weary or enervate your listener. Older versions include the legs of horses and dogs.

Lipstick on a Pig

Higgledy-piggledy Jumbled up in a confused mess. The word first appeared at the end of the 16th century, and may have been inspired by the slovenly reputation of pigs. It is an example of what linguists call a 'reduplicative compound', in which two words are paired on the basis of their sound, and one of them tends to be a fanciful add-on.

Lipstick on a pig 'To put lipstick on a pig' means to make superficial or cosmetic changes to something unattractive in a futile attempt to make it seem more appealing. The phrase dates from the late 20th century, although there are several older expressions with a similar concept; in 1796, Francis Grose's *Classical Dictionary of the Vulgar Tongue* defined a 'hog in armour' as 'an awkward or mean looking man or woman, finely dressed', while the 1889 book of proverbs *The Salt-Cellars* noted that 'a hog in a silk waistcoat is still a hog'.

Pig in a poke, A A blind bargain. The reference is to a former common trick of trying to pass off a cat in a marketplace as a piglet. Opening the poke, or sack, 'let the cat out of the bag', and the trick was disclosed. 'Poke' here is a relative of 'pocket'.

Pig's ear Used in rhyming slang to mean 'beer'. To make a pig's ear of something, however, is to botch it. The ear of a slaughtered pig is its most worthless part, no good for anything.

Pigs might fly The concept of pigs flying as an unlikely occurrence dates from the 16th century but in the 19th century settled to proverbial form as 'Pigs may fly, but they are very unlikely birds'. The current shorter and modified form of this is a 20th-century creation.

Separating the Sheep from the Goats

Black sheep or **Black sheep of the family, The** A ne'er-do-well; a person regarded as a disgrace to the family or community, or as a failure in it. Black sheep were formerly looked on as bearing the Devil's mark.

Count sheep, To To imagine sheep crossing an obstacle and count them one by one as a supposed aid to inducing sleep. The dodge was known to the Victorians but became popular as an insomniac's soporific recourse only in the 20th century. The choice of this particular animal for the purpose may have arisen from a verbal association between 'sheep' and 'sleep'.

Get someone's goat, To To annoy a person. The expression, an old Americanism, is said to relate to a practice among race-horse trainers of soothing a nervous horse by putting a goat in its stall. Someone wanting the horse to lose could sneak in and remove the goat. The horse would again succumb to an attack of nerves and would not run well. But one can irritate a person by constantly butting in, and this may be a more likely reference.

Kid A child, from the kid that is the young of the goat, a very playful and frisky little animal. The related verb 'to kid' means 'to tease', as: 'Only kidding!'

Separate the sheep from the goats To make clear which people in a group are of a higher ability than the others. From the parable in the Gospel of Matthew in which Jesus refers to how judgements will be made on Judgement Day.

Tragedy Literally, a goat song (Greek *tragos*, 'goat', and *ōdē*, 'song'), though why so called is not clear. It may refer to the winner at choral competitions being given a goat as a prize, or to the goat-satyrs of ancient Greek plays.

Yan, tan, tethera, etc. 'Yan, tan, tethera, pethera, pimp' are the numbers one to five in the best known of the many traditional ways of counting sheep in different regions of England. This form is found in parts of Cumbria and Yorkshire, and it is clearly related to the first five numerals in Welsh (*un, dau, tri, pedwar, pump*).

The Cat's Whiskers

Cat's pyjamas, The Something excellent or praiseworthy. A colloquialism of US origin dating from the early 1920s (when the wearing of pyjamas at night was beginning to become popular). 'The cat's whiskers' and 'the bee's knees' have a similar sense.

Cat's whiskers, The An excellent person or thing. The reference is both to whiskers of a cat, since their extreme sensitivity enables it to pass through narrow spaces in total darkness, and to the former use of the term for a very fine adjustable wire in a crystal radio receiver.

Catwalk A narrow pathway or gangway over a theatre stage or along a bridge. Also an extended stage at a fashion show. Cats are able to walk safely along a raised narrow surface such as the top of a wall.

Curiosity killed the cat The original version of this expression was 'care killed the cat'. It is said that a cat has nine lives, but care and worry would wear them all out.

Dead cat bounce In stock exchange jargon, a temporary recovery in share prices after a substantial fall, caused by speculators buying to cover their positions. A live cat on falling will spring up or 'bounce back', but a dead one will not, other than appearing temporarily to rebound because it fell so fast.

Katzenjammer In US slang, anxiety, the jitters, and also an alcoholic hangover. It comes from the German for 'cat's discomfort', a reference to the pain felt on hearing any loud noise on the part of someone suffering the morning after the night before. The term was popularized by the long-running cartoon *The Katzenjammer Kids*, which began in the *New York Journal* in the 19th century and featured two incorrigible children.

Have kittens, To To be extremely nervous or apprehensive. Pregnant cats are sometimes scared into premature kittening.

Let the cat out of the bag, To To disclose a secret. The phrase is said to hark back to medieval markets, where unscrupulous traders might replace a piglet with a less valuable kitten. When the unwary buyer later opened their bag, they would realize the ruse.

Night on the tiles, A An evening or night of merrymaking or debauchery. The allusion is to the nocturnal activities of cats, especially in the mating season.

Rub someone up the wrong way, To To annoy someone; to irritate a person by lack of tact, as a cat is irked when its fur is rubbed the wrong way.

Tabby Originally the name of a silk material with a 'watered' surface, giving an effect of wavy lines. This was later applied to a brownish cat with dark stripes, because its markings resemble this material. The ultimate source of the name is in Arabic *al-'attabiya*, literally 'quarter of (Prince) 'Attab', this being the district of Baghdad where the fabric was first made.

Dog's Dinner

Have a bone to pick, To To have a bone to pick with someone is to have a cause for dispute with them. Two dogs and one bone invariably form a basis for a fight.

Dewclaw A rudimentary inner toe found on some dogs. It is perhaps so called because it only brushes the dewy surface of the grass as the dog walks, whereas the other claws press firmly into the soil.

Dog The word 'dog' is one of etymology's great mysteries, for there are very few records of it in Old English, where the standard term for the animal was 'hound' (from the German *Hund*). Traditionally, given the way the animal was once treated, the dog has been associated in English idioms with a hard life; only more recently has it acquired the more positive associations as 'man's best friend'.

Dog-ears The corners of pages crumpled and folded down. Dog-eared pages are so crumpled, like the turned-down ears of many dogs.

Dog Latin Spurious or 'mongrel' Latin, in which English words are treated like Latin, and Latin words like English, with sometimes embarrassing results. Sometimes also known as 'pig Latin'.

Dogsbody Someone who does all the menial jobs that no one else wants to do, typically a young person or trainee employee. The term dates from the 1920s and was originally applied humorously to peas boiled in a cloth on board ships, and subsequently to a junior officer.

Dog's bollocks, The The very best or most outstanding. The British slang expression emerged in the 1980s, and was initially associated particularly with the humorous magazine *Viz*. The earliest records of the phrase come from printers' slang, where 'the dog's bollocks' represented the colon dash (:–). Probably because of its similarity to 'the bee's knees' and 'the cat's whiskers', it too came to describe something that is the height of excellence.

Dog's dinner or **breakfast, A** A mess or muddle; or dress or adornment that is over-fussy and flashy. The phrase dates from 1902 and refers to the jumbled scraps that a dog might be given to eat.

Dog-tired Exhausted, usually after exercise or hard manual labour, and wanting only to curl up like a dog and go to sleep.

Give a dog a bad name and hang him If you smear a person's reputation they are as good as condemned. In the Middle Ages, animals such as dogs would be brought before courts for alleged 'criminal' behaviour such as biting someone or stealing food, and the punishment frequently meted out was death by hanging. It is this practice that gave us the idea of a 'hangdog', i.e. dejected, expression, and that also has echoes in this 18th-century expression, meaning that a bad reputation, once gained, is very hard to lose.

Jack Russell A small white-coloured sporting terrier first bred by the Rev. John Russell (1795–1883), vicar of Swimbridge in

Devon from 1832 to 1880. Jack Russell, nicknamed 'The Sporting Parson', was much addicted to foxhunting and otter-hunting, and at one time kept his own pack of hounds.

Love me, love my dog If you love someone, you must love all that belongs to them. St Bernard quotes this proverb in Latin, *Qui me amat, amat et canem meum.*

Pavlovian response Ivan Petrovich Pavlov (1849–1936) pioneered the study of the conditioned reflex in animals. In his classic experiment, he first rang a bell when feeding a hungry dog, then trained the dog to salivate on hearing the bell even when there was no sight of food. A Pavlovian response is now generally regarded as any reaction made unthinkingly or under the influence of others.

See a man about a dog, To To excuse oneself; to leave a meeting, party, and so forth, often specifically in order to go to the lavatory. The suggestion is that one is about to place a bet on a dog in a race.

Sirius The Dog Star, so called by the Greeks from the adjective *seirios*, meaning 'hot and scorching'. It gave us the term 'dog days', the hottest part of the summer, associated in ancient times with the rising of Sirius in the Mediterranean area.

Sleuthhound A bloodhound that follows the 'sleuth' (Old Norse *sloth*, Modern English 'slot') or track of an animal. The shortening 'sleuth' was later applied to a detective.

Sold a pup, To be To be swindled. The allusion is to selling something that is worth far less than one expects. A pup is only a small young dog, who will have to be trained.

Terrier A dog that loves to dig or to unearth its prey. It takes its name from the Latin *terra*, 'earth'.

The Horse's Mouth

Cob A short-legged, stout variety of horse, rather larger than a pony, from 13 to nearly 15 hands high (a hand is 4in./10cm). The word 'cob' is of uncertain origin, but it is often used of something big and stout or hard and round. Hence 'cobble', 'cob loaf', and 'cobnut'.

Croupier In French, a *croupier* was a rider who sat behind another, on the horse's 'croup' or rump. The word was transferred in English to the idea of a second standing behind a gambler to back them up, and from there to one who rakes in the money at the gaming table.

Curry favour, To The phrase was originally 'to curry Favel', in which Favel was a chestnut horse in a 14th-century French poem that offered a satire on the corruption of public life. The horse, a conniving stallion and a symbol for cunning and deceit, was also highly amenable to flattery, and people would come and 'curry', or groom, him in order to ingratiate themselves with him. Over time, the legend was lost and Favel was altered to a more meaningful 'favour'.

Hackney Originally (14th century) the name given to a class of medium-sized horses, distinguishing them from warhorses. They were used for riding, and later the name was applied to a horse let out for hire, whence 'hackney carriage'. The name probably comes from the London borough of Hackney, where such horses were formerly raised. A 'hackney cab' is an official term for a taxi.

Hell for leather As fast as possible; at top speed. The phrase originally applied to riding on horseback, the saddle being the 'leather'.

Hobby A favourite pursuit; a pastime that interests or amuses. The origin is in 'hobby' as a small or medium-sized horse, itself probably from the name Robin. From this 'hobbyhorse' the name was transferred to a light wickerwork frame, appropriately draped, in which someone gambolled in the old morris dances. Padstow in Cornwall has its ancient 'Obby 'Oss parade on May Day. The horse is preceded by men clad in white known as 'teazers'. It also came to apply to a toy, consisting of a stick, which a child straddles, with a horse's head at one end. It was from this last, which was the child's pastime, that the name passed to the leisure-time pursuit.

'To get on one's hobby-horse', or for something to be someone's 'hobby-horse', is a reference to someone's (very possibly unhealthy) obsession.

Jade A word of unknown origin applied to a worn-out horse, which also gave us the adjective 'jaded', to describe a tired or downcast individual.

Kick over the traces, To To break away from control or to run riot, as a horse refusing to run in harness kicks over the traces (the two side straps that connect its harness to the swingletree).

Lead someone by the nose, To To make a person do what one wants; to dominate someone. Such a person has no will of their own but tamely follows where they are led, just as a horse is led by bit and bridle. Bulls, buffaloes, camels, and bears are led by a ring through their nostrils.

Long in the tooth Old. The reference is to horses, whose gums recede as they get older, making their teeth look longer.

Look a gift-horse in the mouth, To When one is given a present one should not enquire too minutely into its intrinsic value. The normal way of assessing the age of a horse is to inspect its front teeth: it would be considered very impolite to openly scrutinize an animal one has been given as a present.

Nod is as good as a wink to a blind horse, A However obvious a hint or suggestion may be, it is useless if the other person cannot see it or will not take the hint.

Straight from the horse's mouth Direct from the highest source, which cannot be questioned, parricularly when it comes to the winner of a race.

You can lead (or **take**) **a horse to water but you cannot make him drink** There is always some point at which it is impossible to get an obstinate or determined person to go any further in the desired direction. An Old English version of the proverb translates as 'Who can give water to a horse that will not drink of its own accord?' Dorothy Parker, challenged to produce a sentence using the word 'horticulture', is said to have played on the proverb in the form 'You can lead a horticulture, but you can't make her think'.

Animal Crossings

Pelican crossing A type of road crossing that can be controlled by pedestrians. Hence its name, from 'pedestrian light controlled crossing', with the acronym assimilated to 'pelican'.

Puffin crossing A UK road crossing activated by pedestrians, a development of the pelican crossing. It signals red for drivers to stop when pedestrians are 'sensed' at the crossing or on the road by infrared detectors, with the green 'go' traffic signal appearing when no pedestrians are thus detected. The name is a respelled acronym, by analogy with the pelican crossing, of 'p(edestrian) u(ser) f(riendly) in(telligent) crossing'.

Toucan crossing A dual-use road crossing for cyclists and pedestrians, so named because 'two can' cross on them at the same time. Toucan crossings are usually provided in the UK where cycle routes cross busy roads, and are designed so that cyclists need not dismount to use them.

Zebra crossing A pedestrian crossing consisting of thick black and white longitudinal stripes across the road, parallel to the flow of traffic, and in the UK having a Belisha beacon on either pavement.

Spelling Bee

As snug as a bug in a rug Cosy and comfortable. A whimsical but expressive comparison that dates from the 18th century.

Beeline, A The shortest distance between two given points, such as a bee is supposed to take in making for its hive.

Bee's knees, The Said of something or someone outstanding. The term may have been coined by the US columnist T.A. ('Tad') Dorgan in the early 1920s (it is first recorded in 1922). The reference is perhaps to the pollen baskets on a bee's legs (the process of removing the pollen involves much bending of the bee's knees and is performed with great precision), or maybe it is simply surreal (as with many fanciful formulations of the time, including the 'ant's pants', 'gnat's elbows', 'kipper's knickers', 'elephant's adenoids', and 'cat's pyjamas').

25

Bug An old word for goblin or 'bogy', which probably began with the Middle Welsh *bwg*, 'ghost'. The word survives in 'bogle', 'bogy', and in 'bugaboo', a monster or goblin, and 'bugbear', a hobgoblin said to take the form of a bear and invoked by parents to frighten children into better behaviour.

In common usage the word 'bug' is applied to almost any kind of insect or germ, especially an insect of the 'creepy-crawly' sort, and notably the bed bug. It is colloquially used to refer to an error in software or to anyone 'bitten' with a particular craze or obsession, as well as to a concealed miniature microphone.

Can of worms A complicated matter that is likely to cause problems or even a scandal. The image is of opening a tin of food and finding inside a mass of writhing maggots that will have to be dealt with.

Canopy The word derives from Medieval Latin *canopeum*, 'mosquito net', which is itself from Greek *kōnōpeion*, 'bed with mosquito curtains', from *kōnōps*, 'mosquito'.

Earwig (Old English *ēarwicga*, 'ear beetle') The insect is so called from the erroneous notion that it can enter the ears and penetrate the brain.

Flea market A street market selling second-hand goods and the like, so called because the clutter of bric-a-brac and old clothes is conducive to fleas. The French equivalent is the *marché aux puces*, or simply *les puces*, in Paris, the oldest and best known being that at St Ouen, on the northern edge of the city.

Fleapit Any dingy or dirty place, and conventionally, since the 1930s, an old run-down cinema, where fleas may have been a real hazard.

Ladybird The small red insect with black spots, *Coccinella septempunctata*, called also 'ladybug', 'Bishop Barnabee', and, in Yorkshire, the 'cushcow lady'. The name means 'bird (beetle) of our Lady': the insect's seven spots were understood as corresponding to the seven sorrows of Mary.

Scarab A trinket in the form of a dung beetle, especially *Scarabaeus sacer*. It originated in ancient Egypt as an amulet; the insect was believed to conceal within itself the secret of eternal life.

Sent off with a flea in one's ear, To be To be sent away discomfited by a reproof or repulse. A dog that has a flea in its ear is restless and runs around in distress. The expression dates from at least the 15th century in English, and earlier in French.

Spelling bee A spelling competition, so called as the participants are socially active, like bees.

Tarantella A very quick Neapolitan dance (or its music) in 6/8 time for one couple, said to have been based on the gyrations carried out by those whom the TARANTULA had bitten, either as a result of the poisoning or because the poison was thought to be curable by dancing.

Tarantula A large and hairy spider. Named after Taranto, Latin *Tarentum*, a town in Apulia, Italy, where the spiders abounded. The spider's bite was formerly supposed to be the cause of the dancing mania hence known as 'tarantism'. This was a hysterical disease, common as an epidemic in southern Europe from the 15th to the 17th centuries.

Red Herring

Catch a crab, To In rowing, to fail to put one's oar deep enough into the water, so that one loses one's balance and falls backwards or even overboard. A crab can be scooped out of the water with an oar.

Hook, line, and sinker To swallow a tale hook, line, and sinker is to be extremely gullible, like the hungry fish that swallows not only the baited hook but the sinker (lead weight) and some of the line as well.

Red herring A diversion, usually deliberate but sometimes unintentional, which distracts from a line of inquiry or a topic under discussion. An actual red herring (one dried, smoked, and salted), drawn across a fox's path, was once used to train hounds – the scent might well lead them astray. An alternative theory involves escaped convicts drawing a smelly fish across their tracks in order to put off police dogs.

Whale of A great amount. Colloquially 'whale' is used of something very fine or big, as: 'We had a whale of a time', a fine time, or 'a whale of a job', a very considerable task.

Pebble Worm

As deaf as an adder 'Like the deaf adder that stoppeth her ear; which will not hearken to the voice of charmers, charming never so wisely' (Psalm 58:4–5). All snakes are in a sense 'deaf', having no outer ears, although they do pick up vibrations via the inner ear. As recently as the 1920s, oil made from the melted fat of the adder was sold as a remedy for deafness in some parts of England, capitalizing on the ancient belief that 'like cures like'.

Crocodile A symbol of deity among the Egyptians, because, says Plutarch, it is the only aquatic animal which has its eyes covered with a thin transparent membrane, by reason of which it sees and is not seen, as God sees all, Himself not being seen. The name of the crocodile comes from Greek *krokodilos*, 'worm of the pebbles' – a reference to the crocodile's habit of basking in the sun on the banks of a river.

Frog in the throat, A A temporary loss of voice; hoarseness. The expression is said to allude to the medieval fear of drinking water containing frogspawn, when it was believed frogs would grow inside the body. Hoarseness or 'gagging' was thus allegedly caused by a frog trying to escape from the stomach by way of the throat. More plausible is the idea that hoarseness can induce a very frog-like 'croak'.

Frog-march A method of carrying an obstreperous prisoner face downwards by his four limbs, like a frog. The term is now more generally used, however, for a way of making a person walk somewhere by pinning his arms behind him and hustling him forward.

Toad-eater or **toady** A cringing parasite; an obsequious lick-spittle. Charlatans and mountebanks in 17th-century markets would have their assistant eat a toad, believed at the time to be poisonous, in front of the gathered crowd, only to miraculously 'cure' them with their potion. The assistant gained the name 'toad-eater', used of someone who followed their master or mistress's instructions to the extreme. The story survives still in the idea of 'toadying up' to someone.

VEGETABLE

It seems a little contradictory to talk about 'vegging out' when the root of the word 'vegetable' is the Latin *vegetabilis*, meaning 'animating'. To vegetate, strictly speaking, is to germinate or produce new growth. But by the 18th century, if a person vegetated they were leading a dull and monotonous life, without intellectual or social activity. In other words, vegetables may have the faculty of growth, but they are entirely lacking in the powers of sensation or reason. They simply don't have the fun that animals do.

A browse through the following entries might suggest the opposite: from the 'mandrake' that is said to scream when uprooted, to the 'passion flower' or the floral tribute to the slain 'Hyacinth' – there is plenty of animation here.

Cut and Dried

Agave (Greek *agauē*, feminine of *agauos*, 'illustrious') In classical mythology, Agave was the daughter of Cadmus and Harmonia. Her name has been given to a tropical American plant now well known for the sweet syrup derived from it. One Mexican species (*Agave americana*) is mistakenly called the 'century plant', in the belief that it takes 100 years to flower.

Cut and dried All ready or arranged in advance. The term arose in the early 20th century from an earlier literal sense applied to herbs sold in herbalists' shops, as distinct from fresh, growing herbs.

Frankincense The literal meaning of the word is 'pure' or 'superior incense', from Old French *franc encens*. It was ceremonially used by the Egyptians, Persians, Babylonians, Hebrews, Greeks, and Romans and is an ingredient of the modern incense used in some churches.

Grist to the mill Anything useful or profitable, especially when added to what already exists. Grist is that quantity of grain which is to be ground at one time.

Mandrake The root of the mandrake or mandragora (*Mandragora officinarum*) often divides in two, presenting an approximate appearance of a man. In ancient times human figures were cut out of the root and wonderful virtues ascribed to them, such as fertility. They could not be uprooted without supposedly producing fatal effects, so a cord used to be fixed to the root and around a dog's neck, and the dog, when chased, drew out the mandrake and died. A small dose of the drug was held to produce vanity in one's appearance, and a large dose, idiocy. Famously, the mandrake was said to scream violently when uprooted.

Mistletoe From the Old English *misteltān*, from *mistel*, 'mistletoe', and *tān*, 'twig'. *Mistel* itself may have its origins in an ancient word meaning 'dung', since the plant is propagated in the excrement of birds (potentially undermining its romantic associations). The plant grows on various trees as a parasite, especially the apple tree, and was held in great veneration by the druids when found on the oak. Shakespeare calls it 'the baleful mistletoe' (*Titus Andronicus*, II, iii (1592)), perhaps in allusion to the tradition that it was once a tree from which the wood of Christ's cross was formed, or possibly with reference to the popular belief that mistletoe berries are poisonous.

Peppercorn rent A nominal rent. A peppercorn is of very slight value and is a token rental of virtually free possession without the ownership of the freehold.

Rosemary The herb, which hails from the shores of the Mediterranean, is associated with friendship, loyalty, and remembrance. It takes its name from the Latin *ros marinus*, 'dew of the sea'.

Wormwood The common name for the aromatic herbs of the genus *Artemisia*, from which absinthe and vermouth are concocted. It is said to have been so called because this plant, according to legend, sprang up in the track of the serpent as it writhed along the ground when driven out of Paradise. The word in fact comes from Old English *wormod* and has no connection, except in folk etymology, with 'worm' or 'wood'. 'Vermouth' is directly related.

Cucumber Season

Costermonger A now rare term for a street vendor of fruit, vegetables, and the like. The word properly denotes an apple seller – a 'costard' was a large cooking apple, and 'monger', a dealer or trader (Old English *mangian*, 'to trade'), as in iron-monger or fishmonger.

Couch potato A person who prefers lounging at home watching television to engaging in any purposeful activity, especially if it involves physical effort. The expression is of US origin and appears to pun on 'boob-tuber' as a slang term for a TV addict or someone who watches the 'boob tube' – 'boob' here being a synonym for 'fool', and the potato being a plant tuber.

Cucumber In 18th-century slang, a tailor. Summertime, when cucumbers ripen, was a slack time for tradesmen in towns and cities, when the gentry had left for their country estates, so it came to be referred to as 'cucumber season' or 'cucumber time'. Tailors traditionally took their holidays at this time.

Jerusalem artichoke This plant, which is not an artichoke at all, also has nothing to do with the Holy City. 'Jerusalem' is here a mispronunciation of Italian *girasole*, the sunflower, to which this vegetable is related.

Know one's onions, To To be knowledgeable in one's particular field. The expression is sometimes jokingly said to refer to the lexicographer C.T. Onions, co-editor of the *Oxford English Dictionary* and author of books on English, but it may actually derive from Cockney rhyming slang, with 'onions' short for 'onion rings', meaning 'things'.

Lens From Latin, meaning 'lentil', 'bean'. Glasses used in optical instruments are so called because the double convex lens is shaped like a lentil.

Spill the beans, To To give away a secret. It has long been believed that this expression refers to a voting system of ancient Greece, in which votes were cast by placing one of two different coloured beans in an urn. If someone literally spilled the beans, the election results would be revealed. However, 'spill the beans' only began to emerge in the early 1900s, and it's more probable the idea is a riff on other idioms such as 'upset the apple-cart'.

Sycophant A parasite or servile flatterer. The word comes from Greek *sukophantēs*, literally 'fig shower' (*sukon*, 'fig', and *phainein*, 'to show'), which is said to have described someone who informed against those who exported figs contrary to law, or else to someone who 'showed the fig' (made an insulting gesture) when making an accusation. It's from here that the word shifted from the sense of accuser or informer to fawning flatterer. *See* FICO.

Daisy Chain

Anthology (Greek *anthos*, 'flower', and *legein*, 'to collect') An anthology was a collection of poems or prose extracts, imagined as a bouquet of beautiful flowers.

Daisy The flower's name is really 'day's eye', from Old English *dægesēge*, and the flower is so called because it closes its petals or 'lashes' when the sun sets, but at dawn opens them again to the light.

Forget-me-not According to German legend, this flower takes its name from the last words of a knight who was drowned while trying to pick some from the riverside for his lady. The generic name *Myosotis* ('mouse-ear') refers to the shape of the leaves. To wear the flower is to ensure against being forgotten by one's lover.

Foxglove The flower *Digitalis purpurea* is named from the animal and the glove. It is not known how the fox came to be associated with it, but one suggestion is that it is an alteration of 'folk's glove', 'folk' being the fairies or little people. In Welsh it is called *menig ellyllon* ('elves' gloves') or *menig y llwynog* ('the fox's gloves'), and in Ireland it is called 'fairy thimble'.

Geranium The flower's name comes from Greek *geranos*, 'crane', and the wild plant is called 'crane's bill' from the resemblance of the fruit to the bill of a crane.

Hyacinth According to Greek fable, the son of Amyclas, a Spartan king. The boy was beloved by Apollo and Zephyr but as he preferred the sun-god, Zephyr drove Apollo's quoit at his head and killed him. The blood became a flower, and the petals are inscribed with the signature 'AI', meaning 'woe'.

Iris The Iridaceae is a large family of brightly coloured flowers, including the iris, crocus, and gladiolus. Iris was the goddess of the rainbow.

Lavender The earliest form of the word is Medieval Latin *lavendula*, perhaps from Latin *lividus*, 'bluish'. However, since the plant was used by laundresses for scenting linen, it came to be associated with *lavare*, 'to wash'. The modern botanical name is *Lavandula*. The plant is a token of affection.

Marigold The plant *Calendula officinalis* with its bright yellow or orange flowers is so called in honour of the Virgin Mary.

Mimosa From Modern Latin, from Latin *mimus*, 'mime'. The plant is so called from the notion that it mimics the sensitivity of animals – the leaves of this plant fold upward at the slightest touch.

Passion flower A plant of the genus *Passiflora*. When European missionaries travelled to South America in the 17th century, they used the structure of the native 'passion flower', or *Passiflora edulis*, to illustrate the crucifixion. The flower's five petals and five sepals represented the ten faithful apostles, its corona represented the crown of thorns, while the three stigmas were taken to show the three nails and the five anthers Christ's five wounds. Finally, the plant's tendrils represented the whips used in the flagellation of Christ.

Periwinkle The plant's generic name, *Vinca*, is from Latin *vincire*, 'to bind around'. It is a trailing plant. In Italy it used to be wreathed round dead infants and was thus called *fiore di morto*, 'flower of death'.

Pink The colour takes its name from the flower, which may be so called because the edges of the petals are 'pinked' or notched (although alternatively the name could be from the old phrase 'pink eye', meaning a small eye).

Poppy In medieval art the poppy sometimes represents Christ's blood, from its red colour. After the First World War the Allies adopted the poppy as a symbol of sacrifice. The ultimate origins of the flower's name are unknown. Its recorded history began with the Romans' word for the flower, *papaver*, which may in turn contain an ancient word meaning 'to swell'.

Potpourri (French) A mixture of dried, sweet-smelling flower petals and herbs preserved in a vase. *Pourri* means 'rotten' and *potpourri* is literally the 'vase' containing the 'rotten' flowers.

Primrose The name of the flower is from Medieval Latin *prima rosa*, 'first rose'. The flower is one of the first to appear in the spring, with 'rose' here used generally to mean 'flower'.

Knowing the Wood from the Trees

Against the grain Against one's natural inclination. The allusion is to wood, which cannot be properly planed against the grain.

Bark up the wrong tree, To To waste energy; to be on the wrong scent. The phrase comes from raccoon hunting, which takes place in the dark. The dogs have been trained to mark the tree where the raccoon has fled, but they can mistake the tree in the dark and bark up the wrong one.

Blaze (probably from Middle Low German *bles*, 'white mark', related to English 'blemish') A white marking on the forehead of a horse, also called a star. Similarly, a white mark made on a tree by chipping off a piece of bark is also known as a 'blaze' – 'to blaze a trail' is done by marking trees in this way to signal a route for others to follow, especially when exploring or pioneering.

By hook or by crook By any means, one way or another. The expression derives from an old manorial custom, which authorized tenants to take as much firewood as could be reached down by a shepherd's crook and cut down with a billhook.

Conker A children's name for a horse chestnut, derived from the identical dialect word meaning a snail shell (related to 'conch'), as these were originally used in the game of conkers. The word was popularly associated with 'conquer', and the game was called 'conquerors' for some time.

Hold out the olive branch, To To make overtures for peace. The allusion is to the olive being an ancient symbol of peace.

Horse chestnut John Gerard mentions in his *Herball* (1597) that the tree is so called 'for that the people of the East countries do with the fruit thereof cure their horses of the cough' (despite conkers being poisonous to the animal). Another, less likely, explanation is that when a leaf stalk is pulled off, it leaves behind a miniature representation of a horse's hock and foot with shoe and nail marks.

Loggerheads, To be at To be in a state of disagreement or dispute with someone. 'Loggerhead', an old word for a stupid person, is probably from the dialect word 'logger', a heavy block of wood, plus 'head'. It was also used for an iron implement with a bulbous end that was heated to melt tar, and conceivably the expression originally referred to a fight using these or similar objects as weapons.

Lumber Formerly a pawnshop, named from the province of Lombardy, with which pawnbroking became synonymous after bankers in the area achieved great success using the pawnbroking business model, which for a time was known as 'Lombard banking'. 'Lumber' came to be applied to disused material found in pawnshops, and later to boards and bits of wood. Today it describes timber that has been sawn and split.

Neck of the woods In its original US use, an early settlement in the forest defined by its shape, but now a term for any neighbourhood or area.

Palm The well-known tropical and subtropical tree gets its name from Latin *palma*, 'palm of the hand', from the spread-hand appearance of its fronds.

Perfume The word means simply 'through smoke' (Latin *per fumum*), the first perfumes having been obtained by the combustion of aromatic woods and gums. Their original use was in sacrifices to counteract the offensive odours of burning flesh.

Skid row To be 'on skid row' is to be down on one's luck or penniless. In the US lumber industry, a skid row was a row of logs down which other felled timber was slid or skidded. Early on, Tacoma, near Seattle, flourished thanks to its lumber production. Over time, bars and brothels were established in the area, which during the height of the Great Depression gained a reputation for being down at heel. To 'hit the skids' is equally to be in a rapid decline.

Stock Originally a tree trunk or stem (connected with 'stick'), and so, figuratively, used for something fixed, as in 'stock still'. The word is also used for the 'stem' that is the origin of families, groups, and the like, as: 'He comes of a good stock', i.e. from a good stem, of good line of descent. The village stocks, in which petty offenders were confined by the wrists and ankles, are so called from the stakes or posts at the side. 'Stock' in the sense of a fund or capital derives from part of the wooden 'tally-stick', on which debts would be 'scored' by a knife. The word was then applied to the money that this tally represented, i.e. money lent to the government.

CHIP ON, CHIP OFF

Have a chip on one's shoulder, To To be quarrelsome; to parade or have a grievance. The expression is of 19th-century US origin, and alludes to a form of challenge in which a man or boy dares another to dislodge the chip (piece of wood) he carries on his shoulder.

Chip off the old block, A A person whose behaviour is similar to that of his or her mother or father. A chip is of the same wood as the block from which it comes. The expression was earlier 'chip of the old block'.

Up the Garden Path

Call a spade a spade, To To be outspoken or blunt, even to the point of rudeness; to call things by their proper names without any beating about the bush. Its ultimate source was an ancient Greek expression which meant literally 'to call a fig a fig, a trough a trough'. In the Middle Ages, the Greek word for 'trough', *skaphē*, was replaced by *skapheion*, which denoted a digging tool, and this was translated into English as 'spade'.

Get hold of the wrong end of the stick, To To misunderstand the story or the information. The wrong end of the stick is the dirty or muddy one. In ancient Rome, visitors to communal toilets would use a stick with a sponge at one end to wipe themselves – popular belief holds that picking up the wrong end of this particular stick would have been unpleasant indeed.

Go haywire, To To run riot; to behave in an uncontrolled manner. This US phrase probably arises from the difficulty of handling the coils of wire used for binding bundles of hay, which easily became entangled and unmanageable if handled unskilfully.

Grass The Old English word *græs* is descended from the same root word as both 'green' and 'grow'. In criminal slang 'to grass' is to inform, from Cockney rhyming slang 'grasshopper' for 'copper'. The particular reference was to a plain-clothes officer who 'hopped' from one criminal haunt to another with the aim of gathering intelligence.

Last straw, The The final annoyance or hurt that breaks one's patience or resilience. The expression comes from the proverb 'It is the last straw that breaks the camel's back', itself alluding to the final, minute addition to the burden that makes it literally unbearable.

Lead someone up the garden path, To To deceive or trick someone; to entice a person with false promises of good prospects or the like. The expression may relate to the garden parties of the 19th century, when a male guest with his eye on a particular young lady would at first stroll in the garden with her in full view of her chaperones until an opportunity presented itself for him to lead her up a path screened by shrubs or bushes.

MINERAL

He may not have uttered the precise words, but Sherlock Holmes's 'Elementary, my dear Watson' has happily settled in English idiom to convey something that, though it might seem extraordinary, is actually quite straightforward when broken down into its basic 'elements'. While 'element' today may be a slightly throwaway reference to a constituent part of anything, the word was once fundamental to scientific belief. The very first meaning of 'elementary', in the 16th century, referred to the four elements from which all other substances were believed to be composed: earth, air, fire, and water. To this day, to be 'in one's element' is to be in one's natural surroundings and doing what one does well. The Pythagoreans added a fifth essence, ether – more subtle and pure than fire and said to have flown upwards at creation and formed the basis of the stars. This was the 'quintessence' of life.

The word 'mineral', meanwhile – the third in the famous triumvirate of animal, vegetable, mineral – first referred to the alchemist's use of the 'philosopher's stone' for the purification of metals. What a journey these elementary words in our language have made.

Grindstones and Touchstones

Crop up, To To occur or arise, especially unexpectedly. The verb originates from mining, in which a stratum or vein that comes up to the surface is said to crop up. If it comes out of the side of a slope, it is said to crop out.

Keep one's nose to the grindstone, To To keep hard at work. Tools such as scythes and chisels were formerly constantly sharpened on a stone or with a grindstone.

Make a mountain out of a molehill, To To make a difficulty of trifles. Latin has *arcem e cloaca facere* ('to make a stronghold out of a sewer'), and the French have *faire d'une mouche un éléphant* ('to make an elephant out of a fly').

Plaster of Paris Gypsum, especially calcined gypsum used for making statuary casts, keeping broken limbs rigid for setting and so on. The name derives from the gypsum quarries of Montmartre, Paris.

Touchstone A piece of dark, flinty schist, jasper, or basanite (the *Lapis Lydius* of the ancients), so called because alloys of gold were tested by observing the colour they made on it. 'Touchstone' came to be used to describe any criterion or standard.

Panning for Gold

Bonanza (Spanish, literally 'calm sea', from Latin *bonus*, 'good', and *malacia*, 'dead calm') The term was applied in mining areas of the USA to the discovery of a rich vein or pocket, when the mine was said to be 'in bonanza'. The word is now generally used for an unexpected source of wealth or success. The 'calm sea' of the original sense is one that brings smooth sailing and hence a fortunate passage.

Carat This measure of the purity of gold and a unit of weight for precious stones comes from the Arabic *kīrāṭ*, a unit of weight. The base for that in turn is Greek *keration*, which was used in ancient times for both a carob seed and a unit of weight. Its literal meaning is 'little horn', describing the carob's elongated seed pod.

Diggings or **digs** Lodgings, rooms. A word imported from California and its gold diggings.

Do one's level best, To To do one's utmost. The expression is said to originate in the Californian gold rush, with the level here being an underground seam or level found in a mine.

Hallmark The official mark stamped on gold and silver articles after they have been assayed, so called because the assaying or testing and stamping was done at the Goldsmiths' Hall.

Pan out, To To turn out or to happen, as: 'It has panned out satisfactorily.' The allusion is to the pan used by a prospector to wash out gold from the gravel of streams and riverbeds.

Philosopher's stone The hypothetical substance that, according to the alchemists, would convert all baser metals into gold. Many believed it to be compounded of the purest sulphur and mercury. Medieval experimenters toiled endlessly in the search, thus laying the foundations of the science of chemistry, among other developments.

Ring true, To To appear authentic; to seem likely. The allusion is to the former method of testing coins by dropping them on a hard, cold surface. Those of pure silver or gold had a distinctive ring, i.e. they 'rang true', while those of base metal had a duller sound.

Up to the mark The original reference was to metal that was not up to the standard fixed by the assay office for gold and silver articles.

KISSING THE BLARNEY STONE

Blarney Stone, The A block of rough limestone measuring 4ft (1.2m) by 1ft (30cm) in the wall of Blarney Castle, near Cork, set 83ft (25m) high in the battlements. The tradition is to kiss it, which can be done only by lying on one's back and leaning out over a sheer drop, with a pair of strong arms gripping one's shins. This feat, it is believed, will give the gift of cajolery. The legend surrounding the stone is said to date from 1602, when the smooth-talking Lord of Blarney, Cormac MacDermot MacCarthy, was asked by George Carew, Queen Elizabeth's deputy in Ireland, to give up the tradition by which Irish clans elected their chiefs and to transfer his allegiance to the English crown. MacCarthy constantly procrastinated with blandishments, until the Queen finally exploded: 'Blarney! Blarney! What he says he never means! It's the usual Blarney!' Blarney thus became the laughing stock of the Queen's ministers. The tradition of kissing the stone dates from the 18th century, when the Blarney Castle estate was developed by the Jefferyes family.

Precious

Amethyst (Greek *a-* 'not', and *methuein*, 'to be intoxicated')
A violet-blue variety of quartz supposed by the ancients to
prevent intoxication. Cups and goblets of amethyst were
believed to be a charm against drunkenness, and the stone was
especially cherished by Roman matrons from the belief that it
would preserve the affection of their husbands.

Diamond The gemstone is so called because the diamond,
which cuts other substances, can be cut or polished only by
one of its kind. Its name is from the Medieval Latin *diamas*, a
form of the Latin *adamas*, meaning 'hardest steel', which also
gave us the word 'adamant'.

Jade The fact that in medieval times this ornamental stone was
supposed, if applied to the side, to act as a cure for renal colic
is enshrined in its name, for 'jade' is from the obsolete Spanish
piedra de ijada, 'stone of the side'. Its other name, 'nephrite', is
from Greek *nephros*, 'kidney'.

Onyx (Greek, 'fingernail') The gemstone, a variety of chal-
cedony, is so called because its veined appearance resembles
that of a fingernail.

Opal (Greek *opallios*, probably from Sanskrit *upala*, 'gem')
This semi-precious stone, well known for its play of iridescent
colours, a vitreous form of hydrous silica, has long been deemed
to bring bad luck. Alphonso XII of Spain (1857–85) presented
an opal ring to his wife on his wedding day, and her death
occurred soon afterwards. Before the funeral he gave the ring
to his sister, who died a few days later. The king then presented
it to his sister-in-law, and she died within three months.

Alphonso, astounded at these fatalities, resolved to wear the ring himself, and within a very short time he, too, was dead.

Ruby From the Latin *rubeus*, 'red'. The ancients considered the ruby to be an antidote to poison and to have the power of preserving people from plague, banishing grief, repressing the ill effects of luxuries, and diverting the mind from evil thoughts.

Brass Neck

As right as ninepence Perfectly well, in perfect condition. The expression is said to relate to silver ninepenny pieces formerly given as love tokens.

Brass neck Impudence, cheek. A slang expression of the 20th century, but it is part of a nexus of usages in which impudence or boldness is given the metaphor of brass dating back at least to the mid-16th century – we can also be 'brazen-faced' and as 'bold as brass'.

Cobalt This metal, from which a deep blue pigment is made, was so called by miners partly because it was thought to be useless and partly because the arsenic and sulphur with which it was found in combination had bad effects on their health and on the silver ores. Its name comes from the German *Kobalt*, 'goblin': a nod to the alleged malicious mine demon who miners believed had put it there. *See* NICKEL.

Foil A person or thing that sets off another to advantage. The allusion is to the metallic leaf used by jewellers to set off precious stones.

Magnet A lodestone so called from Magnesia in Lydia, where the magnetic iron ore was said to abound.

Nickel The metal is so called from the German *Kupfernickel*, the name given to the ore (niccolite) from which it was first obtained. *Kupfer* means 'copper', and *Nickel* is the name of a mischievous goblin fabled to inhabit mines in Germany. The name was given to it because, although it was copper-coloured, no copper could be got from it, and so the *Nickel* was blamed.

In the USA a nickel is a coin of five cents, so called from being made of an alloy of nickel and copper.

Gardy Loo

As dry as a Pommie's bath-towel Completely dry. Australians like to believe that English people never take a bath.

Balderdash Nonsense, rubbish. The earliest recorded meaning of the word, in the 16th century, is 'frothy water'. Its origin is uncertain. Certain Scandinavian parallels have been pointed to: Danish *balder*, 'noise, clatter'; Icelandic *baldras*, 'to make a clatter', and Danish *daske*, 'to slap, flap'. There is a striking similarity, too, in Welsh *baldorddus*, 'noisy'. But given the word's original meaning, the most plausible source may be the practice of barbers 'dashing' their 'balls' (spherical pieces of soap) backwards and forwards in hot water to make a froth for shaving.

Divining rod A forked branch of hazel or willow also called *virgula divina*, Aaron's Rod, or the wand of Mercury. When manipulated by the diviner or dowser, it bends towards the place where a concealed spring or a metallic lode is to be found. The Romans used the *virgula divina* in augury, and the forked twig, or *virgula furcata*, was introduced into Cornish mines from Germany in the reign of Elizabeth I. With the decline of mining in the south-west of England, dowsing is now confined to the finding of water.

Loo The word 'loo' has invited more etymological theories than most. They range from a nod to 'Waterloo', a trade name for iron cisterns in the early 20th century, to 'gardyloo', a mangling of the French *gare de l'eau!*, 'mind the water!' This was a cry frequently heard in 18th-century Edinburgh that warned passers-by that bowls of dirty water and even chamber pots were about to be emptied from a window above. Perhaps the most plausible suggestion is another French phrase picked up by British servicemen in France during the First World War: a *lieu d'aisance*, or 'place of ease', was a euphemism for 'lavatory'.

Rival The word originally meant 'person dwelling on opposite sides of a river', and comes from the Latin *rivalis*, 'one who shares the same river'. As water is a precious commodity, it became a frequent source of contention among both animals and humans.

It's a Gas

Gas The word was coined from Greek *khaos*, 'chaos', by the Flemish physician and chemist Jan Baptista van Helmont (1579–1644) as a term for the occult principle supposedly present in all bodies. He was almost certainly influenced by Paracelsus, who used the same Greek word to denote the proper element of spirits such as gnomes. The present technical sense of the word for a fluid that can expand without limit, such as air, arose in the late 18th century. The colloquial expression 'a gas', applied to anything hilarious, probably alludes to nitrous oxide, so-called laughing gas, used in anaesthetics since the 18th century.

Let off steam, To To give vent to pent-up feelings in words; to work off superabundant energy and high spirits in vigorous physical activity. The allusion is to the noisy escape of steam from the safety valve of a steam engine.

Limelight A vivid light, giving off little heat, produced by the combustion of oxygen and hydrogen on a surface of lime. Its main use developed in the theatre, where it was used to throw a powerful beam on one player on the stage to the exclusion of others. Hence the phrase 'to be in the limelight', to be in the full glare of public attention.

Sylph An elemental spirit of air, probably so named from a combination of Latin *silva*, 'wood', and Greek *numphē*, 'nymph'. 'Sylph' subsequently also came to mean a slender woman or girl.

A Pinch of Salt

Mithridate A former concoction named from Mithridates VI, king of Pontus and Bithynia (d. *c*.63 BC), who is said to have made himself immune from poisons by the constant use of antidotes. It was believed to be an antidote against poisons and contained 46 or more ingredients. Mithridates was said, in an account by the historian Pliny the Elder, to take his poison *cum grano salis*, 'with a grain of salt', in order to help it go down. It is from Pliny's account that we adopted the expression 'taken with a pinch of salt'.

Rub salt into someone's wounds, To To make a person's pain or shame even worse. The allusion is to the old sailing days, when errant sailors were flogged on the bare back and afterwards had salt rubbed in their wounds. This was to help heal the lacerations, but it also made them much more painful.

Salt The huge importance of salt in many civilizations accounts for a wealth of words and expressions with connections to it. Famously, the word 'salary' is based on the Latin *salarium* and denoted a Roman soldier's allowance, with which he could buy salt. It is the relative of 'salsa', from the Spanish for 'sauce', and later applied to a 'saucy' dance; 'sausage', or 'salted meat'; and 'salad', originally a plate of salted vegetables.

Sit above the salt, To To sit in a place of distinction. Formerly the family 'saler' (salt cellar) was of massive silver, and placed in the middle of the table. Persons of distinction sat above the 'saler', i.e. between it and the head of the table, while dependants and inferior guests sat below.

ALL AT SEA

Seasoned lexicographers will sometimes jokingly talk of CANOE, the Committee to Ascribe a Nautical Origin to Everything. There is, it seems, a perennial desire to put a large proportion of our vocabulary down to life on the high seas. Consider this habit alongside the very existence of an annual International Talk Like a Pirate Day, and it's clear that there is no shortage of fascination with our oceans. As it turns out, we will never need a secret cabal to invent a nautical story for our expressions, because our language is already awash with words and phrases whose inspiration was born on the waves.

Everything's Shipshape

Between the Devil and the deep (blue) sea Between two evils or alternatives, so that one is in a hazardous or precarious position. It is likely that this expression may be of nautical origin, the 'devil' being a seam in the hull of a ship that ran along the waterline.

Chock-a-block Completely full. This comes from the use of 'chock' for a ship's block (pulley) through which a line or rope passes, so that the sense is essentially 'block against block'.

Clear the decks, To To remove everything not required, especially when making ready for action. The allusion is to a sailing ship preparing for battle, when anything that was in the way of firing the guns was removed from the usually cluttered decks.

Cockpit The arena in which gamecocks were set to fight, also the name of a theatre built around 1618 on the site of a cockpit in Drury Lane. The word was also used for the after part of the lowest deck of an old man-of-war, an armed sailing ship. Hence the modern use of cockpit for the area near the stern of a small yacht where the helmsman sits, the driver's compartment in a racing car and the pilot's compartment in an aircraft.

Cross someone's bows, To To annoy someone and incur their displeasure. It is a breach of good manners for a junior ship to cross the bows of a senior.

Cut and run, To To escape in a hurry; to quit. In the days when a ship's anchor cable was made of hemp the cable was cut, if the occasion demanded it, and the vessel allowed to run before the wind. A classic example of this was when the Spanish Armada was anchored off Calais. Most of the captains cut their cables on the approach of England's fireships.

Cut of someone's jib A person's appearance, attitude, or manner. 'I don't like the cut of his jib' means 'I don't like the look of him'. 'Jib' here is the triangular foresail. Sailors used to recognize a vessel at sea by the cut of her jib.

Cutty sark A Scottish term for a short petticoat or short-tailed shirt, made famous by the *Cutty Sark*, the clipper built at Dumbarton in 1869 for Captain John Willis, shipowner and master mariner. It was badly damaged by fire while undergoing restoration in 2007. The name is taken from Burns's poem 'Tam o' Shanter' (1791), which was illustrated on the carvings round the ship's bows, but the figurehead was of a woman in flowing garments with an outstretched arm.

Fall foul of, To To quarrel with; to make an assault on someone. A rope is said to be foul when it is entangled, and one ship falls foul of another when they run against each other.

Flagship A ship carrying the flag officer. Figuratively, a flagship is something that a company or organization regards as its 'showpiece', such as a particular car model.

Flotsam and jetsam Properly, wreckage and other goods found in the sea. 'Flotsam' designates goods found floating on the sea (Old French *floter*, 'to float'), while 'jetsam' are the things thrown overboard to lighten the load of a ship in distress (a shortening of 'jettison', from Old French *getaison*, related to modern French *jeter*, 'to throw'). The term is now also applied to wreckage found on the shore. 'Flotsam and jetsam' later became a composite phrase meaning 'odds and ends'. 'Lagan', a word of uncertain origin, applies to goods thrown overboard but tied to a float for later recovery.

Forecastle or **fo'c's'le** So called because at one time the fore part of a ship was raised and protected like a castle, so that it could command the enemy's deck. Similarly the after part (now called the 'quarterdeck') was known as the 'after castle'. Soldiers were stationed in these castles to carry on the fighting. It has always been customary to place the crew's quarters in the fo'c's'le and the officers' quarters aft.

Gangway Originally the boarded way (sometimes called the 'gang-plank') in old galleys made for the rowers to pass from stem to stern, and where the mast was laid when it was unshipped (from an old sense of 'gang', meaning 'alley'). The term is now used for the portable bridge or walkway by which passengers enter or leave a ship.

Jolly Roger, The The black flag with white skull and cross-bones; the pirate flag. 'Roger' was originally thieves' cant for a thief or beggar, perhaps based on 'rogue'.

Junk Nautically speaking, 'junk' was originally old or discarded rope. The word is now applied generally to a miscellany of cast-off or unwanted articles, or of food with no nutritious value. It is also a slang term for narcotic drugs such as heroin and cocaine, an addict of which is called a 'junkie'.

Log An instrument for measuring the speed of a ship. In its simplest form it is a flat piece of wood, some 6in. (15cm) in radius, in the shape of a quadrant, and made so that it will float perpendicularly. To this is fastened the log-line, which is knotted at intervals. A logbook on a ship is the journal in which the logs or measurements are entered.

Money for old rope Easy money; money for nothing or very little; something that can be effected easily. In former sailing days, crew members would unpick the odd lengths of rope lying about the ship and sell the strands and strips to shipyards in the next port of call. There they would be hammered into the gaps in the deck planking before being covered in pitch.

Have no room to swing a cat, To To be in a restricted or cramped area. 'Cat' was an abbreviation for the fierce whip with nine lashes known as a 'cat-o'-nine-tails', and this expression may well refer to the restricted space on board old sailing ships where punishment with the cat was often administered.

Plimsoll line or **mark** The mark fixing the maximum load line of a merchant vessel in salt water. It takes its name from Samuel Plimsoll (1824–98), MP for Derby, who from 1870 led a campaign of protest against the overloading and overinsuring of unsafe shipping. The light canvas shoes known as 'plimsolls' probably take their name from the resemblance of the side of the sole to a Plimsoll line.

Port The left-hand side of a vessel when facing forward, with the word perhaps from 'port', 'harbour'. It replaced the earlier 'larboard', which was easily confused with 'starboard', so called from the days when the 'steerboard', or rudder, was carried over the right-hand side. It is presumed that 'port' derives from the fact that the larboard was towards the side of the port.

At the sharp end Directly involved in the action; up where the competition or danger is greatest. The allusion is not to the point of a sword, but to the bows of a ship, which first approach the enemy and any engagement.

Shipshape In proper order; as methodically arranged as things in a ship. When a sailing vessel was properly rigged and equipped she was said to be 'shipshape'. An extended version of the metaphor, 'shipshape and Bristol fashion', refers to the port of Bristol's reputation for efficiency in the days of sail.

Starboard and **larboard** 'Starboard' (denoting the right-hand side of a ship or aircraft facing forwards) is from Old English *stēor*, 'steering paddle', and *bord*, 'side'. 'Larboard' (denoting the left-hand side) is probably from Middle English *laden*, 'to load'.

Tarpaulin (probably from 'tar', 'pall', and '-ing') Properly, canvas sheeting made waterproof with tar; also, in former days, a sailor's hat made of tarred cloth (as were the waterproof jacket and trousers). Hence a colloquial term for a sailor, often abbreviated to 'tar' and so to 'Jack Tar'.

Tight ship, A Literally, a ship in which ropes, rigging, and so on are tied and taut and ready for use; hence a strictly run ship.

Up the pole Slightly mad; in difficulties. The pole is probably a ship's mast, which sailors were popularly judged crazy to climb.

Sailing Orders

Aback 'To be taken aback' is to be shocked or surprised. It originally referred to ships whose sails were pressed backwards against the mast by a headwind.

Bill of health A document given to the master of a ship by the consul of the port from which he comes, certifying that when the ship sailed no infectious disorder existed in the place. This is 'a clean bill of health', and the term is often used figuratively. A 'foul bill of health' means that the place from which the vessel sailed was infected.

Board In sailing, 'to make a board' is to make a distance, leg, or tack when working to windward. To take something on board is to accept or understand instructions, a new situation, or the like. In all its many senses the word derives from Old English *bord*, related to Old Norse *borth*, meaning 'ship's side', 'table'. The verb 'to board', meaning to enter a ship by force, was influenced by French *aborder*, 'to board', from the same word *bord*, meaning the side of a ship, as in 'starboard', 'overboard', etc.

Break the ice, To To be the first to do something; to dispel the stiffness and reserve of a first meeting or conversation. The allusion is to the breaking of a path in the ice to enable a ship to proceed.

By and large Generally speaking; on the whole. To sail by and large is to sail close to the wind and slightly off it, so making it easier for the helmsman to steer and less likely for the vessel to be 'taken aback'.

Dead in the water Unable to function effectively. The reference is not to a drowned person but to a ship that is unable to move for some reason, either because there is no current or no wind, or because her engine has failed.

Dogwatch Two-hour watches (4–6 p.m. and 6–8 p.m.) instead of the usual four-hour watches introduced to enable seamen to vary their daily watch-keeping rota. It is said to refer to the short sleeps traditionally taken by dogs.

Drop the pilot, To To let a ship's pilot leave after they have completed their task of guiding the vessel through a channel. Figuratively, the expression means to dismiss a tried and trusted leader. The phrase was popularized (in the wording 'Dropping the pilot') by John Tenniel's *Punch* cartoon (29 March 1890) showing Count Otto von Bismarck, wearing pilot's uniform, being dismissed by Kaiser Wilhelm II.

Footloose and fancy free Unattached romantically; 'young, free and single'. 'Footloose' refers to a sail on which the restraining ropes at the base (foot) have been slackened off (loosened) so that it flaps about capriciously.

Give a wide berth to, To To avoid; to keep at a distance from. The reference is to giving a ship plenty of room to swing when at anchor. The place where a ship is anchored or tied up is its berth.

Go large, To; to large it The expression received some impetus from the Harry Enfield film *Kevin and Perry Go Large* (2000), recounting teenage high jinks on Ibiza. Previously, 'to go large' had had a blameless but inconspicuous existence as a nautical term meaning 'to proceed at full sail with a favourable crosswind'.

Hail from, To To come from or belong to a place by birth or residence. The expression comes from the custom of hailing (attracting the attention of) passing ships to ascertain their port of departure.

Hand over fist Steadily and rapidly, as: 'He is making money hand over fist.' The allusion is to sailors climbing up or down the rigging. The notion is that one grasps a fistful of coins with one hand while reaching out for more with the other.

Hard and fast Strict; unalterable; fixed. A 'hard and fast rule' is one that must be rigidly kept. It was originally used of a ship run aground.

Hard up Short of money. When a vessel was forced by stress of weather to turn away from the wind, the helm was put 'hard up' to windward to alter course. So, when someone is 'hard up', they must weather the storm as best they can.

Knot As applied to the unit of speed for ships and aircraft, a knot is one nautical mile per hour. The sense of the unit of speed for ships is so called from the knots tied on a log-line formerly used on a ship in conjunction with the sandglass, the speed being the number of knots run out during the time measured by the sandglass.

At large At liberty. The phrase is of French origin, and *prendre le large* is to sail out to sea so as to be free to move.

Offing, In the Said of a ship visible at sea off the land. Such a ship is often approaching port, hence the phrase is used figuratively to mean 'about to happen', 'likely to occur', 'likely to take place', as: 'It looks as if there is a storm in the offing.'

Posh This colloquialism for 'grand' or 'first rate' is traditionally said to have originated in the old days of constant steamship travel between England and India. Passengers travelling by the P&O (Peninsular and Oriental) would, at some cost, book their return passage with the arrangement 'Port Outward Starboard Homeward', thus ensuring cabins on the cooler side of the ship, as it was usually unbearably hot when crossing the Indian Ocean. Passages were booked 'POSH' accordingly, and 'posh' soon came to be applied to a first-class passenger who could afford this luxury. There is, however, no concrete evidence for this explanation, and no mention of it surfaced until several decades after the usage is first recorded. The likeliest source is 19th-century London street slang 'posh', meaning money (probably from Romany *posh*, 'half, halfpenny'), which could easily have evolved to mean upper-class or grand.

Quarantine The period, originally 40 days, that a ship suspected of being infected with some contagious disorder is obliged to lie off port. The term is now applied to any period of segregation to prevent infection. In law the term was applied to the 40 days during which a widow who was entitled to a dower was entitled to remain in the chief house of her deceased husband. The term comes from the Italian *quaranta*, meaning 'forty', as the practice was first used at the port of Venice.

Sail close to the wind, To To keep the vessel's head as near as possible to the quarter from which the wind is blowing yet keeping the sails filled. Figuratively, to go to the verge of what decency or propriety allows, or to take a risk.

Sling one's hook, To To go away; to depart. The expression may allude to the anchor (hook), which must be secured in its sling at the bow before the ship can get under way.

Tell That to the Marines

Buccaneer This name was particularly applied to the sea rovers and pirates of England, France, and the Netherlands who marauded the Caribbean in the 17th century. It is derived through French *boucanier* from Old French *boucan*, a word of Tupi origin used for a frame for smoking meat. The adventurers learned how to prepare smoked meat from the indigenous inhabitants of Hispaniola, and came to combine this trade with their regular piracy. Hence the general use of the word to denote a pirate.

Davy Jones An 18th-century sailor's term for the evil spirit of the sea. Of the many conjectures as to its derivation the most plausible are that 'Davy' is an alteration of the West Indian *duppy* ('devil') and that Jones is an alteration of Jonah, who spent some time in the 'locker' of the whale's belly, or that Davy Jones was a pirate. Consequently, Davy Jones's locker is the sea, especially as the grave of drowned sailors.

Doldrums, The A condition of depression, slackness, or inactivity. The word was applied by sailors to regions where ships were likely to be becalmed and especially those parts of the ocean near the equator that are noted for calms and light winds. The word seems to have originated in Old English *dol*, 'dull', influenced by 'tantrum'.

Elmo's fire, St The luminous phenomenon that is sometimes observed round the masts of ships. 'Elmo', through 'Ermo', is an Italian alteration of 'Erasmus', the name of a 4th-century Syrian bishop who came to be regarded as the patron saint of seamen, and St Elmo's fire was attributed to him.

Landlubber An awkward or inept sailor is so called, as is someone who has had no experience at sea. A 'lubber' is a heavy, clumsy person, and 'lubberwort' is an old synonym for junk food.

Limey In US and (originally) Australian slang, a British sailor or ship, or just a Briton. The nickname derives from the practice of issuing lime juice to a ship's crew to combat scurvy.

Press gang The name formerly given to the naval practice of 'impressment', an ancient and arbitrary method of obtaining men for military service dating back to the early 13th century. The word has nothing to do with 'pressing' in the sense of 'forcing', but derives from the 'prest' or 'imprest' money (French *prêter*, 'to lend') advanced on enlistment, rather like the army's King's Shilling.

Scrape the barrel, To To be reduced to one's last resources; to make the best of what is left. The term is said to allude to the barrels of meat lined and sealed with fat which formed a ship's provisions. When the meat was used up, the crew would gain such sustenance as they could from the layers of fat in the discarded barrels.

Sea change, A An apparently magical change, as though brought about by the sea.

Show a leg Jump out of bed and be quick about it. A naval phrase, from the traditional formula used to call the hands from their hammocks, 'Wakey, wakey, rise and shine, the morning's fine . . . show a leg, show a leg, show a leg.' It comes from the days when women were allowed to sleep on board. They were allowed to 'lie in' and had to 'show a leg' to ensure that no sailor was still turned in.

Slush fund An emergency fund for unforeseen expenditure. The term arose out of Royal Navy slang 'slush' denoting refuse fat, the onshore sale of which (for the making of candles, for example) was a cook's perk.

Son of a gun This dated designation, originally implying contempt but now used with friendly familiarity, derives from the days when women were allowed to come on board. If a baby was born in the ship and paternity was uncertain, the child was entered in the log as 'Son of a gun'.

Spread-eagled A term originally used in the navy for the position of a man when he was lashed to the rigging for flogging, with outstretched arms and legs resembling wings. The word is now used for anyone with arms and legs outstretched, whether lying or standing.

Strike This term is commonly used nowadays to denote a cessation of work by a body of employees in industrial disputes. It is thought to have begun amongst sailors who were unhappy with their working conditions. They would 'strike', or lower, their ships' sails as a way of preventing them going to sea, only agreeing to raise them again once their demands were met.

Swing the lead, To To malinger or make up excuses. The allusion is to a lazy leadsman on a ship who idly swings the line and protracts the job of taking soundings.

Tell that to the Marines! Said of a far-fetched yarn. The story goes that Samuel Pepys, when retelling stories gathered from the navy to Charles II, mentioned flying fish. The courtiers were sceptical, but an officer of the Maritime Regiment of Foot said that he too had seen such. The king accepted this evidence and said, 'From the very nature of their calling no class of our subjects can have so wide a knowledge of seas and lands as the officers and men of Our Loyal Maritime Regiment. Henceforward ere ever we cast doubts upon a tale that lacks likelihood, we will first "Tell it to the Marines".'

Washout, A A fiasco; a failure. 'To wash out' as a verb is 'to cancel', 'to disregard', from the times when naval signal messages were taken down on a slate, which was washed clean when the message had been transmitted to the proper quarters.

Whistle for it, To It was an old superstition among sailors that when a ship was becalmed a wind could be raised by whistling, but to many seamen whistling was 'the Devil's music', which could raise a gale. It was not tolerated, therefore. The phrase 'you can whistle for it' now means 'you won't get it'.

What Shall We Do with the Drunken Sailor?

Grog Traditionally, rum mixed with water, but the term can be applied to any alcohol. It is said to come from Old Grog, the nickname given to the 18th-century Admiral Vernon on account of the coat made of 'grogram' (a heavy fabric) he always wore. It was he who ordered diluted rum to be served out to sailors instead of the traditional neat rum.

Mallemaroking An unusually precise term defined in the 1867 *Sailor's Word-Book* as 'the visiting and carousing of seamen in the Greenland ships'. The word comes from the obsolete Dutch *mallemerok*, a foolish or romping woman.

Pipe down Stop being aggressive or noisy; stop talking. A naval colloquialism derived from the boatswain's instruction of 'lights out', issued on their pipe (a whistle).

Skylark, To To amuse oneself in a frolicsome way; to jump around and be merry; to indulge in mild horseplay. The phrase was originally nautical and referred to the sports of the boys among the rigging after their work was done.

Splice the mainbrace, To A naval expression denoting an extra tot of grog all round, a very rare occurrence. It probably alludes to the issue of an extra rum ration to those who performed the hard and difficult task of splicing the mainbrace, the brace attached to the main yard. It is also used more generally for celebrating and indulging in strong drink.

Sun is over the yardarm, The An expression among naval officers and others indicating that the time has come to have a drink. In home waters and northern latitudes the sun would be over the yardarm – the outer extremity of a ship's 'yard', a spar slung across a ship's mast for the sail to hang from – towards noon.

Three sheets to the wind Very drunk. The sheet is the rope attached to the clew of a sail used for trimming sail. If the sheet is quite free, leaving the sail free to flap without restraint, the sheet is said to be 'in the wind', and 'a sheet in the wind' is a colloquial nautical expression for being tipsy. Thus to have 'three sheets in the wind' is to be very drunk.

Vice Admiral of the Narrow Seas According to Francis Grose, the chronicler of the 18th-century slang of ordinary people – including pickpockets, cardsharps, and taverners – this epithet was naval slang for 'a drunken man that pisses under the table into his companions' shoes'.

Admiral of the Narrow Seas To complete the picture, this individual is 'one who from drunkenness vomits into the lap of the person sitting opposite to him'.

FLYING COLOURS

Nail one's colours to the mast, To To refuse to admit defeat. Colours, or flags, nailed to a ship's mast in battle cannot be lowered as a sign of defeat or capitulation.

Peg To take someone down a peg is to take the conceit out of a braggart or pretentious person; to lower their self-esteem. The allusion is to a ship's colours, which used to be raised and lowered by pegs. The higher the colours are raised, the greater the honour, and to take them down a peg would be to diminish the honour. An alternative explanation refers to the ancient practice of sharing drink from a pegged container down to one's allotted peg.

Sail under false colours, To To pretend to be what one is not, with the object of personal advantage. The allusion is to pirate ships, which approached their prey with false colours at the mast.

With flying colours Triumphantly; easily. The allusion is to a victorious fleet sailing into port with flags still flying at the mastheads.

COLOURFUL

'Red and yellow and pink and green . . .' Despite the children's song, there are no pure colours in a rainbow, for they are all part of a continuous spectrum. But colours are as important to our lives as they are to our imagination, and their cultural histories are embedded in dozens of English expressions – whether we paint the town red, are tickled pink, sing the blues, or pen some purple prose.

Red

Doomfire The poet Gerard Manley Hopkins created 'doom-fire' to describe the vibrant reds and oranges of a sunset, as though the apocalypse is approaching.

Magenta A brilliant red aniline dye derived from coal tar, named in commemoration of the bloody Battle of Magenta (1859), when the Austrians were defeated by the French and Sardinians. This was just before the dye was discovered.

Miniature Originally, a rubrication or a small painting in an illuminated manuscript, which was done with 'minium', or red lead. The word came to express any small portrait or picture.

Paint the town red, To To celebrate without inhibition. The phrase is first recorded in the USA in the 1870s, but a popular story links it with the exploits of the 19th-century Marquess of Waterford, who on the night of 5 April 1837 went on a drunken and vandalizing spree with pots of red paint in the town of Melton Mowbray. The expression doesn't appear until half a century after the event, so the link is not conclusive.

Red-handed To be caught red-handed is to be caught in the act, as if with blood on the hands.

Red rag In the phrase 'like a red rag to a bull', the reference is to anything that is calculated to excite rage. Toreadors' capes are lined with red, although there is no evidence that the colour itself incenses bulls.

Rubric The liturgical directions and titles in a Book of Common Prayer are known as the rubrics because these were (and sometimes still are) printed in red. The directions given on formal examination papers concerning the selection of questions to be answered are also sometimes called the rubrics. The word is from the Latin *rubrica* (*terra*), 'red earth', referring to the use of ochre as a writing material.

Scarlet letter In the early days in Puritan New England a scarlet A, for 'adulteress', was branded or sewn on a guilty woman's dress.

Pink

In the pink In excellent health. The phrase is an abbreviation of the expression 'in the pink of health' or 'in the pink of condition', meaning in the 'flower' or best state.

Porcelain The word comes from Italian *porcellana*, 'cowrie shell', referring to the ceramic material's pale and glossy shell-like finish. This word itself is the adjective of *porcella*, 'little sow', the allusion apparently being to the curve in a pig's back and to its similar colour.

Tickled pink or **to death** Very amused or pleased. A tickled person will often be red in the face from laughing.

Yellow

London particular A colloquial term used in the 19th and early 20th centuries for a London fog. The sulphurous coal smoke of the period gave London smogs a yellowish tinge (whence the name 'pea-souper', after soup made from yellow split peas).

Mellow yellow Dried banana skins, which were widely believed in the 1960s to produce a hallucinatory effect when smoked. The term was popularized by the 1967 song 'Mellow Yellow' by the Scottish folk singer Donovan.

Yellow-bellies A name given to natives of Lincolnshire, in humorous allusion to the frogs found in the fenland districts.

Yellow ribbon A tradition evolved in the US of using yellow ribbons to decorate the home or home town of a person or group of people returning from danger. The song 'Tie a Yellow Ribbon 'round the Ole Oak Tree' (concerning a prisoner returning from jail) was a chart-topping hit (1973) for the pop group Tony Orlando and Dawn, and it made the expression familiar worldwide.

Blue

Blue The colour is traditionally associated in English idiom with sadness or dejection. To have 'the blues' is short for the 'blue devils', demons once believed to visit alcoholics suffering from delirium tremens, or the DTs. The idea crept into human emotion and music – the 'blues' was a kind of music that expressed a singer's struggles as well as passions. A rude joke may be described as blue because sex workers were once made to wear blue gowns in prison, and because a censor's pencil was also blue.

Once in a blue moon Very rarely. On rare occasions the moon does appear to be blue. The cause is minute dust parti-cles in the upper atmosphere, which block the light from the red end of the spectrum and scatter light from the blue end.

True blue A lasting blue, hence a type of constancy. A true blue is one who is constant, steadfast, loyal, and faithful, perhaps from the idea of such qualities being characteristic of blue blood.

Purple

Purple A synonym for the rank of Roman emperor, derived from the colour of the emperor's dyed woollen robe. Purple robes were a mark of dignity among the ancient Greeks and

Romans and were worn by kings, magistrates, and military commanders, hence the colour became a symbol of luxury and power. It was obtained from shellfish (*Buccinum*, *Murex*) and the deep colour was termed *purpura* (from the name of one of these molluscs). Tyrian purple, which was made from a mixture of these shellfish, was particularly costly to produce. From the 16th century, 'purple prose' has been writing that is ornate or over-elaborate.

Light . . .

Candidate A person who seeks nomination for a position or who applies for official acceptance in some way, as by an interview or an examination. The word is from the Latin *candidatus*, meaning 'clothed in white'. Those Roman citizens campaigning for public office would dress themselves in a loose white robe, white being a symbol of integrity and purity.

Silver screen, The An epithet applied to the cinema (as in 'stars of the silver screen'). Originally, cinema screens were given a reflective surface by the application of metallic paint.

White Paper A government publication printed for the information of Parliament. Such a report or statement of policy is not bulky enough to warrant the protective covers of a 'blue book', used for reports issued from Parliament or the Privy Council.

. . . and Dark

As black as Newgate's knocker Very dark, in colour or character. The simile draws on Newgate prison's notoriety as a place of death.

Dimpsy A word from south-west England for the dying of the light, or dusk, and a poetic variation on 'dim'.

Twitter-light A 17th-century term for 'twilight', referring to the tremulous chirruping of birds as dusk descends.

Wolf-light The writer and language collector Robert Macfarlane has documented this as coming from the French phrase *l'heure entre chien et loup*, 'the hour between the dog and the wolf': the time when things move from the familiar to the wild.

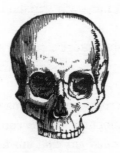

THE BODY

Supercilious, gorgeous, courageous, capricious . . . Expressive adjectives all, but you might not guess that there is a common thread between them. All are based on parts of the body. A 'supercilious' individual might raise an eyebrow (*supercilium*, in Latin) in disdain. A 'gorgeous' one might wear precious jewellery around their throat (the French *gorge*). Any 'courageous' person will demonstrate a lot of heart (Latin *cor*), while a 'capricious' character might flit around so impulsively that their hair will whimsically stand on end – the Italian *capriccio* means 'hedgehog head'.

Beyond such invisible beginnings are many more literal expressions that root our emotions and our behaviour in the physical.

Head over Heels

Achilles tendon (*tendo Achillis*) A strong sinew connecting the heel and calf, which is frequently strained by athletes. Greek myth tells how Thetis took her son Achilles by the heel and dipped him in the River Styx to make him invulnerable – but the heel in her hand remained dry. The hero was slain by an arrow wound in the heel, his only weak spot. The phrase 'Achilles heel' is thus used for a person's small but potentially damaging weakness.

Adam's apple The visible projection of the thyroid cartilage of the larynx at the front of the neck, so called from the story that a piece of the forbidden fruit stuck in Adam's throat. To have a prominent Adam's apple was once described in English dialect as being 'cockthroppled'.

Bowels of mercy Compassion, sympathy. The emotions were once closely associated with a particular organ of the body. The head was regarded as the seat of understanding, the heart was the seat of affection and memory (hence 'learning by heart'), the bowels were the seat of mercy, and the spleen was the seat of passion or anger.

Bum The word has two distinct uses, of different origins. Among the British, the word is first and foremost used for the buttocks or posterior. In the US, it is a term for a vagrant, and hence any worthless person or (adjectivally) thing (e.g. 'a bum deal'). While the British sense is of uncertain origin, the US sense derives from the German *bummeln*, 'to loaf'.

Cold feet A state of fear or apprehension; a 'funk'. It is thought to have originated with the story of a poker player who offered up a feeble excuse for abandoning a losing game, saying his feet were cold.

Eyeteeth The canine teeth, so called because they are located (in the upper and lower jaw) just under the eyes. 'To give one's eyeteeth for' means to go to any length for something or to make any sacrifice for it.

Funny bone A pun on the word *humerus*, the Latin name for the arm bone.

Gall Bile, the bitter fluid secreted by the liver. Hence the figurative use of the word as a symbol for anything of extreme bitterness.

Head over heels Literally, 'turning a somersault', hence 'completely', 'utterly', as: 'head over heels in love', when one is quite 'bowled over'. The expression was originally more logical: 'heels over head'.

Keep your pecker up As the mouth is in the head, 'pecker' (the mouth) means the head, and so 'keep your pecker up' means 'keep your head up'; in other words 'keep your chin up', 'never say die'.

Kow-tow (Chinese *ketou*, literally 'knock head') A Chinese custom of kneeling down and knocking the head on the ground as a sign of reverence, homage, or respect. Hence, in popular usage, to kow-tow is to behave obsequiously to someone, to fawn or to grovel.

Sanguine From Latin *sanguis*, *sanguinis*, meaning 'blood'. It was believed that a person with a good balance of blood had cheeks that were red with good health and well-being. From this it was easy to extend the meaning to a person who was full of vitality, vivacious, confident, and hopeful.

Off Kilter

Bats in the belfry To have bats in the belfry is to be crazy, bats here being the nocturnal kind. The 'belfry' is the human head. In French, someone similarly viewed is said to have *une araignée au plafond* (to have spiders on the ceiling).

Hysteria Generally, a wild uncontrollable emotion or excitement, often accompanied by weeping or laughing. In a narrower medical sense, hysteria is a functional disturbance of the nervous system and of psychoneurotic origin. The word itself comes from Greek *hustera*, 'womb', since it was originally associated with a disturbance of the uterus and its functions. It was thus formerly believed to be a physical disorder confined to women. Even today, 'hysterical' is very rarely used of men.

Lose one's marbles, To To become unhinged. The origin of the phrase (which dates from the 1920s) is uncertain. One suggestion is that it derives from a story about a small boy whose marbles were carried off by a monkey. An unlikely alternative source is rhyming slang: 'marbles and conkers' standing for 'bonkers'.

Give someone the pip, To To make them thoroughly 'fed up', downhearted, and miserable. The word is probably connected with 'pip', the poultry disease that causes birds to pine away.

A Proper Handful

Dab Clever or skilled, as commonly in the phrase 'a dab hand'. The word probably comes from 'dab' in the sense of 'touch lightly'.

Dextrous The original meaning of 'dextrous', from the Latin *dexter*, was 'right-handed'. As that has long been regarded as the favourable side, as opposed to the left (*sinister* in Latin), the adjective came to mean 'skilled'. In heraldry, the term 'dexter' is applied to that side of the shield to the right of the person holding it, hence it is the left side of the shield as seen by the viewer.

Digits (Latin *digitus*, 'finger') The first nine numerals are so called from the habit of counting as far as ten on the fingers. 'Digital' data, expressed as series of digits, is an extension of the same idea.

Fingers crossed An allusion to the superstition that making the sign of the cross will avert bad luck.

Fingerspitzengefühl German for 'fingertips feeling', and used for an intuitive flair or instinct for something.

Knuckle down, To To work away; to be diligent. The expression was first used in the game of marbles, when a player would place their knuckles on the ground in shooting the taw.

Knuckle under, To To acknowledge defeat; to give in; to submit. An allusion to the old custom of striking the underside of a table with the knuckles when defeated in an argument.

Maintenance This is ultimately from the Latin *manu tenere*, meaning 'to hold in the hand'.

Medicinal finger Otherwise known as the 'ring finger', this was so called in medieval times because of the notion that it contained a vein that led direct to the heart.

Middle finger Showing someone the middle finger has been a gesture of obscenity since ancient times. The Romans even called it the *digitus impudicus*, or 'indecent finger', for it was widely interpreted as a suggestion of an erect penis (another obscene hand gesture, the V-sign, might then suggest a double penis).

The historian Tacitus wrote of a battle in which German tribesmen collectively gave advancing Roman soldiers the middle finger.

Palm off, To To pass off fraudulently. The allusion is to a magician, who conceals in the palm of a hand what he pretends to dispose of in some other way.

Thumb In the ancient Roman combats, when a gladiator was vanquished, it rested with the spectators to decide whether he should be slain or not. If they wished him to live, they enclosed their thumbs in their fists. If they wished him to be slain, they turned their thumbs out. The popular saying 'thumbs up', expressive of pleasure or approval, is probably a development from this custom, as is its opposite, 'thumbs down', even though their currrent meaning is a near reversal of the ancient Roman tradition.

Thimble From Old English *thy-mel*, 'thumbstall', so called because it was originally worn on the thumb, just as a handle is operated by the hand.

The Eyes Have It

Eye service Unwilling service, of the sort only done when one's master is looking (by an eye-servant).

Forty winks A colloquial term for a short nap or a doze. The earliest meaning of 'wink' was to close the eyes fully rather than blink – hence 'hoodwinking' someone by pulling a hood over their eyes.

Iris The goddess of the rainbow or the rainbow itself. In classical mythology she was the messenger of the gods, and each rainbow was a bridge or road let down from heaven for her to travel along. The coloured area of the eye surrounding the pupil is also called the iris, because it can be a variety of colours.

Pupil The pupil of the eye – the dark circular opening in the centre of the iris – takes its name from the Latin *pupilla*, 'little doll'. When one looks into the eyes of another, one sees a tiny, doll-like reflection of oneself.

Scare the living daylights out of To frighten badly or startle suddenly. The daylights were originally the eyes, but the term was extended to any vital organ.

Turn a blind eye, To To pretend tactfully not to see; to overlook in order to avoid embarrassment to all concerned. At the Battle of Copenhagen (1801) Admiral Nelson reputedly disregarded an order to disengage by putting his telescope to his blind eye and averring that he saw no signal from Admiral Sir Hyde Parker's ship.

In Your Face

Deadpan Emotionless, expressionless, of a person's face or manner. 'Pan' here is a colloquial word meaning 'face'.

Mug In the 18th century, drinking mugs commonly represented a grotesque human face. This may be the origin of the slang use of 'mug' to mean 'face'. Today's 'mugger' also looks back to this sense: to 'mug' someone in boxing was to punch them in the face.

Mum's the word An admonition to keep what is told you a profound secret. The phrase 'to keep mum' means to keep silent or not to speak to or tell anyone something. The word 'mum' represents a sound made with closed lips.

One's tongue in one's cheek Said of something spoken insincerely or ironically, when one says one thing but means another. In the early 19th century the forcing of the tongue into the left cheek served as a secret signal of disbelief for the speaker at the time.

Sardonic smile or **laughter** The Greek epic poet Homer, of the 8th century BC, used the word *sardanios* to describe bitter, scornful laughter. Later Greeks and Romans interpreted his adjective as *sardonios*, 'Sardinian', and as referring to a 'Sardinian plant' that produced facial contortions resembling horrible laughter, usually followed by death. English adopted 'sardonic' in the mid 17th century with this same idea, to refer to grimly derisive or cynical smiles or laughter.

Shamefaced With a sheepish or guilty expression. The word was originally 'shamefast' (like 'steadfast'), meaning 'bashful', 'modest'.

Stiff upper lip, A A firm resolve coupled with a suppression of the emotions. A supposed traditional characteristic of the British, even though the phrase was originally North American and is first recorded in Harriet Beecher Stowe's *Uncle Tom's Cabin*.

Wet one's whistle, To To have a drink, one's whistle being one's lips.

Paying Through the Nose

Grogblossom The reddened nose that can be the result of long-term alcohol consumption.

Nark or **copper's nark** An antiquated term for a police spy or informer, from a Romany word, *nāk*, 'nose'.

Nosey Very inquisitive; overfond of poking one's nose into the business of others. One who does this is a Nosey Parker, a name popularly said to allude to Matthew Parker, Archbishop of Canterbury (1504–75), who was noted for the detailed articles of inquiry concerning ecclesiastical affairs and the conduct of the clergy. However, the name is first recorded only in the early 20th century, so such a reference seems unlikely. Nosey Parker was the nickname given to a man who spied on courting couples in Hyde Park, London and featured in a popular postcard caption.

On the nose A US expression meaning exactly on time. The nose of a horse was used as an indication of the smallest possible winning margin in a race.

Pay through the nose It is said that in the 9th century the Danes imposed a poll tax in Ireland and that this was called the 'Nose Tax' because those who neglected to pay were punished by having their noses slit. More likely is that paying any hefty price might, metaphorically speaking, give the payer a 'nosebleed'.

Toffee-nosed In its sense of 'supercilious', the word is a pun on 'toff', this being a 'superior' person who looks down his nose at others.

Bad Hair Day

Five o'clock shadow The beginnings of a new beard on a man's clean-shaven face, visible at about this time of day. The expression dates from the 1930s, when it was first used in an advertising campaign for Gem razor blades. Five o'clock shadow is said to have reinforced Richard Nixon's untrustworthy image and scuppered his first bid for the US presidency, when he refused to wear make-up in a televised debate with his opponent John F. Kennedy in 1960.

Sideburns Short side whiskers, originally called 'burn-sides' after the US Federal General Ambrose Everett Burnside (1824–81), who wore such whiskers. As the reference faded, 'sideburns' made more sense.

Widow's peak A V-shaped point of hair over the forehead, reminiscent of the front cusp of the cap formerly worn by widows.

WIGS ON THE GREEN

Wig A shortened form of 'periwig' (earlier, 'perwig'), from French *perruque*. The long flowing wig of Louis XIV's reign (1643–1715) was called the *allonge* ('lengthening'), and in the 18th century there were 30 or 40 different styles and names, including the artichoke, bag, barrister's, bishop's, Blenheim, brush, buckle, busby, bush (buzz), campaigning, cauliflower, chain, chancellor's corded, Count Saxe's mode, crutch, cut bob, Dalmahoy (a bob wig worn by tradesmen), detached buckle, drop, Dutch, full, half natural, Jansenist bob, judge's, ladder, long bob, Louis, pigeon's wing, rhinoceros, rose, she-dragon, small back, spinach seed, staircase, wild boar's back, and wolf's paw.

Wigs on the green A serious disagreement likely to lead to a scrimmage or rumpus. The expression is of Irish origin. Wigs are liable to be pulled off or fall on the grass in a tussle.

ROCK BOTTOM

'A whizpopper!' cried the BFG . . . 'Whizzpopping is a sign of happiness! It is music in our ears!'

ROALD DAHL: *The BFG* (1982)

Buttock-mail A fine once exacted by the church in commutation of sitting on the stool of repentance for sex outside of marriage.

Callipygian Having buttocks that are beautifully proportioned or finely developed. Borrowed from an epithet of Aphrodite, the Greek goddess of love, beauty and desire. *Kallipygos*, from *kallos*, 'beauty', and *pyge*, 'buttock', is one of the more charming nicknames for the goddess.

Dasypygal Having hairy buttocks.

Fart An Old English word related to the German *furzen*. It was originally a more respectable word than it is now. In the 14th century, to 'not give a fart' was to not care at all.

Feisty Spirited and exuberant. Rooted in an obsolete word *feist* or *fist* meaning 'small dog', 'fisting cur' or 'fisting hound' were derogatory terms for a lapdog, deriving from the old verb *fist*, meaning 'to break wind'.

Fizzle The earliest meaning, in the 16th century, was 'to break wind quietly'. It may also go back to the word *fist* which gave us 'feisty'.

Partridge From *perdix*, the Greek name for the bird, which is probably related to *perdesthai*, 'to break wind', in reference to the chirring noise of the bird's wings.

Prat Originally, in the 17th century, a single buttock, and later a person's bottom.

Pratfall A comedy fall onto one's buttocks.

Pygophilia Sexual arousal from seeing or touching the buttocks of another person.

THE CALENDAR

The measuring of time has shaped our history. Every civilization for which evidence survives has tracked it using various methods, from the Neolithic hill chambers through which sunlight would announce the winter solstice, to today's clocks in which time is measured in atoms. No matter whether we measure out our lives with calendars or, as T.S. Eliot put it, with coffee spoons, the language of time trickles through our language as surely as the sand in an Egyptian hourglass.

Red-Letter Days

Calendar The word comes from Medieval Latin *kalendarium*, 'account book', itself from *Kalendae*, Calends, the day at the beginning of each month when interest on debts became due in the Roman calendar. 'Calends' comes from Latin *calare*, 'to proclaim', and is said to have originated in the calling of citizens together on the first day of the month, when the pontifex informed them of the time of the new moon, and the festivals and sacred days to be observed.

Dismal Derived from Latin *dies mali*, 'evil days', in medieval times the word – as part of the term 'dismal days' – referred to 24 specific days of the year that were regarded as unlucky. The meaning became more general as old superstitions faded.

Gaudy (Latin *gaudium*, 'joy') A holiday, a feast day, especially an annual celebration of some event, such as the foundation of a college.

Leap year A year of 366 days, a bissextile year, i.e. in the Julian and Gregorian calendars any year whose date is exactly divisible by four except those that are divisible by 100 but not by 400.

In ordinary years, the day of the month that falls on Monday this year will fall on Tuesday next year, and Wednesday the year after, but the fourth year will 'leap over' Thursday to Friday. This is because a day is added to February, the reason being that the astronomical year (i.e. the time that it takes the earth to go around the sun) is approximately 365¼ days, or more precisely 365.2422, the difference between .25 and .2422 being righted by the loss of the three days in 400 years.

It is an old saying that during a leap year the ladies may propose, and, if not accepted, may claim a silk gown.

Month At one time, a new month started on the day of the new moon or the day after. Hence the name (Old English *mōnath*), which is connected with 'moon'.

Moon The word is probably related to the Sanskrit root *men-*, 'to measure', because time has long been measured by the phases of the moon.

Movable feasts Annual church feasts that do not fall on a fixed date but are determined by certain established rules. Easter Day, which can fall on any date from 22 March to 25 April, is a notable example. Colloquially, the phrase denotes mealtimes (and lifestyles) that are liable to change.

Overmorrow A sadly faded term for 'the day after tomorrow'.

Red-letter day A lucky day; a day to be recalled with delight. In almanacs and more commonly in ecclesiastical calendars, important feast days and saints' days were printed in red, with other days in black.

Se'nnight A week, literally seven nights, on the same lines as 'fortnight' for fourteen nights.

Solstice The summer solstice is 21 June and the winter solstice is 22 December. They are so called because on or about these dates the sun reaches its extreme northern and southern points in the ecliptic and appears to stand still (Latin *sol*, 'sun', and *sistere*, 'to stand') before it turns back on its apparent course.

Vespers The sixth of the canonical hours in the Greek and Roman Churches, with the name sometimes also used of the evening service in the English Church. The word comes from Latin *vesperus*, 'evening', and is a relative of Hesperus, the evening star.

Yonks A slang word meaning 'a long time', especially in the phrase 'for yonks'. It emerged in general use in the 1960s. Its origin is probably a play on 'donkey's years', itself a pun on the length of the animal's ears.

The Year

January The month dedicated by the Romans to JANUS, who presided over the entrance to the year and, having two faces, could look back to the past year and forward to the new. The Dutch used to call this month *Lauwmaand* ('frosty month'), while the Saxons knew it as *Wulfmōnath*, because wolves were very troublesome then from the great scarcity of food. After the introduction of Christianity, the name was changed to *æftera Gēola* ('after Yule').

Handsel A gift for good luck at the beginning of the year. Hence Handsel Monday, the first Monday of the year, when small gifts were given, before Boxing Day took its place. Its name is based on the Old English word *handselen*, meaning 'delivery into the hand'.

February The Dutch used to call the month *Spokkel-maand* ('vegetation month'). The Anglo-Saxons knew it as *Solmōnath* ('mud month').

Groundhog Day In the US, the 2nd of February, from the saying that the groundhog first appears from hibernation on that day. If it sees its shadow, it goes back to its burrow for another six weeks, indicating six more weeks of winter weather. The general idea is that a sunny day (when it sees its shadow) means a late spring, whereas a cloudy day (when it does not see it) means an early spring.

The 1993 film *Groundhog Day*, starring Bill Murray, tells the story of a cynical weatherman made a better person when forced to relive, daily, the Groundhog Day celebrations in a small town.

March The month is named after the god Mars. The old Saxon name was *Hrēthmōnath*, perhaps meaning 'rough month', from its boisterous winds. This subsequently became *Lencten-mōnath* ('lengthening month').

Lent The Saxons called March *Lenctenmōnath* (from Old English *lencten*, 'spring', literally 'lengthening') because in this month the days noticeably lengthen. As the chief part of the great fast, from Ash Wednesday to Easter, falls in March, it received the name *Lenctenfœsten*, or Lent. The fast of 36 days was introduced in the 4th century, but it did not become fixed at 40 days until the early 7th century, thus corresponding with Christ's fast in the wilderness.

Shrovetide The three days just before the beginning of Lent, when people went to confession and afterwards indulged in all sorts of sports and merrymaking. 'Shrove' is the past tense of 'shrive', to confess one's sins and seek penance. Shrove Tuesday, the day before Ash Wednesday, is also known as Pancake Day.

Mardi Gras (French, 'fat Tuesday') Shrove Tuesday, the day before Lent starts. In Paris, a fat ox, crowned with a fillet, used to be paraded through the streets. It was accompanied by mock priests and a band of tin instruments in imitation of a Roman sacrificial procession. Nowadays, New Orleans, Rio de Janeiro, and Venice are perhaps the most famous cities celebrating Mardi Gras.

Maundy Thursday The day before Good Friday is so called from the first words of the antiphon for that day: *Mandatum novum do vobis* ('A new commandment I give unto you', John 13:34). Gifts of 'Maundy money' are given by the sovereign to the number of aged poor men and women that corresponds with the sovereign's age.

Good Friday The Friday before Easter, held as the anniversary of the crucifixion. 'Good' here means 'holy'. Both Christmas and Shrove Tuesday used to be called 'the Good Tide'.

Easter The name was adopted for the Christian Paschal festival from Old English *Ēastre*, a heathen festival held at the vernal equinox in honour of Eastre, a Germanic goddess of the dawn. Her own name relates to 'east'.

April The month when trees unfold and the earth opens with new life. Its Old English name was *Eastermōnath*, 'Easter month'. 'April' is popularly believed to be from Latin *aperire*, 'to open', because it is the month in which trees and flowers open in the northern hemisphere. It is, however, probably of Etruscan origin.

April fool A person fooled or tricked on All Fools' Day (1 April), called in France *un poisson d'avril* ('an April fish') and in Scotland a *gowk* ('cuckoo'). There are many theories as to its beginnings. One involves the Roman festival of Cerealia, held at the beginning of April. The story is that Proserpina was playing in the Elysian meadows and had just filled her lap with daffodils, when Pluto carried her off to the lower world. Her mother, Ceres, heard the echo of her screams, and went in search of the echo. Her search, however, was a fool's errand.

May The Anglo-Saxons called this month *Thrimilcemonath*, because then cows can be milked three times a day. The present name is the Latin *Maius*, from Maia, the goddess of growth and increase.

May Day The 1st of May, celebrated in many countries as a traditional springtime festival. It is unrelated to 'Mayday', the international distress call used by ships and aircraft, which is an alteration of the French *m'aider* in *venez m'aider!* ('come and help me!').

Cast not a clout till May is out An old warning not to shed winter clothing too early in the year. 'Clout' here is a rag or patch, hence a piece of clothing. 'May' is also another name for hawthorn, which blossoms in May. Thus some hold that the proverb means 'do not discard clothing until the hawthorn blossoms'.

June The sixth month, probably named from the Roman *gens* or clan name *Junius*, related to *juvenis*, 'young'. The Anglo-Saxons called it *Sēremōnath* ('dry month').

July The seventh month, named by Mark Antony in honour of Julius Caesar. It was formerly called *Quintilis*, as it was the fifth month of the Roman year. The old Dutch name for it was *Hooy-maand* ('hay month'), while the Anglo-Saxons knew it as *Mœdmōnath* ('meadow month'), because the cattle were turned into the meadows to feed then. Until the 18th century, 'July' was accented on the first syllable, to rhyme with 'ruly'.

Dog days Days of great heat. The Romans called the hottest weeks of the summer *caniculares dies*. Their theory was that the Dog Star, Sirius, rising with the sun, added to its heat, and that the dog days (about 3 July to 11 August) bore the combined heat of both.

Thermidor The eleventh month of the French Revolutionary Calendar, corresponding to the period from 20 July to 18 August. Its name means 'gift of heat', from Greek *thermē*, 'heat', and *dōron*, 'gift'. The dish 'lobster thermidor' (pieces of lobster in a shallot or cream sauce, cooked *au gratin* in the half-shell) is so called because it was apparently created, at 'Chez Marie', a famous Paris restaurant, on the evening of the premiere of *Thermidor*, a play by Victorien Sardou, in 1894.

Silly season A journalistic expression for the part of the year when Parliament and the Law Courts are not sitting (usually August and September), when, through lack of news, the papers have to fill their columns with trivial items, such as news of giant gooseberries and sea serpents.

August Formerly called *Sextilis* in the Roman calendar, as the sixth month from March, when the year began. The name was changed to 'Augustus' in 8 BC in honour of Augustus, the first Roman emperor, whose 'lucky month' it was. The Old English name was *Wēodmōnath*, 'weed month', *wēod* meaning 'grass' or 'herbs'.

September The seventh month from March, when the year formerly commenced. The Anglo-Saxon name was *Hærfestmō nath*, 'harvest month', or after the introduction of Christianity *Hāligmōnath*, 'holy month', the nativity of the Virgin Mary being on the 8th, the Exaltation of the Cross on the 14th, and St Michael's Day on the 29th.

Gossamer The filmy, delicate cobwebs spun by small spiders, which float in the air or settle upon grass particularly in the autumn. The word is believed to to be a shortened version of 'goose summer', because the webs are visible particularly in calm clear weather, and look a little like the down of a goose.

Indian summer A term of US origin now generally applied to a period of fine sunny weather in late autumn. The name may have arisen at a time when such weather was more pronounced in the lands then occupied by indigenous Native American peoples.

Libra (Latin, 'balance') The seventh sign of the Zodiac and the name of one of the ancient constellations, which the sun enters about 22 September and leaves about 22 October. At this time the day and night, being 'weighed', would be found equal.

October The eighth month of the ancient Roman calendar, from Latin *octo*, 'eight'. The Old English name was *Winmonath*, 'wine month', as this was the time of vintage.

November The ninth month in the ancient Roman calendar, from Latin *novem*, 'nine'. The Anglo-Saxon name was *Blōtmō nath*, literally 'blood month', as this was the time when the beasts were slain and salted down for winter use. Another Saxon name was *Windmōnath*, 'wind month', when fishermen beached their boats and stopped fishing until the next spring.

All Hallows Day Another name for All Saints' Day (1 November), 'hallows' deriving from Old English *hālig*, 'holy'.

December (Latin, 'tenth month') The Old English name was *ærra gēola*, 'earlier Yule'. In the French Revolutionary Calendar it was *Frimaire* ('hoarfrost month'), from 22 November to 21 December.

Boxing Day The day after Christmas Day, also known as St Stephen's Day. Boxes placed in churches for casual offerings used to be opened on Christmas Day, and the contents, called the 'dole of the Christmas box' or the 'box money', were distributed next day by priests. Apprentices also used to carry a box around to their masters' customers for small gratuities. Postmen received such gifts until after the Second World War.

Noel In English, a Christmas carol, or the shout of joy in a carol, and also, as in French, an alternative name for Christmas (as 'The first Nowell'). Noël (or Noel) is a traditional name given to a person born at Christmas-time. The word ultimately comes from Latin *dies natalis*, 'birthday'.

Yule or **Yuletide** The Christmas season. From Old English *geōla*, related to Old Norse *jōl*, the name of a pagan festival at the winter solstice.

THE DAYS OF THE WEEK

Our names for days of the week are based on translations of Latin terms. Days of the week in ancient Rome were named after the gods, but the equivalent Germanic gods were substituted in some cases.

Sunday For centuries the first day of the week, anciently dedicated to the sun, but in many modern diaries and calendars, the seventh day.

Monday The second day of the week, called by the Anglo-Saxons *mōnandæg*, 'day of the moon'.

Tuesday The third day of the week, or popularly the second, named after Tiu (the son of Odin and a younger brother of Thor), who was identified with Mars, the Roman god of war.

Wednesday Originally, the day dedicated to Woden, or Odin, of Scandinavian mythology, the supreme god and creator, god of victory and the dead. In French it is *mercredi*, 'Mercury's day'.

Thursday The day of the god Thor, called by the French *jeudi*, i.e. 'Jove's day'. Both Jupiter (Jove) and Thor were gods of thunder, and Thursday was sometimes called Thunderday.

Friday The sixth day of the week (or fifth counting from Monday). In ancient Rome it was called *dies Veneris*, 'day of Venus', hence French *vendredi*. The northern nations adopted the same idea and the nearest equivalent to Venus was Frigg or Freyja, hence Friday (Old English *frīgedæg*).

Saturday Known by the Anglo-Saxons as *Sæternes dæg*, after the Latin *Saturni dies*, the day of Saturn.

Sabbath The day of rest, which is considered by Jews to be Saturday, and by Christians, Sunday. The Law of Moses dictated that every seventh year should also be observed as a 'sabbath', during which the land lay fallow. This became known as the 'sabbatical' year, in which 'sabbatical' means 'of the sabbath'. In the late 19th century, US universities borrowed the idea to give academic staff every seventh year free to research or travel. 'Sabbath' ultimately comes from the Hebrew *sabat*, 'to rest'.

WEATHER STATION

It's the stereotypical British obsession: the subject that can inspire both small talk and in-depth conversations about everything from climate change to party contingency plans. (In particular, rain, which demands its own special category here.) Much of our lives is as circumscribed by the weather as it ever was, and it follows therefore that we have hundreds of words and expressions with which to describe it. It also provides an enduring metaphor for our emotional state – whether we are simply 'under the weather' or 'on cloud nine'.

Bolt from the Blue

Brass monkey A phrase commonly used in expressions denoting extreme coldness, such as 'cold enough to freeze the balls off a brass monkey'. It is often said that the reference is to a type of brass rack or 'monkey' in which cannonballs were stored and which contracted in cold weather, so ejecting the balls. However, hard evidence for this story is lacking. More probably it refers to a notional or real brass figure of a monkey

– especially one of the 'three wise monkeys', which were often embodied in such a form and used as ornaments.

Bolt from the blue, A A sudden and wholly unexpected event or catastrophe, like a thunderbolt from the blue sky, or a flash of lightning without warning.

Cat's paw A pattern of ripples on a surface of water, caused by a light wind. In nautical parlance, a cat's paw is a hitch in the form of two loops in the bight of a line, used to attach it to a hook.

On cloud nine Elated; very happy. One theory as to the origin of this involves a meteorological guide published in 1896 called the *International Cloud Atlas*. The guide classified ten basic types of cloud, in which cloud nine is 'cumulonimbus', a cumulus cloud of great vertical extent, topped with shapes of mountains or towers. The expression 'on cloud nine' was then popularized by a 1950s US radio show in which a character called Johnny Dollar, a fictional insurance investigator, was continually coming unstuck through various misadventures. Every time he was knocked unconscious, he was taken to 'cloud nine', where he recovered.

Groundswell A long, deep rolling or swell of the sea, caused by a recent or distant storm, or by an earthquake. The expression is also used figuratively of a strong public opinion that can be detected even though it is not expressed openly.

Lee (Old English *hlēow*, 'shelter') Nautically, the side or quarter opposite to that against which the wind blows; in other words, the sheltered side.

Mackerel sky A sky dappled with detached rounded masses of white cloud, resembling the markings on the back of a mackerel.

Mare's-tail sky A sky with wisps of trailing clouds, indicating winds at high altitudes.

Monkey's wedding (Translating Portuguese *casamento de macaco*) An expression used in parts of southern Africa to denote a situation in which rain is falling and the sun is out at the same time. A parallel Portuguese usage is *casamento de rapôsa*, literally 'vixen's wedding'.

Pathetic fallacy A term coined by John Ruskin (1819–1900) in the third volume (1856) of his *Modern Painters* to describe the figure of speech that attributes human feelings to nature.

Smog A linguistic and literal blend of 'smoke' and 'fog', as an insidious form of polluted air. The word appears to have been first used in 1905 by H.A. des Voeux of the Coal Smoke Abatement Society to describe atmospheric conditions over British towns.

Pea-souper A 19th-century phrase for a particularly dense smog, and especially that associated with London before the Clean Air Acts of the 1950s and 1960s. The reference is to the dense consistency of pea soup.

Trade winds Winds that blow 'trade', i.e. regularly in one track or direction. This sense of the word comes from the Low German *Trade*, 'track', which gave us the Modern English 'tread'. In the northern hemisphere they blow from the north-east, and in the southern hemisphere from the south-east, about 30° each side of the equator. In some places they blow six months in one direction, and six months in the opposite.

Under the weather Unwell or out of sorts, as if affected by the weather. The most popular suggestion as to the expression's story involves sailors who, when ill, would recuperate under the weather deck, the deck that was exposed to the elements.

Rain Check

Petrichor The distinctive smell of rain after a long dry spell. This word was coined in the 1960s from *petro-*, meaning 'of rocks', and *ichor*, the ethereal fluid believed to flow through the veins of the Greek gods.

Rain cats and dogs, To To rain very heavily. In northern mythology the cat is supposed to have great influence on the weather, and 'The cat has a gale of wind in her tail' is a seafarers' expression for when a cat is unusually frisky. Witches that rode on storms were said to assume the form of cats. The dog is a signal of wind, like the wolf, both of which were attendants of Odin, the storm god. From these facts it has been speculated that the cat may be taken as a symbol of the pouring rain, and the dog of the strong gusts of wind accompanying a rainstorm – hence 'rain cats and dogs'. However, it is also the case that the descent of various bizarre objects (e.g. pitchforks and stair-rods) from the sky has been cited in English and other languages as evidence of abnormally heavy rainfall, and it may well be that cats and dogs are simply two further examples of this. There is no evidence for the popular belief that cats and dogs, asleep in thatched roofs, would be washed down by the rain in medieval times.

Rain check In the USA a receipt or the counterfoil of a ticket entitling one to see another baseball game if the original match for which the ticket was purchased is rained off. The phrase is now in general use for a promise to accept an invitation at a later date.

Red sky at night, shepherd's delight; red sky in the morning, shepherd's warning An expression dating from the 14th century, indicating the likelihood of fair or foul weather based on the colour of the evening or dawn skies. The original allusion is to Matthew 16:2:

> When it is evening, ye say, It will be fair weather: for the sky is red. And in the morning, It will be foul weather today: for the sky is red and lowering.

Swithin, St According to the old adage, if it rains on St Swithin's Day (15 July), there will be rain for 40 days. The saying is based on the legend that St Swithin, 9th-century bishop of Winchester and adviser of Egbert of Wessex, desired to be buried in the churchyard of the minster, that the 'sweet rain of heaven might fall upon his grave'. At his canonization, the monks thought to honour the saint by transferring his body to the cathedral choir and fixed 15 July 971 for the ceremony, but it rained day after day for 40 days, thereby, according to some, delaying the proceedings.

Umbrella The device was used in ancient China, Babylon, Egypt, and elsewhere to keep off the sun, but it was not commonly found in England until after the philanthropist Jonas Hanway (1712–86) publicized it from about 1750 by carrying one regularly in the streets of London to keep off the rain. He incurred a good deal of ridicule in the process. The origin of the name reflects the umbrella's earliest use, as it comes from the Latin *umbra*, 'shade'.

STEAL SOMEONE'S THUNDER

Steal someone's thunder, To To forestall a person or to adopt another's own special methods as one's own. The phrase comes from an event on 5 February 1709. That year the critic and playwright John Dennis had invented an effective device for producing stage thunder for his new play *Appius and Virginia*. Despite its dramatic effects, the play was a failure and was withdrawn. Shortly after, when attending a production of *Macbeth* in the same theatre, Dennis heard the sound of his own machine booming out from the stage. Accounts by those attending the same performance relate how Dennis stood up and exclaimed, 'My God! They will not let *my* play run, but they steal my thunder!'

NUMBER-CRUNCHING

The US writer Nathanael West believed that 'numbers constitute the only universal language'. Dr Seuss, meanwhile, told us that 'You have to be odd to be number one'. Numbers are everywhere in life and so, it follows, in our vocabulary. Often they wear their hearts on their sleeves – we are 'in seventh heaven', 'dressed to the nines', 'at sixes and sevens', or 'a nine-day wonder'. Just as frequently, though, our desire to calculate is hidden behind the most everyday words, such as 'umpteen' and 'scruples', while our methods of counting have given us the double meanings of 'digit' (a finger and a number) and 'calculate' (from the Latin for a small pebble). Meanwhile, on one particular afternoon quiz show, solving an often fiendish numbers game is a joyful challenge for us all.

Figure It Out

Cardinal numbers The natural basic numbers, which denote quantity, such as 1, 2, 3, 4, and 5. (1st, 2nd, 3rd, etc. are 'ordinal' numbers, since they denote order.) 'Cardinal' comes from the

Latin *cardo*, 'hinge', and all its senses – of a church dignitary, a sin, or a number – share the idea of something being of pivotal importance, on which everything else turns or depends. The colour 'cardinal' is so called because of the deep scarlet of a cardinal's cassock.

Fibonacci sequence An infinite sequence of numbers – 0, 1, 1, 2, 3, 5, 8, 13, 21 . . . – in which each after the first two is the sum of the two numbers preceding it. Such a sequence is reflected in many natural phenomena, such as the number of spirals of seeds in the head of a sunflower. The numbers are known as 'Fibonacci numbers'. It is named after the Italian mathematician Leonardo Fibonacci (*c*.1170–*c*.1250), who is said to have devised it in 1225 to solve a problem relating to the breeding rate of rabbits.

Google A US company formed in 1998 that runs the Google internet search engine. Google resulted from a research project in 1996 by two postgraduate students from Stanford University, Larry Page and Sergey Brin. Such is its dominance over other search engines that 'to google' has become a generic verb meaning to search for something or someone on the internet. The story goes that Page and Brin thought they were naming their company after 'googol', the vast number represented by a 1 followed by 100 zeroes, but got the spelling wrong.

Hecatomb In ancient Greece, the sacrifice of 100 head of oxen, from Greek *hekaton*, 'hundred', and *bous*, 'ox'. Hence any large sacrifice or large number. It is said that the ancient Greek philosopher Pythagoras offered up 100 oxen when he discovered that the square of the hypotenuse of a right-angled triangle equals the sum of the squares of the other two sides.

Sesquipedalian A word sometimes applied with heavy irony to cumbersome and pedantic words. It comes from Horace's *sesquipedalia verba,* 'words a foot-and-a-half long'.

Sudoku A puzzle that involves filling in a 9×9 matrix with numbers. Every digit from 1 to 9 must be inserted once into each of nine vertical columns and nine horizontal rows, and into each of nine 3×3 boxes (known as 'regions'). It first appeared in Japan in 1984 under the slogan *Suuji wa dokushin ni kagiru,* meaning 'The numbers must be single'. The rather unwieldy name was subsequently shortened to *sudoku* (often mispronounced as 'suduko').

Countdown

Algebra A branch of mathematics in which formulae and equations, using alphabetical symbols as well as numbers, are studied. The word's original meaning in English (as used during the 16th century) related to bone-setting and the treatment of fractures; this sense came from the Arabic *al-jabr,* 'the reunion of broken parts'. The mathematical sense that is now more familiar had been used in connection with mathematics as early as the 9th century by the Persian mathematician and astronomer al-Kwarizmi.

Calculate, To From the Latin *calculus,* meaning 'pebble', and referring to the small stones used by the Romans for counters. On an abacus, the round balls were called *calculi.* The Greeks voted by pebbles dropped into an urn, a method adopted both in ancient Egypt and Syria. To count these pebbles was to 'calculate' the number of voters.

Cater-cornered Placed diagonally, as of a badly parked car in a parking space. 'Cater' is an old word for the four dots on dice, which form diagonals, from French *quatre*, 'four'. Other spellings of the term are 'catty-cornered' and 'kitty-cornered', but the expression is unrelated to cats.

Ell An old measure of length, which, like 'foot', was taken from a part of the body (the forearm) and was originally 18in. (45.5cm), as the approximate measurement from the elbow to the fingertips. The word is related to Latin *ulna*, now used as the name for the inner and longer of the two bones of the forearm.

Minute A minute of time (one-sixtieth part of an hour) is so called from Medieval Latin *pars minuta prima*, 'first small part', which, in the old system of sexagesimal fractions, denoted one-sixtieth part of the unit. A 'second' is from *minuta secunda*, 'second minute'. In the same way, the mathematical minute is one-sixtieth part of a degree. From the same Latin word as above, 'minute' also denotes something very small. Hence the minutes of a speech, meeting, or the like are brief notes taken down during the proceedings to be subsequently written up as a summarized record of what was said and of any decisions taken.

Nail A nail was formerly a measure of weight of 8lb (3.6kg). It was used for wool, hemp, beef, cheese, and other provisions. It was also a measure of length of 2¼in (6cm). In ancient Rome a nail was driven into the wall of the temple of Jupiter every 13 September. This was originally done to tally the year, but subsequently it became a religious ceremony for warding off calamities and plagues from the city.

Nip of whisky, A 'Nip' is short for 'nipperkin'. This was a small measure for wine and beer, containing about half a pint (about 285ml), or a little under.

Quarter or **quarters** Most ancient Roman cities were divided into four parts, called quarters, by their two main avenues: the Cardo and the Decumanus Maximus. The *Quartier Latin* ('Latin quarter') of Paris is the university area. Although popularly renowned as the bohemian quarter, it derives its name from its ancient fame as a centre of learning when Latin was the common language for the students, who came from all over Europe. The military sense of 'quarters', where an army lodges, is from this sense of a portion of a town.

Quorum (Latin, 'of whom') The lowest number of members of a committee, board, or the like whose presence is necessary before business may be transacted. The word comes from the stock formula used when forming Latin commissions: *quorum vos* [. . .] *duos* (etc.) *esse volumus*, 'of whom we wish you [. . .] to be two (etc.)', the ellipsis standing for the persons' names and the number being variable.

Scruple The name of the weight (20 grains; 1/24oz; 1.296g) and the term for care or hesitation (as in 'a scruple of conscience') both come from Latin *scrupulus*, meaning 'a sharp little pebble'. Pebbles were frequently used as counters, while if one gets into a shoe, it will make the wearer tread very carefully indeed.

Curious Numbers

Zero The figure 0, nothing. From Arabic *sifr*, meaning 'empty', also giving English 'cipher' and French *chiffre*, 'number'.

Naught, nought These are merely variants of the same word, and both come from Old English, meaning literally 'no thing'. 'Naught' was formerly applied to things that were bad or worthless, which produced the adjective 'naughty'.

One basket had very good figs, even like the figs that are first ripe: and the other basket had very naughty figs, which could not be eaten, they were so bad.

Jeremiah, 24:2

Trivium (Latin, 'place where three ways meet', from *tres*, 'three', and *via*, 'road') In the Middle Ages, the three roads that led to learning, i.e. grammar, rhetoric, and logic. 'Trivial' first related to these basic, low-level studies.

Three golden balls The once familiar pawnbroker's sign is said to have been taken from the coat of arms of the Medici family and first introduced to London by Lombard bankers and moneylenders. The positioning of the balls was popularly explained in that there were two chances to one that what was brought in would be redeemed.

Seven A mystic or sacred number. It is composed of four and three, which have long been considered lucky numbers. Among the Babylonians, Egyptians, and other ancient peoples there were seven sacred planets, and the Hebrew verb 'to swear' means literally 'to come under the influence of seven things'. There are seven days in creation, seven days in the week, seven virtues, seven divisions in the Lord's Prayer, seven ages in the life of man, and the seventh son of a seventh son was always held notable. Among the Hebrews, every seventh year was 'sabbatical', and seven times seven years was the 'jubilee'.

In seventh heaven The most exalted level of heaven in Jewish and Islamic theology. According to the Talmud, the seventh heaven is the place where God dwells over the angels, the souls of the righteous, and the souls of those yet to be born.

Nine From ancient times the number nine has been held to be of particular significance. There are nine orders of angels;

there were nine Muses; the abracadabra amulet was worn for nine days, and then flung into a river. The weird sisters in Shakespeare's *Macbeth* (I, iii (1606)) sing as they dance around the cauldron, 'Thrice to thine, and thrice to mine, and thrice again to make up nine', and then declare 'the charm wound up'. In the modern world, leases are sometimes granted for 999 years, i.e. three times three-three-three. Many run for 99 years, the dual of a trinity of trinities.

Nine days' wonder Something that causes a great sensation for a few days, and then passes into the limbo of things forgotten. An old proverb is 'A wonder lasts nine days, and then the puppy's eyes are open', alluding to dogs, which (like cats) are born blind.

Whole nine yards, The The complete package, everything. The phrase, which emerged in the USA in the 1960s, has been explained with reference to all manner of bizarre measurements and quantities, from the length of a hangman's noose and the capacity (in cubic yards) of a ready-mixed cement truck, to the dimensions of a nun's habit and the length of a Spitfire's ammunition belt, none of which stands up to close examination. A plausible derivation remains tantalizingly out of reach.

Thirteen Thirteen was regarded as an unlucky number even among the Romans, who held it as a sign of death and destruction. The origin of the idea that sitting down 13 at a table is unlucky is said to stem from Norse mythology and the story of a banquet in Valhalla, upon which the god and shape-shifter Loki once intruded, making 13 guests, and at which Balder (son of Odin and Frigg, and chief of the gods) was slain. The superstition was confirmed in Christian countries by the Last Supper of Christ and the 12 Apostles. In the Middle Ages witch covens were believed always to have 13 members. A fear of the number 13 is known as 'triskaidekaphobia'.

Score From Old English *scora*, related to Old Norse *skor*, meaning 'notch'. The word was originally applied to a notch on a piece of wood known as a 'tally' or 'tally-stick', hence a reckoning or account. As the term for the quantity of a set of twenty, the allusion is probably to the special score or mark made on a tally-stick to indicate that figure. Drovers passing their animals through a tollgate always based their counting on twenties or scores.

Twenty-twenty vision Perfect vision. The term alludes to the Snellen chart used when measuring visual acuity. The patient reads rows of letters printed in successively decreasing sizes. Twenty-twenty (20/20) vision means that a row of letters near the bottom of the chart can be read at a distance of 20ft (6.1m). Measurements are now metric, so that the chart is placed 6 metres from the patient and normal vision is expressed as 6/6.

Umpteen Signals regiments in the army once called the dash in Morse code by the name 'umpty', while the dot was known as the 'iddy'. In mainstream English, 'umpty' came to mean an indefinite large number, and eventually developed into 'umpteen', following the pattern of 'thirteen' etc.

AT SIXES AND SEVENS

At sixes and sevens Higgledy-piggledy; in a state of confusion, or, of people, unable to come to an agreement. The phrase probably comes from an old dicing game called 'hazard', and may have arisen as a mistranslation of Old French *cinque et sice*, 'five and six'. However, it is also traditionally held that the expression arose out of a dispute between two of the great livery companies, the Merchant Taylors and the Skinners, as to which was sixth and which seventh in the order of the companies appearing in processions in the City of London, both companies having been chartered in 1327 within a few days of each other. In 1484 they submitted the matter to the judgement of the then mayor, Sir Robert Billesden, and the aldermen. The award was that the master and wardens of both companies should entertain each other to dinner annually and that the Skinners were to precede the Taylors in that year's procession. The next year the Taylors were to take the sixth place and this alternation was to continue 'ever more'. The story is colourful, but chronologically speaking – sadly – it is very unlikely.

COLLECTIVE NOUNS

The majority of group terms that we know and love today sprang from the medieval imagination. Created by the elite for the elite, they surfaced in the Middle Ages, written down in books of etiquette aimed at instructing the nobility on how not to embarrass themselves while out hunting, hawking, or fishing. For the medieval nobleman, knowing that the correct term for a group of ferrets was a 'busyness', for hares a 'flick', and for hounds a 'mute' would not only avoid humiliation but act as a marker of class and status.

Our primary source for such terms is the 15th-century *Book of St Albans*, a three-part compendium on aristocratic pursuits. Its authorship is attributed to Dame Juliana Berners, prioress of the Sopwell nunnery in Hertfordshire. Not only did her work contain over 160 group names for beasts of the chase and characters on the medieval stage; it also boasted the first images to be printed in colour in England. It was an instant success, reprinted and reissued many times by both William Caxton and the printer and publisher Wynkyn de Worde. Its popularity extended far beyond the nobles for whom it was originally intended.

Many of these terms – 'a murmuration of starlings', 'an unkindness of ravens', 'a superfluity of nuns' – endure to this day. There is no authority on the 'correct' collective noun for any given group; rather, they are established by usage. Below is a selection of some of the most revealing.

Abomination of monks, An This collective noun pithily reflects a prevailing view that monks were greedy and licentious, as well as oblivious to the poverty suffered beyond monastery walls.

Crash of rhinoceri, A These animals were a popular exotic pet in royal menageries. It is said that the Portuguese king Manuel I arranged a fight between an elephant and a rhino to establish their respective dominance. The rhino charged, the elephant fled, and the aggression of the rhino became entrenched in popular belief.

Impertinence of peddlers, An As medieval farms began to switch from agriculture to livestock, many labourers were forced to make ends meet by becoming itinerant peddlers. The high taxes imposed upon them meant they had to sell their wares at high prices, gaining a reputation for dishonesty in the process.

Misbelief of painters, A A misbelief of painters reflects the fact that the portrait artist's job was to flatter their subject – to suspend disbelief, if you like – in those who viewed his work.

Murmuration of starlings, A Prior to the choice of 'murmuration' for a gathering of starlings, inspired by the sound of the birds when flocking together, the collective noun was 'mutation', thanks to the belief that the bird shed a leg at the age of 10 and then promptly grew a new one.

Superfluity of nuns, A In the 13th century, a nunnery was the expected refuge for spinsters of the nobility. Bequests would be made to these religious institutions when they accepted an unmarried daughter, but many of them were severely over-crowded. An alternative theory reflects the emerging view, leading up to the Dissolution of the Monasteries in the 16th century, that there were far too many monasteries and nunneries.

Unkindness of ravens, An The black, brooding, noisy birds were believed to show cruelty to their young and were regarded as bringers of bad luck.

Worship of writers, A Making a living from writing in the Middle Ages was tricky, and any author must look for a wealthy patron to fund their endeavours. In return, writers were frequently compelled to pen fawning dedications in every new work. Geoffrey Chaucer was bound in this way to Henry IV.

SPELLING IT OUT

'Don't you just love the Oxford Dictionary? When I first read it, I thought it was a really really long poem about everything.' David Bowie (of course) wasn't wrong. Dictionaries rely on an alphabet, the foundation of many of the world's writing systems to this day. Most of them can be traced back to Egypt, where evidence unearthed by archaeologists dates from around 1850 BC. And letters have always been threaded into 'texts' – a relative in language of the word 'textile', because we weave our words as we weave our cloth. Equally, they can be used solo and still be invested with meaning. We 'catch a few zzzs' in order to feel 'A-OK', or we may even use a 'four-letter word' without 'minding our Ps and Qs'.

The Alphabet

Alphabet The word goes back to Greek *alphabētos*, combining *alpha* and *beta*, the first two letters of the Greek alphabet. The number of letters in an alphabet varies in different languages. Although the English alphabet is capable of innumerable combinations and permutations, there are no means of differentiating the vowel sounds. For example, 'a' sounds differently in 'fate', 'fat', 'Thames', 'war', 'orange', 'ware', 'abide', 'calm', 'swan'. So with 'e', as in 'era', 'the', 'there', 'prey', 'met', 'England', 'sew', 'herb', 'clerk'. The other vowels are equally variable.

A This letter evolved from the Hebrew and Phoenician character known as *aleph*, 'ox', supposedly because it originally represented an ox head.

A1 First class. In *Lloyd's Register of Shipping*, the state of a ship's hull is designated by letters and that of her equipment by figures. A1 thus generally means 'excellent'.

A-OK Excellent; in good order. A US space-age expression, allegedly standing for 'all systems OK'. It is said to have been the invention of a NASA public-relations officer, Colonel 'Shorty' Powers, who used it during the suborbital flight on 5 May 1961 of the astronaut Alan Shepard. Powers misheard a simple 'OK' from Shepard as 'A-OK' and relayed it to reporters and radio listeners.

C The form of the letter is a rounding of the Greek *gamma* (Γ), which was a modification of the Phoenician sign for *gimel*, 'camel', although not actually representing this animal.

D This letter is the outline of a rude archway or door. It is called in Phoenician and Hebrew *daleth* ('door') and in Greek *delta*. In the latter language it has a triangular shape (Δ). In Egyptian hieroglyphics it is represented by a hand.

D-Day In the Second World War the day appointed for the Allied invasion of Europe and the opening of the long-awaited second front. It was eventually fixed for 5 June 1944, but owing to impossible weather conditions, it was postponed at the last moment until 6 June. D simply stands for 'Day'.

E This letter is derived from an Egyptian hieroglyph and the Phoenician and Hebrew sign called *he*. The following legend is sometimes found in churches under the two tables of the Ten Commandments:

PRSVR Y PRFCT MN
VR KP THS PRCPTS TN
The vowel E
Supplies the key.

F The Egyptian hieroglyph represented a horned asp and the Phoenician character a peg.

F is written on his face 'Rogue' is written on his face. The letter F used to be branded near the nose, on the left cheek of felons, on their being admitted to 'benefit of clergy'. The same was used for brawling in church. The custom was not abolished by law till 1822.

G This letter is a modification of the Latin C, which was a rounding of the Greek *gamma*. Until the 3rd century BC the 'g' and 'k' sounds were both represented by the letter C. In the Hebrew and old Phoenician alphabets G is the outline of a camel's head and neck, and Hebrew *gimel* means 'camel'.

H The form of the capital H is through the Roman and Greek from the Phoenician (Semitic) letter *Heth* or *Cheth*, which, having two crossbars instead of one, represented a fence. The corresponding Egyptian hieroglyph was a sieve, and the Anglo-Saxon rune is called *hægl*, 'hail'.

I represents the Greek *iota* and Semitic *yod*. The written and printed 'i' and 'j' were for long interchangeable. In Samuel Johnson's *Dictionary* of 1755, 'iambic' comes between 'jamb' and 'jangle'. Hence in many series, such as the signatures of sheets in a book or hallmarks on plate, either I or J is omitted.

The dot on the small 'i', known as the 'tittle', was introduced about the 11th century as a diacritic in cases where two 'i's came together (e.g. *filii*), to distinguish between these and 'u'. The expression 'to a T' is thought to be a shortening of 'to a tittle', i.e. to the tiniest degree.

J is a modern introduction, differentiated from 'i' only in the 17th century and not completely distinguished from it until the 19th. In Dr Johnson's *Dictionary*, 'joyous' is thus followed by 'ipecacuanha', and 'itself' is followed by 'jubilant'.

Jot A tiny amount. 'Jot' is an anglicization of the Greek *iota*, the smallest letter of the alphabet. To care 'not one jot' is to not care very much at all.

K The 11th letter of the alphabet, representing the Greek *kappa* and the Hebrew *kaph*. The Egyptian hieroglyphic for K was a bowl. The Romans, after the C was given the K sound, used the latter only for abbreviated forms of a few words from Greek. Thus, false accusers were branded on the forehead with a K for *kalumnia* (English 'calumny'). As the recognized abbreviation for the prefix 'kilo-', K is used colloquially for 'a thousand', and particularly (mainly in quoting salaries) for multiples of £1,000.

L The 12th letter of the alphabet. In Phoenician and Hebrew it represents an ox goad, *lamed*, and in the Egyptian hieroglyphic a lioness.

Letter The name of a character used to represent a sound; also a missive or written message. The word came into English from Old French *lettre*, itself from Latin *littera*, 'letter of the alphabet'. Its relatives include 'literature', 'literal', and 'alliteration'.

M The 13th letter of the English alphabet. M in the Phoenician character represented the wavy appearance of water, and in Hebrew it is called *mem* ('water'). The Egyptian hieroglyphic represented the owl.

N The 14th letter of the English alphabet, represented in Egyptian hieroglyphics by a waterline (~~). It was called *nun* ('fish') in Phoenician.

O The 15th letter of our alphabet, the 14th of the ancient Roman, and the 16th of the Phoenician and Semitic (in which it was called *ain*, 'eye').

O' An Irish patronymic (Irish ó, 'grandson', 'descendant'). In contexts such as tam-o'-shanter, five o'clock, and CAT-O'-NINE-TAILS, 'o' stands for 'of', but in such now-obsolete phrases as 'He comes home late o' night', 'they go to church o' Sundays', it represented Middle English *on*.

P The 16th letter in the English alphabet, called *pe*, 'mouth', by the Phoenicians and ancient Hebrews, and represented in Egyptian hieroglyphics by a shutter.

Mind one's Ps and Qs, To To be careful; to be circumspect in one's behaviour. The expression probably derives from an admonition to children learning to write to be careful to distinguish between the forms of 'p' and 'q', or to printers' apprentices when handling and sorting type. More fancifully, it is suggested that in public houses accounts were scored up for beer, with P for pints and Q for quarts, and a customer needed 'to mind his Ps and Qs' when the reckoning came. Another is that in the France of Louis XIV (r.1643–1715), when huge wigs were fashionable, dancing masters would warn their pupils to 'mind your Ps [*pieds*, 'feet'] and Qs [*queues*, 'wigs']', lest the latter fall off when bending low to make a formal bow. There is little evidence that the letters stand for 'pleases' and 'thank yous'.

Q The form of this letter may have originated in Egyptian hieroglyphics, and have pictorially represented the eye of a needle or even a monkey with its tail hanging down.

R The 18th letter of the English alphabet (17th of the Roman). As a medieval Roman numeral, R stood for 80 and R̃ for 80,000. In England it was formerly used as a branding mark for rogues. It has been called the 'snarling letter' or 'dog letter', because a dog in snarling utters a sound resembling *r-r-r-r* or *gr-r-r-r*.

Three Rs, The Reading, writing, and arithmetic. The phrase is said to have been originated by Sir William Curtis (1752–1829), an illiterate alderman and lord mayor of London, who gave this as a toast, i.e. 'Riting, Reading, and Rithmetic'.

SOS The Morse code signal (3 dots, 3 dashes, 3 dots: ··· ––– ···) used by ships and planes in distress to summon immediate aid, hence any urgent appeal for help. The letters are simply a convenient and distinctive combination and are not an abbreviation, although they have been popularly held to stand for 'save our souls' or 'save our ship', or humorously 'save our sausages'.

U The 21st letter of the English alphabet, in form a modification of V, with which for many centuries it was interchangeable.

Words beginning with U and V (like those beginning with I and J) were not separated in English dictionaries until about 1800 and later.

U and Non-U A former semi-humorous mark of distinction between social classes in England based on the usage of certain words. 'U' is Upper Class and 'Non-U' is non-Upper Class. It is U to say 'luncheon' for what Non-U folk call 'lunch'; U to say 'napkin' instead of 'serviette'; and U to prefer 'cycle' to 'bike'. The terms owe their popularity to Nancy Mitford (1904–73), who quoted them in an article in the magazine *Encounter* in September 1955, but they were actually invented by Professor Alan Ross in 1954.

V The 22nd letter of the alphabet, formerly sharing its form with U. In the Roman notation it stands for 5 and represents ideographically the four fingers and thumb with the latter extended.

W The 23rd letter of the English alphabet. The form is simply a ligature of two Vs (VV). Hence the name, for V was formerly the symbol of U as well as of V.

X The 24th letter of the alphabet, representing the 22nd letter of the Greek alphabet (*chi*), and denoting in Roman numeration 10. In algebra and mathematics generally x denotes an unknown quantity. The reason for this is that algebra came into use in Europe from the Arabian peninsula and the Arabic *shei*, 'a thing', 'a something', used to designate the mathematically 'unknown', was transcribed as 'xei'. X as an abbreviation stands for 'Christ', as in 'Xmas'.

Y Derived from the Greek Y (upsilon), added by the Greeks to the Phoenician alphabet. It is used to represent both consonantal and vowel sounds, as respectively in 'yew and 'fly', and as such is often called a 'semivowel'.

Ye An archaic way of writing 'the'. Early printers used 'y' as a substitute for the Old English letter þ, the character representing modern 'th', hence the use of 'ye' for 'the' and 'yt' as an abbreviation for 'that'. It was always pronounced 'the'. It is found in modern pseudo-historical use in some quaint contexts, such as 'Ye Olde Tea Shoppe'.

Z The last letter of the alphabet, called 'zed' in England, but in the USA 'zee' (following the pattern of B, 'bee', and C, 'cee', etc.). Its older English name was 'izzard'. It was the sixth letter of the Greek alphabet, zeta (ζ).

> Thou whoreson zed! thou unnecessary letter!
> SHAKESPEARE: *King Lear*, ii, ii (1605)

In mathematics it denotes the third unknown quantity, and as a medieval numeral it represents 2000. It is also used as a contraction mark, as in 'viz' (for 'videlicet') and 'oz' (for 'ounce').

Reading the Runes

Ampersand The character '&' for 'and'. Its origins lie in the hornbook – a single-sided alphabet tablet protected by a transparent covering of horn and used as an educational primer from medieval times. After reciting the 26 letters, pupils would add the character '&' (. . . x, y, z, &), and this was called 'Ampersand', an alteration of 'and *per se* and', i.e. the symbol '&' by itself represents 'and'. The symbol '&' is an adaptation of *et* (Latin 'and').

Criss-cross Although often thought of as a reduplicated form of 'cross', the word actually evolved from 'Christ-cross', i.e. 'Christ's cross'. This was originally a cross that was placed before the alphabet in a hornbook. The Christ-cross row was thus the alphabet.

Italic type or **italics** Italic lettering was first used in 1501 by Aldus Manutius (*c*.1450–1515), being the work of his type designer, Francesco Griffo of Bologna, and based on the *cancelleresca corsiva* of the papal chancery. Its name is from the Greek *Italikos*, 'from Italy'.

Rune A letter or character of the earliest alphabet in use among the Gothic tribes of northern Europe. Runic inscriptions most commonly occur in Scandinavia and parts of the British Isles. Runes were employed for purposes of secrecy, charms, or divination, and the word is also applied to ancient lore or poetry expressed in runes. 'Rune' is related to Old Norse *rūn*, 'secret'.

Swastika An elaborate cross-shaped design, known as the Gammadion or Fylfot, used as a charm to ward off evil and bring good luck. It was adopted by Hitler as the Nazi emblem about 1920, probably from the German Baltic Corps, who wore it on their helmets after service in Finland, where it was used as a distinguishing mark on Finnish aeroplanes. It is this Nazi symbolism that defines the swastika in the minds of most people today. The word is from Sanskrit *svasti*, 'good fortune'.

QWERTY

QWERTY The standard layout on English-language typewriter keyboards, representing the first six letters from the left on the top row. The layout, still found even on modern computer keyboards, was originally designed to slow down typing and so prevent jamming of the keys on the early manual machines. The idea was to keep alternating between opposite sides of the keyboard to prevent adjacent keys tangling. It so happens that all the letters needed to type the word 'typewriter' are in the top line of the layout (QWERTYUIOP), but the theory that this was intended to help non-skilled sales staff demonstrate the machine is a myth. The French equivalent is AZERTY.

FIGHTING TALK

For all its destruction, war is surprisingly productive when it comes to language. Each major war and military campaign has left its mark, sometimes buried beneath layers of use so that the origins have become unrecognizable. Much of this language conveys the adrenaline, fear, and hopeless destruction of the battlefield. Then again, much of military life consists of hurrying up and waiting, and that too is reflected in its vocabulary – most famously of all, in 'going doolally'.

Having a Field Day

Bite the bullet, To To endure pain with courage; to behave stoically. The expression probably originated in field surgery in the days before anaesthesia. A surgeon about to operate on a wounded soldier would give him a bullet to bite on to distract him from the pain and reduce his ability to scream, which would otherwise distract the surgeon.

Chivy or **chivvy, To** To chase or urge someone on. The word probably originated in the ballad of Chevy Chase, which tells of the battle of Otterburn, in 1388, on the Scottish border. 'Chivy' was originally a noun meaning a hunting cry, and later came to describe a chase or pursuit.

Cross the Rubicon, To To take an irrevocable step, as when the Germans crossed the Belgian frontier in August 1914, which led to war with Great Britain. The Rubicon was a small river (possibly the present-day Fiumicino) which separated ancient Italy from Cisalpine Gaul, the province allotted to Julius Caesar. When Caesar crossed this stream in 49 BC he passed beyond the limits of his province and became an invader in Italy, thus precipitating war with Pompey and the Senate.

Curfew The ringing of a bell every evening as a signal to put out fires and go to bed; also the hour for this and the bell itself. The word is from Old French *cuevrefeu*, literally 'cover fire'. William the Conqueror instituted the curfew in England, in 1068, at the hour of 8 p.m. The word is now extended to mean the period commonly ordered by occupying armies or government authorities in time of war or civil commotion when civilians must stay indoors.

Deadline The final date or time when a task or assignment must be completed. This sense of a strict boundary derives from the 'deadline' round a military prison camp. The phrase was coined in the notorious Confederate prisoner-of-war camp, Andersonville, during the American Civil War (1861–65). Some distance from the peripheral wire fence, a line was marked out and any prisoner crossing this line was shot on sight.

Face the music, To To brave the consequences of one's actions or to put on a bold front in an unpleasant situation. The expression may derive from the stage, although some authorities take it from the military ceremony in which an officer being cashiered was required to face the drum squad while his charges were read out.

Field day A military term for a day when troops have manoeuvres or exercises. Generally, a field day is a day or time of exciting activity and success. In the US Navy it is a day devoted to cleaning the ship and preparing for inspection.

Full monty, The Everything; the lot; 'the works'. Said of anything done to the utmost or fullest degree. The origin of the expression is uncertain. One explanation traces the term to Field Marshal Bernard Montgomery, nicknamed 'Monty' (1887–1976), said to have begun every day with a full English breakfast when campaigning in the African desert in the Second World War. Another links it with the tailor Montague Burton, whose firm made a quarter of British uniforms in the Second World War and a third of the demob suits at the end of the war. The full monty is said to refer to the option of buying a two-piece suit together with a waistcoat and spare pair of trousers.

Reveille (French *réveiller*, 'to awaken') The bugle call used in the armed forces announcing that it is time to rise.

Run the gauntlet, To To be attacked on all sides, to be severely criticized. The word came into English as 'gantlope' but is ultimately from Swedish *gatlopp*, literally 'passageway'. The reference is to a former punishment among soldiers and sailors. The company or crew, provided with rope ends, were drawn up in two rows facing each other, and the delinquent had to run between them, while every man dealt him as severe a blow as he could. The spelling 'gauntlet' is due to confusion with *gauntlet*, 'glove' (Old French *gantelet*, a diminutive of *gant*, 'glove').

Shape up or ship out, To Used in injunctions to improve performance or remove oneself/another from the scene. The expression originated in the US military in the mid-20th century. It often occurs as the imperative 'Shape up or ship out!'

Tattoo The beat of the drum at night to recall soldiers to barracks is from Dutch *taptoe*, from the command *tap toe!* ('turn off the taps'), meaning to close the barrels of beer. The other meaning of 'tattoo', as the indelible marking of the skin, represents Tahitian *tatau*, 'mark'. The word was introduced by Captain Cook in 1769.

Wakey, wakey! A brisk instruction to wake up. It became familiar to generations of 20th-century British squaddies (often in the extended form 'Wakey, wakey, rise and shine!') as their caring NCOs sought to rouse them from their slumbers at reveille.

CHANCE ONE'S ARM

Chance one's arm or **luck, To** To run a risk in the hope of succeeding and obtaining a profit or advantage. The phrase may have begun as tailors' jargon, and an army connection has also been suggested: a non-commissioned officer who offended against service regulations risked demotion and the loss of a stripe from his sleeve. More colourfully, the Earl of Kildare is said to have sought to end a quarrel between his family and the Ormondes at the end of the 15th century by sticking his arm through a hole cut in the door of St Patrick's Cathedral, Dublin, in the hope that the Ormondes would simply seize it rather than chop it off. They did, and the feud was ended.

Over the Top

Alarm The word 'alarm' was originally a military order meaning 'to arms!' It comes from the Italian phrase *all' arme!*, 'to arms!', just as the word 'alert' was an instruction to be on the lookout, from the Italian *all' erta*, 'to the watchtower'.

Beat retreat, To Originally, in the military sense, to summon men by drum beat to withdraw to camp or behind the lines when hostilities temporarily ceased at the approach of darkness. It was also to give warning to the guards to collect and be posted for the night. The drums were later augmented by fifes and, more recently, with the advent of military bands, beating retreat became an impressive ceremonial display.

Flash in the pan, A A failure after a showy beginning. The allusion is to the attempt at firing an old flintlock gun that ends with a flash in the priming pan but nothing more, the gun itself 'hanging fire'.

Gung-ho Excessively or unthinkingly eager, especially in the context of patriotism and military aggression. The term dates from the Second World War when it was adopted as a slogan by US Marines as a Pidgin English form of Mandarin Chinese *kung*, 'work', and *ho*, 'together'.

Here's mud in your eye A jocular drinking toast dating from the First World War and perhaps originating among army officers, with reference to the mud of the trenches.

KBO A humorously euphemistic abbreviation of 'keep buggering on', an injunction to persist in spite of all obstacles. It was reputedly, and fittingly, a favourite of Winston Churchill.

Keep one's powder dry, To To be prepared for action. The phrase comes from a story told of Oliver Cromwell. During his campaign in Ireland, he is said to have concluded an address to his troops, who were about to cross a river before attacking, with the words 'Put your trust in God, my boys, and keep your powder dry.' The reference is to the gunpowder used in muskets.

Kilroy was here During the Second World War, a phrase found written up wherever the Americans (particularly Air Transport Command) had been. One suggestion is that a certain shipyard inspector at Quincy, Massachusetts, chalked up the words on material he had inspected. Pictorially, Kilroy was a wide-eyed, bald-headed face peering over a fence.

Marseillaise The hymn of the French Revolution and the national anthem of France. It was first made known in Paris by troops from Marseilles, hence the name.

Over the top Excessive; gross. The allusion is to troops going 'over the top' of the trenches in battle.

Parting shot A telling or wounding remark made on departure, giving one's adversary no time to reply. This was originally a 'Parthian shot', alluding to the strategy of horsemen from the ancient kingdom of Parthia to turn in flight as if in retreat, only to discharge arrows and missiles backwards at their pursuers.

Pitched battle A battle that has been planned, with the place and time chosen beforehand.

Slogan The first slogan was not in the world of advertising or politics, but was rather the Scottish Gaelic word for a battle cry or war cry, *sluagh-ghairm*, from *sluagh*, 'army', and *gairm*, 'shout'. An early attempt to anglicize *sluagh-ghairm* produced the spelling 'slughorn', but 'slogan' had more traction. It came to mean any war cry, and later, a political party cry or advertising catchphrase.

Great Guns

Blockbuster Anything of great power or size, such as an epic film or a bestseller. The term derives from the heavy high-explosive bombs dropped in the Second World War, which were capable of destroying a whole block of buildings.

Exocet A French-made guided anti-ship missile. The British public first became aware of it in 1982 when it was launched by Argentina against British ships in the Falklands War. Its name derives from Greek *exōkoitos*, 'flying fish' (literally, 'fish that gets out of bed').

Go off at half-cock, To To fail as a result of doing something prematurely or without proper preparation. The allusion is to a gun that goes off when the hammer is set at half-cock and supposedly secure.

Great guns With great zest and success. The term 'great gun' emerged in the 15th century, denoting a large artillery piece (as distinguished from a 'small gun', which was a musket, rifle, etc.). In nautical parlance of the 19th century, 'blow great guns' denoted the wind blowing with great violence, presumably making a noise resembling heavy artillery. The expression has now faded from use, but the more general 'go great guns', first recorded in the early 20th century and originally associated with horse-racing, is still going great guns.

Gun This word was formerly used for a large stone-throwing military device of the catapult or mangonel type. It is probably a shortened form of the Scandinavian female name *Gunnhildr*, itself from Old Norse *gunnr*, 'war', and *hildr*, 'battle'. The bestowing of female names on arms is common – other weapons include 'Big Bertha' and 'Mons Meg'.

Hang fire, To To delay; to be irresolute; to be slow in acting. The expression derives from gunnery. A gun could be slow in firing the charge if it had not been properly loaded and primed, or if the powder was damp.

Hoisted by one's own petard, To be To be beaten with one's own weapons or caught in one's own trap. The 'petard' was both a small bomb made of a box filled with powder, used to blast down a door or to make a hole in a wall, and a kind of firework that explodes with a sharp report. The risk is that the person laying the petard may be blown up by its explosion. The metaphor is first recorded in Shakespeare's *Hamlet* (1604).

Jeep The registered name of a small all-purpose car first developed by the USA during the Second World War and based on the initials GP, for General Purpose, the US Army designation for this type of car. The name probably derives from this, although it was influenced by 'Eugene the Jeep', a versatile cartoon character that had a cry of 'Jeep', produced by the creator of Popeye.

Jerrycan A 4½-gallon (20.5-litre) petrol or water container, which would stand rough handling and stack easily, developed by the Germans for the Afrika Korps in the Second World War. It was borrowed by the British in Libya and became the standard unit of fuel replenishment throughout the Allied armies. The name is an allusion to its origin.

Lock, stock, and barrel The whole of anything; in entirety. The lock (firing mechanism), stock (butt), and barrel comprise a complete gun or rifle.

Moaning Minnie A Second World War term for a six-barrelled German mortar. The first word alludes to the rising shriek when it was fired; the second was based on the German word for 'mortar', *Minenwerfer* (literally 'mine thrower'). The name was also given to the air-raid warning siren because of its repetitive wail.

Molotov The alias (meaning 'hammer') of the Russian diplomat Vyacheslav Mikhailovich Skryabin (1890–1986) inspired the name of the Molotov cocktail, a home-made anti-tank bomb, invented and first used by the Finns against the Russians in 1940 and developed in Britain as one of the weapons of the Home Guard. It consisted of a bottle filled with inflammable liquid, lit with a slow match protruding from the top.

Point-blank Direct. A term from gunnery. When a cannon is so placed that the line of sight is parallel to the axis and horizontal, the discharge is point-blank, and was supposed to go direct, without curve, to an object within a certain distance. In French *point blanc* is the white mark or bullseye of a target; in order to hit it, the ball or arrow must not deviate by the least amount.

Pommel The pommel of a sword is the rounded knob terminating the hilt, so called from its apple-like shape (French *pomme*, 'apple'), and to 'pummel' someone, meaning to pound them with one's fists, was originally to beat them with the pommel of one's sword.

Smoking gun A piece of incontrovertible incriminating evidence. The allusion is to a gun that has obviously only just been fired after being used to commit a crime. The expression is particularly applied to the incriminating tape of 23 June 1973 in the Watergate affair. President Nixon would almost certainly not have been threatened with impeachment if the tape had remained undiscovered.

Tank The heavily armoured combat vehicle running on caterpillar tracks was first introduced on the battlefield by the British in the Battle of the Somme (1916). It was called by the code name 'tank' in order not to arouse enemy suspicions. The term came about partly because the vehicle resembled a water tank, partly because it was supposedly designed for use in desert warfare.

Swan about or **swan around, To** To move around aimlessly. A phrase popular among troops in the Second World War to describe a tank moving apparently aimlessly across the battlefield, like a swan swimming idly about the waters or meandering with others in an aimless convoy. The long gun barrel additionally evokes the bird's long neck.

Win or Lose

Carte blanche (French, 'blank paper') Originally, a paper with only the signature written on it, so that the recipient may write their own terms upon it, knowing they will be accepted. The expression is of military origin, referring to unconditional surrender, but it is now used solely in a figurative sense, so that to give someone carte blanche is to grant them absolute freedom of action.

Have someone's number on it, To An expression used by members of the armed forces to refer to a bullet or other missile destined to hit a particular person, since it is supposedly marked by fate for their extinction.

Havoc From the Old French word *havot*, meaning 'pillage', 'cry havoc' was originally the signal from a victorious army commander for soldiers to start plundering. The sense of plunder gradually passed into an idea of destructive devastation or chaos.

Kiss me, Hardy These famous words, often used facetiously, were uttered by the dying Lord Nelson when taking leave of his flag captain, Thomas Masterman Hardy (1769–1839), in the moment of victory at the Battle of Trafalgar (1805). Hardy knelt down and kissed his cheek. They were preceded by the request, 'Take care of poor Lady Hamilton.' According to some, the words actually spoken by Nelson were 'Kismet, Hardy', i.e. 'Fate, Hardy'.

My number's up I have been caught or am about to die. A soldier's phrase. In the US Army a soldier who has just been killed or has died is said to have 'lost his mess number'. An older phrase in the Royal Navy was 'to lose the number of his mess'.

Ovation An enthusiastic display of popular favour, so called from the ancient Roman *ovatio*, 'exultaton', which was an entrance by a victorious commander who entered the city on horseback or on foot. A greater victory deserved a grander entry known as a 'triumph', which gave us our modern sense of the word for victory.

Pass under the yoke, To To make a humiliating submission; to suffer the disgrace of a vanquished army. The Romans made a yoke of three spears, two upright and one across on top. When an army was vanquished, the soldiers had to lay down their arms and pass under this archway.

Prang RAF slang in the Second World War meaning to bomb a target with evident success, to shoot down another or to crash one's own aircraft, and generally to collide with, or bump into, any vehicle. According to Eric Partridge, *A Dictionary of RAF Slang* (1945), the word may be a blend of 'paste' and 'bang', but it is more likely to be simply imitative.

Push up the daisies, To To be dead and buried. The idea is that the dead body fertilizes the soil, so stimulating the growth of the daisies in the churchyard. The expression is first recorded in a poem by Wilfred Owen written in the First World War. Keats had earlier written of 'daisies growing over me' in a letter of 1821, the year of his death.

Pyrrhic victory A victory won at too heavy a price, like the costly victory won by Pyrrhus, king of Epirus, at Asculum in 279 BC. ('One more such victory and we are lost.') Pyrrhus lost all his best officers and many men.

Trophy Originally the arms of a vanquished foe, collected and set up by the victors on the field of battle. The captured standards were hung from the branches of an oak tree, a portion of the booty being laid at the foot of the tree and dedicated to a patron deity. The Romans frequently bore their trophies to Rome. The word relates to Greek *tropē*, 'turning', referring to the act of turning back an enemy.

Home Thoughts

Blighty A colloquial name for England used by soldiers serving abroad in the First World War but originating among those who had served in India some years before. It represents Urdu *bilā yatī*, 'foreign land', from Arabic *wilāyat*, 'country'. The term became popular during the First World War in several songs, including 'Take me back to dear old Blighty, put me on the train for London town'.

Dear John A letter ending a personal relationship. The expression dates from the Second World War, when US servicemen were separated from their partners, who then wrote to terminate the relationship. The words were used as a typical opening to such a letter.

Doolally An army expression for an unbalanced state of mind or mental derangement. Formerly, time-expired soldiers in India were sent to Deolali, a town near Bombay, to await passage home. There were often long, frustrating delays, when boredom and the climate may have led to some odd behaviour, which caused some of them to become 'doolally'. The full phrase was 'doolally tap', the latter word being of Malaysian/Indonesian origin and meaning 'malarial fever'.

Jingoism Aggressive British 'patriotism'. The term derives from the popular music hall song by G.W. Hunt, which appeared at the time of the Russo-Turkish War (1877–78), when anti-Russian feeling ran high and Disraeli ordered the Mediterranean fleet to Constantinople.

> We don't want to fight, but by Jingo if we do,
> We've got the ships, we've got the men, and got the
>   money too.
> We've fought the Bear before, and while we're Britons
>   true,
> The Russians shall not have Constantinople.

The Russophobes became known as Jingoes, and any belligerent patriotism has been labelled jingoism ever since.

Rank and File

Beefeaters The popular name of the Yeomen Warders of the Tower of London, a body of ceremonial guardians established by the new king Henry VII in 1485. The term is sometimes also incorrectly applied to the Yeomen of the Guard, a similarly long-established but distinct corps of royal bodyguards. The meaning of the term 'Beefeaters' is literally 'eaters of beef', and is thought to refer to the supposed historical practice of paying the Warders partly in rations including beef.

Caddie This word is now solely used for the person who carries a golfer's clubs on the course. In the 17th century it was the term for a gentleman who learned the military profession by serving in the army without a commission. Hence, from the 18th century, it came to be applied in Scottish use to a person looking for employment or an apprentice.

Constable In the Byzantine Empire, the constable was master of the imperial stables and a great officer of state, hence the use of the name for an official of a royal household or a military commander. It was adopted by the Frankish kings, and the office grew steadily more important under their successors. The name is from the Latin *comes stabuli*, 'count of the stable'.

Diehards, The At the Battle of Albuera (1811), the 57th Foot, later the 1st Battalion Middlesex Regiment, and afterwards the 4th Battalion the Queen's Regiment, had three-quarters of their officers and men either killed or wounded. Colonel Inglis was badly wounded, but refused to be moved. Instead he lay where he had fallen crying, 'Die hard, my men, die hard.'

Digger An Australian. The name was in use before 1850, when it was applied to those mining for gold, and was later applied to Anzac troops fighting (and digging in) in Flanders in the First World War and again in the Second World War.

Dogface Originally, in 19th-century US slang, an ugly-looking person. In the 20th century the word was applied as an insult by members of the US Marine Corps to infantrymen in the US Army, whom they looked down on.

Dragoon The name was originally that of a mounted infantry-man, hence its inclusion in the present names of certain cavalry regiments, such as the Royal Scots Dragoon Guards. It is taken from the carbine called a 'dragon', which breathed forth fire like a fabulous beast.

Fanfaron A swaggering bully or cowardly boaster who blows his own trumpet. From Spanish *fanfaronada*, from *fanfarron*, meaning 'to boast'. Sir Walter Scott uses the word for finery, especially for the gold lace worn by military men. Hence the now rare word 'fanfaronade' for boastful or ostentatious behaviour.

Gurkhas A Nepalese people whose men have volunteered to serve in the British Army since the 19th century. They are respected for their martial spirit, and have built a reputation as some of the finest soldiers in the world. Their name is Sanskrit for 'cow protectors', the cow being a sacred animal to the Hindus.

Jerry (from 'German') Since the First World War a nick-name for a German or Germans collectively. Also an old collo-quialism for a chamber pot, said to allude to the shape of an upturned German helmet.

Lieutenant The military rank below a captain. The word derives from Old French and means literally 'place-holding', that is, standing in for an officer of higher rank. The word is usually pronounced 'leftenant' in the British Army, 'lootenant' in the US. The British pronunciation may have come from a misreading of the 'u' for a 'v' before the 19th century, which later became an 'f'.

MI5 The British intelligence service was organized by Captain Vernon Kell (1873–1942) when, in 1909, the Admiralty established the Secret Service Bureau to counter the threat posed by the expanding German fleet. Kell became responsible for counter-espionage within the British Isles, and in 1915 his service was incorporated in the Directorate of Military Intelligence as MI5, Military Intelligence section 5. The number originally indicated Europe as its area of operations, as distinct from MI1, MI2, MI3, and MI4, which covered the other continents.

Rank and file Soldiers and non-commissioned officers as distinct from commissioned officers, hence the followers in a movement as distinct from its leaders. 'Rank' refers to men in line abreast or side by side, 'file' to men standing one behind the other.

Rascal This word, originally a collective term for the rabble of an army, was later applied to a member of the mob, or *mobile vulgus*, 'excitable crowd'. The word itself ultimately goes back to Latin *radere, rasus*, 'to scrape'.

Rookie In army slang, a recruit, a novice. In the USA the name is given to a raw beginner in professional sport. It is an altered form of 'recruit'.

Smersh The popular name for the Russian counter-espionage organization responsible for maintaining security within the Soviet armed and intelligence services during the Second World War. An organization known as Smersh also features as the villains in some of Ian Fleming's James Bond novels. The name is a shortening of Russian *smert' shpionam*, 'death to spies'.

Soldier Originally a hireling, one paid a wage, especially for military service, from Late Latin *solidus*, 'gold coin', hence 'pay'.

Tommy or **Tommy Atkins** A British Army private soldier, just as a Jack Tar is a British sailor. From 1815 and throughout the 19th century Thomas Atkins was the name used in the specimen form accompanying the official manual issued to all army recruits, supplied to show them how details of name, age, date of enlistment, and the like should be filled in on their own form.

Gone for a Burton

Ace The number one on a playing card or on dice based on the Latin *as*, meaning 'unit'. Since an ace is the card with the highest value in many card games, the word moved to describe excellence in a field. During the First World War the French word *as*, applied to an airman who had brought down ten enemy aeroplanes, was imported in its English equivalent 'ace'.

Boffin A nickname used by the RAF in the Second World War for a research scientist, one of the backroom boys. It passed into general use in the 1940s. Its origin is uncertain, but it may derive from an obsolete torpedo bomber, the Blackburn Baffin, itself named after the navigator William Baffin (*c.*1584–1622), discoverer in 1616 of Baffin Bay in the North Atlantic. The word passed into slang to mean a studious person or 'swot'.

Bridge too far, A A position reached that is too risky; a step that is 'one too many'. The phrase comes from the title of Cornelius Ryan's book *A Bridge too Far* (1974), made into a memorable film, about the 1944 Allied airborne landings in the

Netherlands. These were intended to capture 11 bridges needed for the Allied invasion of Germany but the enterprise failed grievously at Arnhem. In advance of the operation General Frederick Browning is said to have protested to Field Marshal Montgomery, who was in overall command, 'But, sir, we may be going a bridge too far.'

Burton, Gone for a Of a person or a thing, absent, missing, or lost, and of a person alone, dead, or presumed dead. The expression was common among service personnel in the Second World War, when it was held to be bad luck to say bluntly that a pilot had died or was missing in action. The 'burton' here may well refer to Burton upon Trent, a centre of beer production for over a century. To have 'gone for a Burton' might then have been a darkly humorous riff on ending up 'in the drink' after a crash.

Flat spin To be in a 'flat spin' is to be very flurried and in a panic. In flying, a flat spin is when the longitudinal axis of an aircraft inclines downwards at an angle of less than 45°. In the early days this inevitably involved loss of control. It later came to be an aerial manoeuvre performed at low level in air combat as an evasive action.

Go pear-shaped, To To go wrong. The term became current in the 1980s but was earlier found in RAF slang with humorous reference to the shape of an aircraft that has crashed nose first.

Kamikaze A Japanese word meaning 'divine wind', referring to the providential typhoon that on a night in August 1281 foiled a Mongol invasion. In the Second World War it was applied to the 'suicide' aircraft attacks organized under Vice Admiral Onishi in the Philippines between October 1944 and January 1945. Some 5,000 young pilots gave their lives when their bomb-loaded fighters crashed into their targets.

Milk run An RAF expression of the Second World War for any sortie flown regularly day after day, or a sortie against an easy target on which inexperienced pilots could be used with impunity. It was as safe and simple as a milkman's early morning round.

Piece of cake Something easy, or easily obtained. The allusion is to the ease with which a slice of cake is taken and eaten. The RAF appropriated the expression in the Second World War, and a cartoon at the time of the Berlin airlift in 1948 depicted a pilot saying, 'Piece of Gatow, old boy' (Gatow was a strategic Berlin airfield used for this operation).

On a wing and a prayer With only a small hope or chance of success. The phrase comes from a Second World War song based on the words that the pilot of a damaged aircraft radioed to ground control as he prepared to come in to land:

Tho' there's one motor gone, we can still carry on
Comin' in on a wing and a pray'r.

INSULTS

An insult was once a very physical attack. At its heart is the Latin *insultare*, 'to jump on or trample', i.e. to leap on the prostrate body of a foe. The dictionary bears out the belief that humans are far more adept at trading kicks in the teeth than compliments.

Bespawler A person who spits when he talks.

Cumberworld A useless person who merely takes up space.

Dew-beater An 18th-century slang word for a very large shoe – by extension, a clumsy or awkward person.

Fopdoodle An insignificant or foolish man.

Fustilugs A ponderous, clumsy person; especially a fat and slovenly woman.

Gillie-wet-foot An old Scots word for a swindling businessman, or someone who gets into debt and then flees.

Gnashgab An 18th-century northern English word for someone who only ever seems to complain.

Gobemouche A gullible person who is always open-mouthed in gullibility or astonishment. From the French for 'fly-swallower'.

Goldenballs An old abusive appellation, recorded in the Domesday Book (1086), which lists a Humfrid Aurei Testiculi (Humphrey Goldenbollocks). Victoria Beckham famously used it, presumably affectionately, for her husband, the footballer David, and once she revealed it in 2001, it was widely trumpeted in the British press.

Ipse dixit (Latin, 'he himself said so') The dogmatic insistence that something is true based on the assertion of one person. *Ipse dixit* was first used by the Roman orator Cicero as a translation of a Greek motto with the same meaning, *autos epha*, repeated by devoted followers of the philosopher Pythagoras whenever they presented his teachings. In their eyes, if their master said it, it must be fact. *Ipse dixit* found its way into the law courts as a criticism of any argument that was based on the say-so of only one authority. From there, 'ipse-dixitism' was formed to mean any unfounded political opinion, and then more generally any assertion made without a shred of evidence to back it up.

Jerk An early US term for a small train on a branch railway, also a small township of little consequence, so generally anything of trifling importance. In such remote places a locomotive had to 'jerk' water from a stream or water tower into its tender. The township became known as a jerk town, and 'jerk' eventually broadened to describe someone obnoxious.

Klazomaniac Someone who predominantly shouts when speaking.

Lickspigot A parasite; one who only drinks other people's alcohol.

Lickspittle A toady; a sycophant; a flatterer.

Lobcock A large, relaxed penis, hence a dull and inanimate individual.

Lubberwort A 16th-century nickname for a lethargic, fuzzy-minded person.

Muck-spout A dialect word for someone who swears a huge amount.

Mumpsimus One who insists they are right, despite clear evidence they are not. The original meaning was 'an erroneous doctrinal view obstinately adhered to', and was put into currency by Henry VIII in a speech from the throne in 1545. He remarked, 'Some be too stiff in their old mumpsimus, others be too busy and curious in their sumpsimus.' He referred to a familiar story of a priest who always incorrectly read out the Communion prayer as *Quod ore sumpsimus, Domine* ('What we have taken in our mouth, Lord'), by substituting *sumpsimus* with *mumpsimus*. When his mistake was pointed out, he said that he had read it with an 'm' for forty years, 'and I will not change my old mumpsimus for your new sumpsimus'. The word slipped into figurative use to describe an obstinate individual who refuses to accept the truth despite hard evidence.

Nincompoop A fool or simpleton. The word dates from the late 17th century, but its origins remain obscure. An early variation was 'nickumpoop', and a connection has been suggested with French *nicodème*, 'a simpleton' (perhaps an allusion to the Pharisee Nicodemus, who in St John's Gospel puts naive questions to Jesus), with possibly a riff on English 'ninny' and Dutch *poep*, both meaning 'fool'.

Off one's trolley Crazy; demented. The trolley here is a trolley car, an electric-powered vehicle that runs along metal tracks set into the roadway. After the havoc caused by the Great Blizzard of 1888, New York's Manhattan trolleys no longer used overhead cables, and instead picked up their supply from an electrified third rail. If the car became derailed, its power was lost. The analogy is between a vehicle that has literally come off the rails and can't function, and a person who is no longer acting sanely.

Parwhobbler One who monopolizes conversation so no one else can get a word in.

Rakefire A visitor who outstays his or her welcome, so that the dying coals in the fireplace would need to be raked over just to keep it burning.

Scobberlotcher An old English dialect word for someone who can never be bothered to work hard.

Slubberdegullion A scoundrel. *Slubber*, an English dialect word, means to 'stain' or 'tarnish', and probably comes from an old Dutch word meaning 'to walk through the mire'.

Slugabed A habitually late riser.

Smell-feast Someone who turns up uninvited at a meal or party and expects to be fed.

Smellfungus A capricious critic: a fault-finder (after Smelfungus, a hypercritical traveller in *A Sentimental Journey through France and Italy* (1768) by Laurence Sterne).

Snoutband Someone who constantly interrupts a conversation, typically only to contradict or correct someone else.

Trumperiness This 19th-century word describes a state of being extremely showy but utterly worthless – in other words, trashy. It is first cousin to 'trumpet', from French *trompe*, 'trumpet'.

Whiffle-whaffler An indecisive time-waster. When a wind 'whiffles' it blows fitfully in short gusts or puffs.

PLAYING THE GAME

The world of sport has given us hundreds of metaphors to live by. We aim to be 'up to scratch', 'a safe pair of hands', 'have a game plan', 'cover all bases', 'step up to the plate', and 'be a big hit'. Conversely, we try to avoid being 'on the ropes', 'blind-sided', 'down and out', or 'behind the eight ball'. Whether it's an emotion, a dilemma, or a victory you need to express, sporting idioms will always knock it out of the park.

Cut and Thrust

All over bar the shouting Success is certain. The earliest uses of the phrase involve the throwing of hats up into the air, suggesting that the shouting is a form of celebration and applause, particularly at a victory in a sporting event.

Argue the toss, To To dispute a decision already made. Once the coin has been tossed, with the result for all to see, there is no point in disputing the throw.

Back to square one Right back to the beginning. This expression has inspired dozens of theories as to its origin. Most popular of all is the explanation that football commentaries would often refer to the area of pitch where the ball was in play according to numbered grids. While this system certainly existed, its grids were more rectangular than square, and no evidence has been found as yet of players going 'back to square one'. More likely is a nod either to the children's game of hopscotch or a snakes and ladders board.

By a long chalk By far; easily. The allusion is probably to the chalk marks made on a floor to record the score of a player or team. A 'long chalk' would mean a high score.

Cut and thrust A lively argument or spirited discussion. The allusion is to fencing.

Early doors At an early point in the proceedings. The expression originally referred to the early opening of the doors of a theatre and began to be more widely disseminated through television sports commentaries in the 1970s.

From scratch A person starting from scratch in a sporting event is one starting from the usual starting point (i.e. the line marked, originally scratched out), whereas his fellow competitors would be starting ahead of him with handicaps awarded to their respective merits. 'To start from scratch' in general usage means to start from nothing or without particular advantages.

Knock into a cocked hat, To To beat in a contest by a wide margin; to defeat easily. In the game of ninepins, three pins were set up in the form of a triangle, and when all the pins except these three were knocked down, the set was said to be 'knocked into a cocked hat'. The idea is that of a hat being knocked out of shape.

Knock spots off someone, To To beat them soundly; to get the better of them. The allusion is probably to pistol-shooting at a playing card, when a good shot will knock out the pips or spots.

Like a hog on ice Supremely confident; cocky; self-assured. A phrase used in the USA, but it may have originated in Scotland, having connection with the hog used in curling.

No holds barred Anything goes. An allusion to a wrestling match in which normal rules are set aside.

Play fast and loose, To The inspiration was probably an old cheating game once practised at fairs. A belt or strap was doubled and rolled up with the loop in the centre and placed on edge on a table. The player then had to catch the loop with a skewer while the belt was unrolled, but this was done in such a way by the trickster as to make the feat impossible.

Shoot one's bolt, To To exhaust one's efforts; to do all that one can. The bolt here is that of the archer.

Slam dunk Something reliable or certain; a foregone conclusion. The imagery is from basketball, in which a slam dunk is a forceful shot ('dunk') in which the player thrusts ('slams') the ball down through the basket with both hands from above the rim.

Stadium This word comes, via Latin, from Greek *stadion*, an altered form of *spadion*, 'racecourse', from *span*, 'to pull', referring to the drawing of chariots. The *stadion* was also a measure of length, 600 Greek feet, the equivalent of about 607 English feet (185m).

There are no flies on him He is no fool; he won't be caught napping. The term derives from angling. A person was formerly said to be 'no fly' if they failed to rise to the bait.

In the Right Ballpark

Ballpark figure An approximate figure, especially of a financial amount. A ballpark is a US baseball stadium. Since the playing area is large, a ballpark figure (or a figure that is 'in the right ballpark') will not be narrowly defined. The term, which dates from the 1950s, equally relates to the practice of estimating the crowd attendance at a baseball game.

Knock it out of the park, To In baseball, to hit a home run, because any ball hit beyond the boundaries of the park is uncatchable. Figuratively, therefore, this is to perform stupendously well.

Left field In baseball, the part of the playing area to the left of the batter, beyond third base, which rarely sees any action and from which the ball rarely arrives. Hence, metaphorically, something that is 'out of left field' is out of the ordinary, unexpected, eccentric, unorthodox, or experimental.

Play hardball, To To take ruthless and uncompromising action in pursuit of one's goal. 'Hardball' is baseball played with a hard ball, as contrasted with softball.

Southpaw In US usage, a left-handed baseball player, especially a pitcher, or any left-handed person in general. In both US and British usage the term describes a boxer who leads with his right hand.

Children's Games

Cat's cradle A game in which a loop of string is wound around and between the fingers to make patterns. The origins of the name are elusive, but in some versions it was called 'scratch-cradle'.

French skipping Also known as 'jumpsies' and 'elastics', this game combines the skills of both cat's cradle and hopscotch, in requiring its players to make elaborate moves by jumping with and threading a piece of elastic stretched around two other players' ankles.

Here we go round the mulberry bush An old game in which children take hands and dance round in a ring, singing the song of which this is the refrain. The rhyme was first recorded by James Orchard Halliwell-Phillipps, an English Shakespearean scholar and antiquarian, as an English children's game in the mid-19th century. It has been suggested that the original mulberry bush was at HM Prison Wakefield, West Yorkshire, and that the song records female Victorian prisoners dancing around the tree with their children during their exercise time.

Hopscotch The children's game, in which each player takes turns to hop into and over squares marked on the ground to retrieve a marker, is so called because the squares are 'scotched' or 'scored' into the earth or ground.

Lego A construction toy consisting of interlocking plastic building blocks. It came out of a business set up in 1932 at Billund, Denmark, by Ole Kirk Christiansen, a master carpenter and joiner, who originally made and sold stepladders, ironing boards, and wooden toys. In 1934 he named the last Lego, from Danish *leg godt*, 'play well', a name which it was later realized was also Latin for 'I collect'.

Ping-pong The game of table tennis took on its popular name at the turn of the 20th century, 'ping' representing the sound made when the bat strikes the ball and 'pong' the sound when the ball hits the table. According to the *Daily Chronicle* of 2 May 1901, the inventor of ping-pong was one James Gibb, a former Cambridge athlete. The game was originally sold under various names, such as 'Gossima', 'Whiff Whaff', and 'Flim Flam', and like these 'Ping Pong' was a proprietary name, registered in Britain in 1900 and in the USA in 1901.

Subbuteo A brand of table football. It dates from 1947 as the creation of Peter Adolph, who originally wanted to call it 'Hobby'. This name was not acceptable for registration purposes, however, so instead he took the Latin name of the hobby hawk, *Falco subbuteo*, adopting the second word of this by default.

Tic-tac-toe A game of noughts and crosses, in which two players take turns to try to complete a row, a column, or a diagonal with either three O's or three X's drawn in the spaces of a nine-squared grid. The name was first used for games in which the pieces made clicking noises, and imitates this sound.

Tom Tiddler's ground A place where it is easy to pick up a fortune or make a place in the world for oneself. The name comes from the old children's game in which a base-keeper, who is called Tom Tiddler, tries to keep the other children from crossing the boundary into his base. As he does so, they sing:

Here we are on Tom Tiddler's ground
Picking up gold and silver.

Join the Cue

Behind the eight ball In a dangerous position from which it is impossible to escape. The phrase comes from the game of pool, in one variety of which all the balls must be pocketed in a certain order, except the black ball, numbered eight. If another ball touches the eight ball, the player is penalized. Therefore, if the eight ball is in front of the one which he intends to pocket, he is in a hazardous position.

Billiards The name is from the French *billard*, 'little tree trunk'. It was originally used for the cue, but was soon transferred to the game itself.

Call the shots, To To have control over a situation; to be the one who is in charge. The allusion is to a game of pool, in which the player nominates which ball must go into which pocket, so avoiding fluke scores.

Cue The long stick used in billiards and snooker is a relative of 'queue', French for the tail of an animal and later for a line of people. In the 18th and 19th centuries it also referred to a pigtail, when it was alternatively spelled as 'cue'. It is from there that the sense of the long thin rod used in the table games emerged.

Snooker The game and name of snooker emerged among the British Army serving in India in the 19th century, when it was played amongst officers as a fast-moving version of billiards. The word may rest on existing army slang in which 'snooker' meant 'a new or green cadet', and later as a joking reference to the inept play of a fellow officer. In the game itself, if the balls are so arranged by one player as to make potting impossible, their opponent is said to be 'snookered', i.e. put in a difficult position.

Up to Scratch

Below the belt Unfairly, unscrupulously. It is prohibited in the Queensberry rules of prizefighting to hit below the waist belt.

Haymaker In boxing a vicious, swinging blow, like a man wielding a heavy pitchfork of hay.

On the ropes On the verge of ruin or collapse. The allusion is to the boxing ring, where a fighter who is driven back against the ropes is often close to defeat.

Saved by the bell Extricated from an unpleasant or undesirable situation by the intervention of someone or something. The reference is to the bell at the end of a round in a boxing match, rescuing the loser from further punishment.

Set-to, A A fight or a tussle, literally or verbally. In pugilism opponents were 'set to the scratch' or line marked on the ground.

Throw in the towel, To To concede defeat. The allusion is to boxing, in which a second or trainer would throw the towel into the ring to admit that his man had lost.

Throw one's hat into the ring, To To enter a contest or to become a candidate for office. There was an old custom of throwing one's hat into the ring as the sign of accepting a pugilist's challenge.

Throw up or **in the sponge, To** To give up; to confess oneself beaten. The metaphor is from boxing matches, for when a second tossed a sponge (used to refresh a contestant) into the air it was a sign that his man was beaten.

Up to scratch, To come To be ready or good enough in any test; to make the grade. Under the London Prize Ring Rules, introduced in 1839, a round in a prizefight ended when one of the fighters was knocked down. After a 30-second interval, this fighter was allowed eight seconds in which to make his way unaided to a mark scratched in the centre of the ring. If he failed to do so, he 'had not come up to scratch' and was declared beaten.

On a Roll

Blue chip Applied to the stock of highly reputable and well-established companies, which is considered to be a reliable investment. The metaphor comes from the blue chip used in roulette and other gambling games, which is usually assigned a high value.

Devil's bones Dice, which were made of bones, and often led to ruin.

Die is cast, The The die of chance has been thrown, a step is taken, and there is no drawing back. So said Julius Caesar when he crossed the Rubicon with the Latin words *Iacta alea est*.

Mumchance Silence. Mumchance was a game of chance with dice, in which strategic silence was indispensable. 'Mum' here is connected with 'mumble'.

No dice Nothing doing; out of the question. An expression of US origin dating from the 1930s and presumably referring to the refusal of a gambling-house proprietor to allow a player to start or continue gambling.

On a roll Experiencing luck; enjoying success; doing well. The US expression originates from gambling (specifically crap-shooting), and dates from the 1970s. The roll is that of the dice, which keep falling favourably.

Call My Bluff

Above board In the open, without dishonesty or fraud, as when a card or poker player has their hands above the table (board).

Busted flush, A A person or thing that shows signs of great promise and fulfilment but that ultimately lets one down as a failure. The term comes from the game of poker, in which a busted flush is a flush (a hand of five cards all of the same suit) that one fails to complete.

Call someone's bluff, To To challenge someone to prove their claims. A poker player sometimes bluffs by exaggerating the strength of his or her hand, betting large sums on it in the hope that others will withdraw. At some stage, however, an opponent matching the stake has the right to call on the player to show his or her hand.

Dead man's hand In the western states of the USA, a combination of aces and eights in poker, so called because when Sheriff Wild Bill Hickok was shot in the back at Deadwood, South Dakota, he held such cards in his hand.

Pass the buck, To To evade blame or responsibility and to shift it on to someone else. A US phrase, coming from the game of poker, the term is said to refer to the buckhorn knife that was placed in front of a player to indicate that he was the next dealer. When he had dealt, he 'passed the buck' to another player. The knife itself was so called because its handle was made from the horn of a buck. The earliest recorded use of the phrase is by Mark Twain in 1872.

Marking Someone's Card

Chicane A term used in bridge or whist for a hand containing no trumps. Its general meaning is the use of petty subterfuge, especially in legal dodges and quibbles. On a motor-racing circuit, a chicane is a short section of sharp bends formed by barriers, designed to serve as a test of driving skill. Again the idea is of 'dodging' or weaving in and out.

Jackpot In poker, a pot that cannot be opened until a player has a pair of jacks or better. The word is generally applied to the 'pool' disgorged by a gaming machine or to the top prize in a contest, draw, or lottery. To hit the jackpot is to win any great prize or unexpected 'bonanza'.

Leave in the lurch, To To desert a person in a difficulty. In cribbage a player is left in the position called the lurch when his or her adversary has run out a score of 51 holes before the player has turned the corner or pegged out the 31st hole. 'Lurch' itself is from the French *lourche*, a 16th-century game resembling backgammon.

Level pegging Equality in a contest or rivalry with another person. The expression is from those games, such as cribbage, in which a pegboard is used for scoring.

Mark someone's card, To To provide them with information; to tip them off; to put them right. The expression dates from the 1960s and derives from horse-racing, in which the 'card' is the programme of events that the punter or tipster will annotate ('mark') to indicate possible winners.

Peg out, To To die. The allusion is to the game of cribbage, in which the game is ended by a player pegging out the last holes.

Rubber In whist, bridge, and some other games, a rubber is a set of three games, the best two of three, or the third game of the set. By extension, in cricket the term is applied to a Test series, whether the number of matches is odd or even. Its origin is uncertain, but it may be a transference from bowls, in which the collision of two woods is a rubber, because they rub against each other.

Slam A term in card-playing denoting winning all the tricks in a deal. In bridge this is called a grand slam, and winning all but one, a little or small slam. The word itself was originally the name of a card game, and is perhaps from obsolete *slampant*, 'trickery'.

Spade The spade of playing cards is so called from Italian *spada*, 'sword', the suit in Italian packs being marked with short swords. In French and British cards the mark, largely through similarity in name, has been altered to the shape of a pointed spade.

In spades To the greatest degree or number; very much (as in 'You deserved that in spades'). A phrase of US origin, alluding to the status of spades as the highest-ranking suit in the card game bridge.

Turn-up for the book or **books, A** A completely unexpected result or occurrence, especially a welcome one. 'Turn-up' alludes to the turning up of a particular card in a game, while the 'book' is a book of bets, such as the one kept by a book-maker at a racecourse.

Whist The card game originated in England (16th century). It was first called 'triumph' (whence 'trump'), then 'ruff' or 'honours', and then, early in the 17th century, 'whisk', in allusion to the sweeping up of the cards. 'Whist', the later name, appears in Samuel Butler's *Hudibras* (1662–80), and was adopted through confusion with 'Whisht!' meaning 'Hush!' or 'Silence!'

Yarborough A hand at bridge in which there is no card higher than a nine. It is so called because the 2nd Lord Yarborough (1809–62) used to lay 1000 to 1 against such an occurrence in any named hand. The actual mathematical odds are 1827 to 1 against.

Par for the Course

Birdie A score of one under par. It is based on the use in US slang of 'bird' to mean 'excellent' – a birdie is a 'bird of a shot'. Other bird metaphors were added for various other golf shots, including an eagle (two under par) and an albatross (three under par).

Bogey One stroke above par in golf. The word was first recorded in the 1890s. The story goes that in 1890 Dr Thomas Browne, honorary secretary of the Great Yarmouth club, was playing against a Major Wellman, the match being against the 'ground score', i.e. the scratch value of each hole. This system was new to the major, and he exclaimed, thinking of a popular song at the time, that his invisible and apparently invincible opponent was a regular 'bogey man'.

Golf The sport is not, as is popularly believed, based on the acronym Gentlemen Only, Ladies Forbidden – a reference to the fact that women were long prohibited from joining the most prestigious golf clubs. Intead it is likely to come from the Dutch *kolf*, a 'club' or 'bat'.

Par The number of strokes a first-class player should require for a particular hole or course. Derived from the use in the Stock Exchange of 'par' to mean a level that a stock may be above or below. It comes from the Latin, meaning 'equal'.

Links The word 'links' in its use as a field of play for golf derives from Old English *hlinc*, 'ledge'. This came to apply in Scotland to a narrow strip of coastal land with coarse grass and sand-dunes.

Par for the course As expected or predicted, given the circumstances, as: 'He's half an hour late but that's par for the course, knowing him.' The phrase dates from the 1940s and alludes to a golf player's expected score for a particular course.

Horses for Courses

Canter An easy gallop, originally called a Canterbury trot, from the supposed gait adopted by mounted pilgrims to the shrine of St Thomas à Becket at Canterbury.

Cinch A certainty. A word of US origin derived from the Mexican saddle girth (Spanish *cincha*), which was strong, tight, and safe.

Come a cropper, To To fall heavily or fail badly. The expression came from horseriding, and its origin probably lies in 'neck and crop', meaning 'altogether', 'completely'.

Dark horse, A A racing term for a horse of possible promise, but about which nothing is known. The allusion is not to a dark-coloured horse but to one about which the public has been 'kept in the dark'.

Derby The Derby is the name of the premier horse race in England, founded by the 12th Earl of Derby in 1780. Since at least as early as 1840, 'derby' has been used to denote any kind of sporting contest – a local derby is a sporting contest between local rivals.

Desultory Roman circus riders who used to leap from one horse to another were called 'desultores', from Latin *desilire*, 'to jump down'. Hence the use of 'desultory' in English to denote someone who figuratively flits from one thing to another.

Down to the wire Said of a situation in which the outcome is not known until the last minute. The allusion is to the imaginary line marking the end of a horse race, where the winners notionally pass 'under the wire'. The phrase is also heard in the variant 'up to the wire'.

Gee-up! A call to a horse to encourage it to move off or go faster. The word may simply imitate the sound of the instruction.

Give and take, To To be fair; to practise forbearance and consideration. In horse-racing a 'give and take plate' is a prize for a race in which the runners that exceed a standard height carry more than the standard weight and those that fall short of it less.

Home and dry Safe and successful, having satisfactorily completed some endeavour. The allusion is to a horse race, when the winning rider has such a good lead that he can rub down his mount before the rest of the field arrive.

Horses for courses A course of action or policy that has been modified slightly from the original to allow for altered circumstances. A horse that runs well on a dry course will run less well on a damp course and vice versa. The expression came into use in the late 19th century.

Steeplechase Originally a horse race across fields, hedges, ditches, and other obstacles, now run over a prepared course. The term is said to have originated from the frolic of a party of fox-hunters in Ireland (1803) who decided to race in a straight line to a distant steeple. The term is also applied to a cross-country race of this kind on foot, and to an athletics track event, run over 2000 or 3000 metres and involving hurdles and a water jump.

Tod, To be on one's To be alone, a contraction of 'Tod Sloan' in Cockney rhyming slang. James Forman 'Tod' Sloan (1874–1933) was a famous US jockey, who fell from favour thanks to a suspicion he had been betting on races in which he competed. Later historians cleared his reputation, but it is said he died a lonely death of cirrhosis of the liver.

Win hands down, To To win easily. A jockey rides with hands down and his reins loosened when he is winning comfortably and easily.

Checkmate

Checkmate A term in chess for the situation in which an opponent's king is threatened and unable to escape. This wins the game. Figuratively, to checkmate is to thwart someone, or make them powerless. The word comes from the Persian *šāh māt*, 'the king is dead'.

Chess 'The game of kings' derives its name from Old French *esches*, the plural of *eschec*, meaning 'check'. Its use in chess has led to the many senses of 'check' in English, from 'stopping' or 'controlling' something to the squared pattern that is a check or chequered cloth.

Endgame The final stages of a game, especially chess, when few pieces remain.

Mah-jongg A Chinese game played with 'tiles' like dominoes, made of ivory and bamboo, with usually four players. The game was introduced to the USA by Joseph P. Babcock about 1919 under the trade name Mah-jongg, which he coined. It is Chinese for 'sparrows', referring to the mythical 'bird of 100 intelligences' that appears on one of the tiles.

Turn the tables, To To reverse a situation by bringing forth a countercharge. The phrase probably comes from the game of backgammon, which until the 18th century was commonly known as 'tables'. The specific reference may be either to swapping over the pieces on the board, or to reversing the players' positions (a backgammon board is divided into four sections known as 'tables'). In either case a reversal of fortune may follow.

Zugzwang A situation in chess in which whichever move one makes – and the player has to make one – will lead to a serious, often decisive, disadvantage. From the German for 'move compulsion'.

On a Sticky Wicket

Cricket The name of the game may come from an Old English word meaning a 'stool' perhaps used as a 'wicket'. This word is first recorded in an official document of 1598, in which a man in his fifties swears that when he was a schoolboy he played cricket and other games on a field in Guildford, Surrey, which would date the sport to at least the reign of Henry VIII.

Duck's egg Now always used in the shortened form of 'a duck', meaning in cricket no score at all. It arose from the resemblance of 'o' on the scoreboard to a duck's egg. In US usage 'goose egg' is used for no score at all in a game.

Hat trick In cricket, the taking of three wickets with three successive balls. A bowler who accomplished this formerly earned the right to take his hat round the ground for a collection. The phrase is now also applied to any success achieved three times in a row.

Silly In cricket, 'silly' is used to indicate fielding positions close to the battter's wicket; thus 'silly mid-on' and 'silly mid-off' (fielding positions in front of the batter respectively on the on and off sides of the wicket) are considerably closer to the batsman than 'mid-on' and 'mid-off'. 'Silly' itself comes from Old English _sælig_, 'happy', related to modern German _selig_, 'blessed', 'happy', so that the original sense was 'happy through being innocent'. As the innocent are easily taken in by worldly cunning, the word came to signify 'gullible', 'foolish'.

Sledging In cricket, the heaping of insults on an opposing batter so as to break their concentration. The analogy is with giving them a battering with a sledgehammer.

Sticky wicket, A A difficult or awkward situation. The allusion is to cricket, when a pitch that is drying after rain causes difficulties for the batter when the ball is bowled.

Yorker In cricket, a deceptive ball delivered so that it pitches directly beneath the bat and is thus likely to be missed by the batter. It is perhaps so called from its first being developed by a Yorkshire bowler.

Roaring Games

Cornish hug A special grip in wrestling. Cornish men were noted wrestlers and tried to throttle their antagonist with a particular grip or embrace called the Cornish hug.

Croquet The garden game probably takes its name from a French dialect variant of *crochet*, 'little hook', because the early croquet mallets were shaped like hockey sticks.

Dwile flonking An English pub game that involves propelling a beer-soaked rag with the aid of a broom handle in an attempt to hit a member of the opposing team. Despite attempts to invest it with a spurious antiquity, it appears to have been invented in 1966 by a pair of Suffolk printers. *Dwile* is an old East Anglian dialect word for 'dishcloth', and *flonk* is probably an invention based on 'fling'.

Marathon A long-distance race. In the modern Olympic games the marathon race was instituted in 1896, the distance being standardized at 26 miles 385 yards (42.195km) in 1924. It is famously named after the Battle of Marathon (490 BC), the result of which was announced at Athens by an unnamed courier who fell dead on his arrival, having run nearly 23 miles (37km). This runner is sometimes cited as Pheidippides (or Philippides), who actually ran from Athens to Sparta to seek help against the Persians before the battle.

Pall Mall The smart West End thoroughfare in the centre of London takes its name from the old 'alley' where 'pall mall' was first played long before Charles II introduced it in St James's Park. 'Pale-maille,' says Randle Cotgrave, 'is a game wherein a round box ball is struck with a mallet through a high arch of iron, which he that can do at the fewest blows, or at the number agreed upon, wins.' The name comes from Italian *palla*, 'ball', and *maglio*, 'mallet'.

Pilates A system of gentle exercises performed lying down that stretches and lengthens the muscles, designed to make the body long, lean, supple, and strong. Although it came into vogue on both sides of the Atlantic in the 1990s, it had been invented in the 1920s by Joseph Pilates (1880–1967), a German entrepreneur who studied different exercise routines to strengthen his body after a sickly childhood.

Pole position In motor racing, the starting position in the front row and on the inside of the first bend, usually regarded as the best and most advantageous. The reference is to the pole as the term for the inside fence on a racecourse and also the starting position closest to it. A horse was said to 'have the pole' if the jockey had drawn this position. Hence, 'to be in pole position', meaning to have the advantage generally.

Regatta A boat race, or organized series of boat races. The name was originally given to the races held between Venetian gondoliers, from obsolete Italian (Venetian dialect) *rigatta*, meaning 'strife', 'contention'.

Ringer A term applied on the racecourse, running track, and the like to a runner who is fraudulently entered for a race as a substitute for another in order to provide an unfair advantage. It is also used of a person or thing which closely resembles another. Hence, 'dead ringer' for someone who bears an exact resemblance to another.

Roaring game, The Curling, so called because the Scots when playing or watching support their side with noisy cheering, and because the stones, which are made of granite or whinstone, roar as they cross the ice.

Tennis

Love The word is from Old English *lufu*, connected with Sanskrit *lubh*, 'to desire', and Latin *lubere*, 'to please'. In the sense 'nil score in tennis', as 'forty-love' (40–0), 'love-all' (0–0), love probably comes from the phrase 'to play for love', i.e. without stakes. It is not likely to be an alteration of French *l'œuf*, 'the egg', as often stated, on the grounds that a figure o resembles an egg, even though this is the sense of a 'duck' (duck's egg) in cricket.

Real tennis The original form of the game of tennis, as played since the Middle Ages on an irregularly shaped indoor court divided by a net. It is popularly believed (probably because of the game's association with Henry VIII) that 'real' is a survival of an old word meaning 'royal'. The game is sometimes even alternatively called 'royal tennis', especially in Australia. In fact it was termed 'real', in the 1880s, simply in order to distinguish it from the new outdoor game called 'lawn tennis'.

Seeded players Those players regarded by the organizers of a tournament (e.g. lawn tennis at the All England Club, Wimbledon) as likely to reach the final stages, and who are so placed in the order of play that they do not meet each other until the closing rounds. The allusion is to sowing seeds in such a way that those of the best plants are not 'weeded out' before their time.

!?

TERMS FOR THINGS YOU DIDN'T KNOW HAD A NAME

What do you call the projecting part of your chin, or the groove about your lip? How about the plastic tag at the end of your shoelace, or the metal tip of an umbrella? We can all be thankful that there are words for every one of these things, even if we never knew we needed them.

Aglet The plastic coating on the end of a shoelace.

Agraffe The wire cage that holds the cork in a bottle of champagne.

Crapulence The sick feeling you get after eating or drinking too much.

Dysania The state of finding it hard to get out of bed in the morning.

Ferrule A ring or cap, especially made of metal, which strengthens the end of a handle, stick, or umbrella and prevents it from splitting or wearing.

Glabella The space between the eyebrows.

Griffonage Unreadable handwriting.

Nibling Non-gender-specific term for a niece or nephew.

Nurdle The perfect swish of toothpaste seen in toothpaste adverts.

Philtrum The groove between the nose and upper lip.

Phloem Long, fibrous, vascular tissue on the inside of banana skins; by extension, the strings on the fruit itself.

Pogonion The foremost point on the midline of the chin.

Purlicue The space between thumb and forefinger.

Scurryfunge Time spent frantically cleaning just before guests come.

Zarf The cardboard sleeve for a coffee cup.

REAL PLACES

Language and landscape have always been intertwined. English pays tribute to hundreds of venues in its words and expressions, from being 'sent to Coventry' to London's 'bedlam' and on to Wiltshire's 'moonraker' and Oxford's 'toff'. In the same way, our local dialects, pub names, and slang continue to shape the language of our identity – whether we talk about being 'wisht as a winnard' or 'bostin fittle', count our sheep in Old Norse, are called Marchant or Fletcher, drive past the Elephant and Castle, prepone a meeting on the streets of Bradford, and take our pints in Ambleside's Drunken Duck while swapping tales that are all 'cock and bull'.

Sent to Coventry (and Elsewhere)

Albion An ancient and poetic name for Britain, probably of Celtic origin and a reference to the white (Latin *albus*) cliffs of Dover.

Banbury Cross A market cross in Banbury, celebrated in the nursery rhyme 'Ride a cock-horse to Banbury Cross / To see a fine lady on a white horse'. As a toy, a 'cock-horse' was a stick with a wooden horse's head on it, on which a child pretended to ride like a horse. In the days when the rhyme was composed, 'horse' would have rhymed with 'cross'. The original cross was destroyed by Puritans in 1602. The present-day one is a replica, erected in 1859.

Bedlam A corruption of 'Bethlehem' and a reference to the Hospital of St Mary of Bethlehem, also known as Bethlem Royal Hospital, in London, set up as an asylum. 'Bedlam' subsequently became a term for any hospital dealing with mental illness, and from there, insultingly, for any scene of 'mad' confusion.

Carry coals to Newcastle, To To do what is superfluous; to take something where it is already plentiful. The French say: *porter de l'eau à la rivière* ('to carry water to the river'). The Germans say: *Eulen nach Athen tragen* ('to carry owls to Athens', for the owl was the bird of the Greek goddess Athene). Russians say: *yekhat' v Tulu so svoim samovarom* ('to go to Tula with one's own samovar'; Tula was a major centre of samovar production).

Cornwall (Cornish, *Kernow*) The county's name goes back to the tribal name Cornovii, meaning 'horn people', referring to the long peninsula that is Cornwall. The first part of the name was adopted by the Anglo-Saxons, who called the Britons who lived here *Cornwalas*, 'Corn-foreigners'. This eventually became modern 'Cornwall'.

Croakumshire A name given to the county of Northumberland, whose inhabitants were alleged to speak with a peculiar croak. It was said to be particularly noticeable in Newcastle and Morpeth, where the people were believed to be born with a burr in their throats that prevented them from voicing the letter 'r'.

Devonshire The name is derived from the early Celtic inhabitants, the Dumnonii, whose own name may mean 'deep ones', in that they were valley dwellers.

Epsom salts Hydrated magnesium sulphate, used as a purgative and to reduce inflammation. It is so called because it was originally obtained by the evaporation of the water of a mineral spring at Epsom in Surrey. According to Thomas Fuller's *Worthies* (1662), the spring was discovered by a farmer in 1618, who noticed that, in spite of the drought, his cows refused to drink water from the spring. On analysis, it was found to contain the bitter purgative, sulphate of magnesia. Epsom Wells developed, like Tunbridge Wells, as a favourite London spa. Aubrey, Pepys, Nell Gwyn, and Queen Anne's consort were among its visitors.

Geordie A Tynesider or the dialect spoken by the native inhabitants of this north-eastern region of England. The name is a local form of 'George', used as a generic nickname for local miners, sailors, and others. It is specifically associated with, if not actually derived from, the name of George Stephenson (1781–1848), the Newcastle engineer who built the first successful steam locomotive in 1814 and who became manager of the world's first public railway, the Stockton and Darlington, in 1821. Linguists trace the Geordie dialect back to Northumbrian, one of the three divisions of Old English.

Hundred A former division of the English shire, corresponding to the 'wapentake' of Danish areas. Originally the hundred probably consisted of 100 hides (a hide was typically equal to between 60 and 120 acres).

Isle of Man One explanation of the name is that given by Richard of Cirencester (d. *c.*1401): 'Midway between the two countries [Britain and Ireland] is the island called Monoeda, but now Monavia', i.e. deriving the name from Gaelic *menagh* or *meanagh*, meaning 'middle'. The Manx name of the island is Ellan Vannan, 'island of Mann', and in Irish it is Oileán Mhanannán, 'Manannán's isle'. Caesar recorded the name of the island as Mona in the 1st century BC.

John o'Groats The site of a legendary house 1¾ miles (2.8km) west of Duncansby Head, Caithness, north-eastern Scotland. The story is that Malcolm, Gavin, and John o' Groat (or Jan de Groot), three Dutch brothers, came to this part of Scotland in the time of James IV (r.1488–1513). There came to be eight families of the name, and they met annually to celebrate. On one occasion a question of precedence arose. Consequently John o' Groat built an eight-sided room with a door to each side and set an octagonal table in it so that all were 'head of the table'. This building went ever after by the name of John o' Groat's House.

Manchester The name of the city was recorded in the 4th century AD as Mamucio, from a Celtic root word *mamm*, meaning 'breast', referring to the rounded hill on which Manchester arose. To this was added *ceaster*, the Old English form of Latin *castra*, 'camp', referring to its former status as a Roman walled town. A native of Manchester is a Mancunian, from *Mancunium*, the Medieval Latin name of the city.

Martello towers Round towers about 40ft (12m) high and of great strength. Many of them were built on the south-eastern coasts of England in about 1803 against the threat of French invasion. They took their name from Cape Mortella, Corsica, where a tower, from which these were designed, had proved extremely difficult to capture in 1794.

Mersey A river that flows through Liverpool. The geographical name itself derives from the Old English words for 'boundary river'.

Moonraker A nickname for a resident of Wiltshire. The name alludes to a story involving Wiltshire yokels who were caught by some excisemen raking a pond for kegs of smuggled brandy. They feigned stupidity and claimed that they were trying to rake out the moon that was reflected in the water.

Pommy or **Pommie** An Australian and New Zealand term for a Briton, used both affectionately and disparagingly. Evidence suggests that it arose as a blend of 'pomegranate' and 'immigrant', the former word referring to the ruddy or sunburnt complexions of the British when they arrived on shore.

Pompey The nickname of the English city and seaport of Portsmouth, applied to it particularly as a Royal Navy base and (perhaps originally) to its football club. Various ingenious or fanciful suggestions have been made as to its origin, including the local fire brigade, known as the Pompiers (from French *pompier*, literally 'pumper'), who used to exercise on Southsea Common, closely adjacent to Portsmouth.

Riding One of three former administrative divisions of Yorkshire, which takes its name from the Old Norse *thrithjungr*, 'third part', from *thrithi*, 'third'.

Scouse A name applied to the vocabulary and accent of people from Liverpool. The word is a shortened form of 'lobscouse', a sailor's name for a stew, particularly of meat, vegetables, and ship's biscuit. Hence 'lobscouser' as a former name for a sailor.

Send to Coventry, To To ostracize a person or to ignore them. Royalist prisoners captured in Birmingham were sent to Coventry, which was a Parliamentary stronghold.

Shropshire The Old English name for the county was *Scrobbesbyrigscir*, literally 'Shrewsbury-shire'. The Norman name was *Salopescira*, hence 'Salop' as a synonym for the county (and its official name from 1974 to 1980) and 'Salopian' for a native.

Stonehenge The most famous prehistoric monument in Britain. It is situated on Salisbury Plain about 8 miles (13km) north of Salisbury. The second half of the name is from Old English *hengen*, 'hanging place', so that the overall meaning is 'stone gallows', from its resemblance to such.

Maybe It's Because I'm a Londoner

Born within (the) sound of Bow Bells, To be Said of a true Cockney. St Mary-le-Bow, Cheapside, has long had one of the most celebrated bell-peals in London. John Dun, a textile dealer in 1472 gave two tenements to maintain the ringing of Bow Bell every night at nine o'clock, to direct travellers on the road to town. In 1520 William Copland gave a bigger bell for 'sounding a retreat from work'. An air raid destroyed the bells and the interior of the church in 1941. On 20 December 1961 the restored bells rang out to mark the start of the church's rebuilding.

Cockney A Londoner, especially one born within sound of Bow Bells. In Middle English, *cokeney* meant both a 'cock's egg' (a small, malformed egg and hence, loosely, some kind of oddity) and a pampered, 'cockered' child. One theory as to the use of Cockney for a Londoner is that the term came to be applied by country folk to those living in town, as an insult towards their reputed ignorance of country life and customs.

Cockney rhyming slang A coded language that evolved among street traders in the mid-19th century, and grew in popularity as a successor to 'back slang', which was widely used by London's thousands of costermongers. It works by replacing an everyday word, usually a noun, with a rhyming phrase. The rhyming part of the phrase is then usually dropped, making it difficult for the uninitiated to determine the meaning. So to 'have a butcher's' by taking a look derives from 'butcher's hook/look. A more recent form of rhyming slang is 'Mockney', which plays on the names of well-known figures. 'Going for a Britney' means 'going for a Britney Spears/beer', for example, while 'I haven't a Scooby' decodes as 'I haven't a Scooby Doo/ clue'.

Elephant and Castle The sign of a public house at Newington Butts that has given its name to an Underground station and to a district in south London. A popular but completely erroneous explanation is that the name is an alteration of 'Infanta de Castile', referring to Eleanor of Castile, wife of Edward I. Instead it is likely to have come from the crest of the Cutlers' Company – which traded extensively in ivory – which featured an elephant bearing a howdah shaped like a castle.

Get on someone's wick, To To annoy them. The final word is rhyming slang, 'wick' being short for 'Hampton Wick' (a locality in south-west London), representing 'prick'.

Isle of Dogs, The A peninsula on the left bank of the Thames between Limehouse and Blackwall reaches, opposite Greenwich and part of Docklands. The name (first recorded in 1520) may well originally have been applied facetiously in contrast to more elegant names such as 'Isle of Man', but it has also been speculated that it may have been suggested by the Canary Islands, etymologically the 'isle of dogs', wines from which were no doubt landed at the Isle of Dogs in the early days.

Mall, The A broad thoroughfare in St James's Park, London, so called because the game of 'pall mall' used to be played there by Charles II and his courtiers. The 'mall' was the mallet with which the ball was struck.

Mayfair A fashionable district in the West End of London. There was an annual fair in the area from the reign of Edward I, called St James's Fair, which was renewed by James II to commence on 1 May, hence the name.

Middlesex The original territory of the Middle Saxons, which seems to have included the area of the later counties of Middlesex and Hertford, between Essex and Wessex. It became a shire in the 10th century, and was finally absorbed by Greater London, Surrey, and Hertfordshire in 1965.

Old Bailey The Central Criminal Court of the City of London and of (approximately) the Greater London area, situated in the thoroughfare of this name. 'Bailey' comes from Old French *baille* ('enclosed court'), referring to the enclosure of the City wall between Ludgate and Newgate.

Piccadilly The London street takes its name from Piccadilly Hall, which existed in the vicinity in the early 17th century, the home of Robert Baker, a tailor. The name is derived from 'pickadills' or 'peccadilloes', the round hems about the edge of a skirt or garment, also a kind of stiff collar or band for the neck and shoulders. The name may be in allusion to the tailor's source of wealth or the fact that it was the 'skirt house' or outermost house in the district.

Ritzy In colloquial usage, fashionable and luxurious; ostentatiously smart. The allusion is to one or other of the Ritz-Carlton Hotel, New York, the Ritz Hotel, Paris, or the Ritz Hotel, London, which became identified with wealth. The last of these was established in 1906 by the Swiss hotelier César Ritz (1850–1918).

Soho This cosmopolitan area of London apparently derives its name from the old hunting grounds it now stands on, where the hunting cry 'Soho!' would frequently have been heard. It is a very old call, dating from at least the 13th century. New York's SoHo area of Manhattan may have been named with the London enclave in mind, but it is formally an acronym for '*so*uth of *Ho*uston Street'.

Vauxhall A part of Lambeth, London, so called from Falkes de Bréauté, who was lord of the manor in the early 13th century. The Russian word for 'station', transliterated as *voksal* or *vokzal*, is thought to derive from Vauxhall or its pleasure gardens. Some suggest that visiting Russian dignitaries may have mistaken the name of the railway station at Vauxhall for the generic name of the building itself.

All Roads Lead to Rome

All roads lead to Rome All efforts of thought converge in a common centre. From the centre of the Roman world roads radiated to every part of the empire, so any road, if followed to its source, must lead to the great capital city, Rome.

Barbarian The Greeks and Romans called all foreigners 'barbarians' since they were 'babblers', speaking a language not understood by them. The word is thus imitative of speech that is unintelligible as in 'ba ba ba'.

Beyond the pale Outside the limits of what is acceptable, especially in terms of civilized behaviour. 'Pale' in this context is a wooden fence surrounding and demarcating a piece of territory (from Latin *palum*, 'stake'), with the implication that those who live outside it are barbarians.

Fiddle while Rome burns, To To trifle during an emergency or crisis. An allusion to Nero's reputed behaviour during the burning of Rome in AD 64, when it is said that he sang to his lyre and enjoyed the spectacle from the top of a high tower.

Graffiti A name applied originally to the wall drawings and inscriptions found at Pompeii and other Italian cities. The name reflects the fact that these were originally scratched on – it comes from the Italian *graffito*, 'a scratch'.

Laconic This originated with the Laconians and Spartans of ancient Greece, known for their austere lifestyle and concise speech. When Philip of Macedon wrote to the Spartan magistrates, 'If I enter Laconia, I will level Lacedaemon to the ground,' their answer contained the single word 'If'.

Palace Originally a dwelling on the Palatine Hill of Rome, where Augustus, and later Tiberius and Nero, built their mansions. The word was then transferred to other royal and imperial residences and subsequently to similar buildings.

Romance languages Those languages that are the immediate offspring of Latin, the language of the Romans, such as Italian, Spanish, Portuguese, French, and Romanian.

When in Rome, do as the Romans do Conform to the manners and customs of those among whom you live. St Monica and her son St Augustice of Hippo wrote in a letter to St Ambrose, 'At Rome they fast on Saturday, but not at Milan.

Which practice ought to be observed?' St Ambrose replied, 'When I am at Milan, I do as they do at Milan, but when I go to Rome, I do as Rome does!' (*Epistle* xxxvi).

La-La-Land

Alcatraz A notorious US prison on the rocky island of the same name in San Francisco Bay, whose inmates included such figures of infamy as Al Capone and Robert Stroud, the 'Birdman of Alcatraz'. It takes its name from the Spanish *Isla de los Alcatraces*, 'island of the pelicans'.

Big Apple, The New York City. The name was first popularized in the 1920s by John J. FitzGerald, a reporter for the *Morning Telegraph*, who used it to refer to the city's racetracks and who claimed to have heard it used by stable-hands in New Orleans in 1921. The idea is that of a prize fruit sought by those looking for fame and fun.

Big Easy, The The nickname of New Orleans, Louisiana, referring to the city's laid-back, easy-going lifestyle.

Gotham New York. The name of Gotham was given to the city by Washington Irving in his *Salmagundi* (1807), in which are recounted 'the chronicles of the renowned and ancient city of Gotham'. The name is actually from the Old English for 'goat home'. Irving is said to have been inspired by a folk tale set in the village of Gotham in Nottinghamshire, called 'The Wise Men of Gotham', in which residents of the village decide to feign madness in order to avoid the chaos of a prospective visit by the king. To prove it, they perform all manner of bizarre stunts, including building a fence around a bush to prevent a cuckoo from escaping. The ruse works and the king passes them by. The writer and artist Bob Kane used 'Gotham City' as the name of the dark, crime-ridden city where his creation Batman lived and operated.

Ground zero Originally, the point on the earth's surface either at or immediately above or below the centre of a nuclear explosion. Latterly it has been applied more broadly to the seat of any cataclysmic blast – notably the site of the World Trade Center in Lower Manhattan, New York City, destroyed by the terrorist action of 9/11.

La-La Land A humorous US nickname, first recorded in the 1970s, for the city of Los Angeles, California. 'La-La' is mainly a reduplication of its initial letters, but it may also contain implications of dreamy abstraction, which come to the fore in the subsequent figurative use of the name for a fantasy land: someone who is 'in la-la land' is out of touch with reality.

Las Vegas The self-styled 'Gambling Capital of the World', in Nevada, USA. Its first settlers were Mormons, attracted by the springs in the dry valley along the Old Spanish Trail. Hence its name, Spanish for 'the meadows'.

Montezuma The Aztec emperor (d.1520) who was overthrown in Mexico by the invading Spaniards. His wealth was legendary, and his name is a byword for cruel human sacrifice.

Montezuma's revenge One of several colourful euphemisms for diarrhoea suffered by visitors to Mexico or abroad in general, in allusion to the emperor's supposed reprisal after his defeat.

Motown A shortening of 'Motor Town' as a nickname for Detroit, Michigan, a city that, thanks to the enterprise of Henry Ford, became the 'automobile capital of the world' for some decades during the 20th century. The record company Tamla Motown was established in Detroit during the 1950s.

Philadelphia The first city of the state of Pennsylvania, founded in 1682 by William Penn (1644–1718) and others of the Society of Friends, and so named from the Greek *philadelphia*, 'brotherly love'.

Plug ugly A thug or violent criminal, especially one whose function is to command acquiescence by a threatening appearance. The term seems to have originated as the name of street gangs (the 'Plug-Uglies') in New York City and Baltimore in the middle of the 19th century. One suggestion is that it came from the large 'plug hat' (a sort of top hat) stuffed with paper which members wore for protection from the clubs of such rival gangs as the 'Dead Rabbits' or the 'Bowery Boys'.

Route 66 The major highway that formerly ran across America for some 2,448 miles (3,940km), from Chicago, Illinois, through Missouri, Kansas, Oklahoma, Texas, New Mexico, Arizona, and California to Los Angeles. Its highway number was chosen because it was thought that 66 sounded good and would be easy to remember.

Uncle Sam A nickname for the collective citizens of the USA. It arose in the neighbourhood of Troy, New York, in about 1812, partly from the frequent appearance of the initials US on government supplies to the army and others.

Pardon My French

Dutch This word, properly relating to Holland, is directly related to German *Deutsch*, 'German', and was formerly used in English to denote the people of Germany or German descent, not merely the Netherlanders. The Anglo-Dutch wars in the 17th and 18th centuries resulted in many expressions that take a swipe at the Dutch. Courage that is only achievable through alcohol became known as 'Dutch courage'; unintelligible gobbledygook became known as 'Double Dutch'; 'I'm a Dutchman' was used to express disbelief; and a 'Dutch treat', or to 'go Dutch', whereby each person pays for themselves, was seen as the result of a host's stinginess. A Dutch concert is one in which singers sing their different songs at the same time, hence any great noise and uproar, like that supposedly made by a party of drunken Dutchmen.

French disease, The An old euphemism for venereal disease, especially syphilis, relying on crude national stereotyping (it was customary in the past to associate sexually transmitted diseases with foreigners of every sort). Syphilis has also been 'the French pox' and 'the Frenchman' while the French retaliated with *mal de Naples*.

French leave Leave or absence without permission or without announcing one's departure. The reference is to the French custom of leaving without saying goodbye to one's host. The French associated the habit with the English, however. Hence their equivalent for 'to take French leave', which is *s'en aller* (or *filer*) *à l'anglaise*, 'to go away in the English way'.

Greenland Discovered by Eric the Red of Iceland in 982, who reputedly chose the name 'for he said it would make men's minds long to go there if it had a fine name'. The name was actually not inappropriate for the point where he landed, a smooth grassy plain at the head of the Igaliku fjord, near the modern settlement of Julianehåb (Qaqortoq), at a latitude equal to that of the Shetland Islands. For the ice-clad country as a whole, however, it is a clear misnomer.

Iceland The island state received its name from the Viking Floki, who landed here in 960. A century earlier, another Viking had named the island Snjoland, 'snow-land'. The name was more appropriate then than now, when the climate was colder.

Ireland The name effectively means 'Eire land', with the first word being the country's Irish name. According to legend, this may originally have been the name of an ancient goddess, but it has also been derived from 'Érainn', the name of an ancient people of Ireland. The Greek form of 'Érainn' was *Iernoi* (later *Ierne*), which was transformed into the Latin name for Ireland, *Hibernia*.

Lesbian Inspired by Lesbos, one of the islands of the Greek Archipelago, or to Sappho, the poetess of Lesbos. The remaining fragments of her poems express her affection and admiration for women, hence her inspiration for the terms 'lesbian' and 'sapphic'.

Lido An outdoor bathing place, usually with sunbathing facilities and often providing entertainments. The name is taken from the sandy island called the Lido, facing the Adriatic outside Venice, long a fashionable bathing resort. Its own name comes from Latin *litus*, 'shore'.

Mediterranean The midland sea, the sea in the middle of the (Roman) earth, from Latin *medius*, 'middle', and *terra*, 'land'. The Romans called it *Mare Nostrum*, 'our sea'.

Milliner An alteration of 'Milaner', so called from Milan in Italy, which at one time led the way in Europe on all matters of taste, dress, and elegance.

Moulin Rouge The Paris dance hall, with its cancan dancers, opened in Montmartre in 1889 and took its name from another hall nearby that had closed. Over its entrance it had a model of a red windmill (French *moulin rouge*), with working sails and the figures of a miller and his wife at different windows. When the sails turned, the couple waved to each other.

Pardon my French Excuse my swearing. Real French is unlikely to be involved. The French are unfairly associated with anything 'naughty' in the British mind, hence also 'French kiss' and 'French letter'.

Slave The word 'slave' came to English from the Old French *esclave* in the Middle Ages. It is a close relative of 'Slav', for during the 9th century the Slavic peoples of eastern and central Europe had been conquered and reduced to a servile state.

Vatican The palace of the pope, so called because it stands on the *Vaticanus Mons* (Vatican Hill) of ancient Rome, which got its name through being the headquarters of the *vaticinatores* ('soothsayers').

Vaudeville An alteration of French *val de Vire* or Old French *vau de Vire*, 'valley of the Vire', the native valley of Olivier Basselin, a Norman poet (d.1418) and author of convivial songs, which were so named from the place where he composed them. It is now applied to variety entertainment made of songs, dances, sketches, etc.

And Beyond

Black Hole of Calcutta, The On 20–21 June 1756 Siraj-ud-Dawlah, Nawab of Bengal, reputedly confined 146 British prisoners in the extremely small prison – 18 × 14ft 10in. (5.5 × 4.5m) – of the East India Company's Fort William after its capture. Only 23 people escaped suffocation. A military punishment cell or guardroom is often nicknamed the Black Hole, and dark, stuffy places are sometimes said to be 'like the Black Hole of Calcutta'.

Black Sea, The Formerly called the Euxine Sea, and probably given its present name from its dangers and lack of shelter rather than from the colour of its waters.

Dead Sea, The The Palestinian Salt Sea or Sea of the Plain of the Old Testament, in the ancient Vale of Siddim, known to the Romans as *Mare Mortuum*. It is fed by the River Jordan, and its salt content is about 25 per cent, while normal sea water is usually between 3 and 4 per cent. It supports no life other than microbes and a few very low organisms, hence its name.

India The country is so named from its main river, the Indus, itself from Sanskrit *sindhu*, 'river'.

Pacific Ocean So named by the Portuguese navigator Fernão de Magelhães (Ferdinand Magellan, *c*.1480–1521) in 1520, because there he enjoyed calm weather and a placid sea after the stormy and tempestuous passage of the Strait of Magellan. 'Pacific' comes from the French *pacifique*, 'peaceful'.

Pakistan The name of this state formed in 1947 was coined in 1933 by a Cambridge student, Chaudarie Rahmat Ali, to represent the units that should be included when the time came: P for Punjab, A for the Afghan border states, K for Kashmir, S for Sind and 'stan' for Baluchistan. At the same time the name can be understood to mean 'land of the pure', from Iranian or Afghani *pāk*, 'pure', and Old Persian *stān*, 'land' (as in Afghanistan itself).

Sierra The word is Spanish for 'saw' and is used for the name of a chain of mountains with jagged peaks, especially in the USA or Spain itself. Some of the best-known such chains are the Sierra Madre, 'mother chain', in Mexico, and the Sierra Nevada, 'snowy chain', in both California and south-eastern Spain. The word also gave the name of the West African state of Sierra Leone, 'lion chain'.

Spice Islands An archipelago in the eastern part of Indonesia, whose chief products are traditionally spices of all kinds, much sought after by 15th- and 16th-century navigators and traders when spices were highly prized commodities in Europe. They were once so significant that 'visiting the Spice Islands' was a euphemism for going to the toilet.

Taj Mahal The mausoleum in Agra, India, was built in 1632 by the jewel-loving Emperor Shah Jahan in memory of his favourite wife, Arjumand Banu Begam (1592–1631). She was known as Mumtaz Mahal, 'exalted one of the palace', and the name of the mausoleum is an alteration of this with *taj* meaning 'crown'.

TRANSPORT

Travel wasn't always easy. The very word is an offshoot of 'travail', meaning hardship and woe. A simple trip out on horseback might involve any number of perils; although they look very different on paper, 'road', 'ride', and 'raid' are all close relatives. A road was a track along which one could ride and also risk a raid. For all their lack of punctuality, crowdedness, and expense, today's transport options seem positively cheery by comparison.

Busman's holiday There is a story that in the old days of horse-drawn buses a driver spent his holiday travelling about on a bus driven by one of his mates. Hence the phrase, which means a holiday or free time spent doing the same sort of thing that one does at work, so that it is a holiday in name only.

Cab A contraction of 'cabriolet', a small one-horse carriage, from French *cabriole*, 'goat-like leap'. The reference is to the lightness of the carriage, which seemed to 'caper' by comparison with its lumbering predecessors. Cabs were introduced in London in the 19th century.

Emmets and grockles Two West Country expressions applied to tourists and holidaymakers. 'Emmet' is an old word for an ant, with the idea that these insects swarm everywhere. The word 'grockle' is said to derive from a clown called Grock, implying someone to be laughed at. It arose in 1963 from comments made about holidaymakers at the Globe Inn, Brixham, and was used by Peter Draper in his film *The System* (1964), made at Brixham, Torquay, and other parts of Devon.

Journey (Old French *journee*, 'day') The word originally applied to a day's travel, which in medieval times was usually reckoned as 20 miles (32km). It later came to apply to travel of any distance or length of time from one place to another.

Mile A measure of length, in the British Commonwealth and the USA, 1760 yards (1609m). It is so called from Latin *mille*, 'thousand', the measure being 1,000 paces by a Roman soldier.

Ocean The first mention of the word 'ocean' in English looks back to the classical world. The ancient Greeks believed the world was surrounded by a single great river, which they called *ōkeanos*. 'Ocean' originally described what was thought to be the 'Great Outer Sea' running around the disc of the entire earth and enclosing Europe and Asia, the only lands thought to exist at that time.

Omnibus The name, from the Latin meaning 'for all', was first applied to the public vehicle in France in 1828. In the following year it was adopted for the vehicles that started to run on the Paddington (now Marylebone) Road, London. The plural is 'omnibuses', and the word is now normally abbreviated to 'bus'. Other vehicles gained similarly abbreviated names, such as 'cab' from cabriolet, 'van' from caravan, and 'truck' from truckle.

Portmanteau word A portmanteau is a type of leather travelling bag which opens out flat into two parts. A 'portmanteau word' is thus a word made up of two others 'folded together'. This sense of the term was coined by Lewis Carroll in *Through the Looking-Glass* (1871). His own creations included 'chortle', a blend of 'chuckle' and 'snort'; 'galumph', from 'gallop' and 'triumph'; and 'frabjous', from 'fabulous' and 'joyous'.

Push the envelope, To To go beyond normal limits; to pioneer. The phrase comes from aviation, in which an 'envelope' is the known limit of an aircraft's range and powers, so called from their appearance on a graph. 'Pushing' such an envelope could thus mean flying fast enough to break the sound barrier.

Radar A term formed from *ra*dio *d*etection *a*nd *r*anging, as a means of detecting the direction and range of aircraft, ships, and the like by the reflection of radio waves.

Rickshaw The two-wheeled passenger vehicle drawn by one or two men in Asian countries has a name that is a shortened form of the Japanese *jinricksha*, literally 'man strength vehicle'.

Ride shotgun, To To guard a person or thing in transit. The US expression alludes to the armed assistant on a stagecoach who sat beside the coachman to protect him from attack by bandits. The term was later used of any person riding in the front passenger seat of a motor vehicle.

Vis à vis (French, 'face to face') The term is properly applied to people facing one another, as in a railway carriage. It is also an old name for a carriage or coach that enables the occupants to face one another. The phrase is now often used in the sense of 'in relation to', 'as regards'.

Whole caboodle, The The whole lot; the whole collection. The word probably originates from a shortened form of the more general US phrase 'kit and boodle', in which 'boodle', from Dutch, means 'possessions'.

MONEY

Money doesn't just make the world go round, it is a major impetus for our phrases, too. Slang, in particular, has embraced money – or the lack of it – from the beginning. Whether it is the root of true happiness or all evil, perhaps we should take note that 'money's' linguistic beginnings rest on the goddess Moneta, whose name may well derive from the Latin *monere*, 'to warn'.

All in Completely exhausted. The expression probably derives from stock market jargon. Dealers would cry 'All in!', meaning that all stock should be held in, when prices were falling and the market was depressed, and conversely 'All out!' when they were rising and the market buoyant.

Bankrupt In Italy, when a moneylender was unable to continue business, his bench or counter was broken up, so that he was literally quite 'bankrupt' – the word comes from the Italian *banca rotta*, meaning 'broken bench'.

Bear (noun) In stock exchange parlance, a bear is a speculator for a fall in the price of shares. Thus 'to operate for a bear' or 'to bear the market' is to use every effort to depress prices so as to buy cheap and profit on the rise. The term probably derives from the proverb to 'sell the skin before one has caught the bear'. One who sold stocks in this way was formerly called a bearskin jobber.

Blackmail 'Mail' here is the old Scottish word for a rent or tax payment. Blackmail was originally money paid by farmers in the border counties in return for protection or immunity from harassment.

Bull In stock exchange language, a bull is a speculative purchase for a rise, or the buyer who makes such a purchase. In this sense it is the opposite of a 'bear'. Since the early 18th century, the terms 'bull' and 'bear' have been broadly used on the stock exchange to describe an optimist or pessimist in share dealing.

Dollar The sign $ is possibly a modification of the figure 8 as it appeared on the old Spanish 'pieces of eight', which were of the same value as the dollar. It was in use in the USA before the adoption of the Federal currency in 1785. The word is a variant of 'thaler' (Low German *daler*), which historically means 'valley' (English 'dale' is related). At the close of the 15th century the Counts of Schlick coined pieces from the silver extracted from the mines at Joachimsthal ('Joachim's valley', now Jáchymov, in the Czech Republic). These pieces, called 'Joachimsthaler', gained such repute that they became standard coin. Other coins made like them came to be called 'thalers', which was later mangled to 'dollar'.

Exchequer The title derives from the chequered cloth once used for calculations of royal revenues. The Exchequer was originally the office or department that dealt with the Crown's income and expenditure.

Fee A word from Old French *fie*, of Germanic origin, related to Old English *fēo*, 'cattle', 'goods', 'money', which itself gave modern 'fief'. A similar relationship exists in Latin between *pecunia*, 'money', and *pecus*, 'cattle'. English 'capital' shares the development, since it derives from Latin *capita*, 'heads' (of cattle), and its own related word, through French, is 'chattels'.

Hammered, To be A stock exchange term, used of a broking firm in the 'House' that cannot meet its commitments. This is done by the 'Head Waiter', who approaches the rostrum and attracts the attention of the members present by striking the desk with a hammer before making the announcement. Today, it is more likely to refer to someone who is extremely drunk.

Make ends meet, To To spend no more money than is necessary; to manage to live without getting into debt. The 'ends' are probably the final figures on a balance sheet.

Mint, The A place where money is coined gets its name from the Latin *moneta*, 'money', itself from the temple of Moneta (a nickname of the goddess Juno), used as a mint in ancient Rome.

Monkey Slang for £500 or (in the USA) $500, and among sailors the vessel that contained the full allowance of 'grog'. The use may refer to an Indian 500 rupee note of that era, which featured a monkey on one side.

On the nail Immediately or on the spot, as: 'to pay on the nail'. One meaning of nail (possibly from medieval times) was a shallow vessel mounted on a stand, and business was concluded by payment into the vessel. It may have been so named from the rough resemblance of the stand to a nail's shape. Outside the Corn Exchange at Bristol such 'nails' can still be seen in the form of four bronze pillars, and it is said that if a buyer was satisfied with the sample of grain shown 'on the nail', he paid on the spot.

Nest egg Money put by. The allusion is to the custom of placing a china egg in a hen's nest to induce her to lay her eggs there. If a person has saved a little money, it serves as an inducement to increase the store.

In the nick of time Just in time; at the right moment. The allusion is to tally-sticks marked with nicks or notches at close intervals.

Pay The English word comes from Old French *payer*, ultimately from Latin *pax*, 'peace', the allusion being to the pacifying of a creditor.

Penny (Old English *pening*) The English coin, before decimalization worth one-twelfth of a shilling, was originally made of silver and was used by the Anglo-Saxons. The old symbol 'd' for a penny is derived from the Roman *denarius*, an ancient silver coin.

Pound A unit of weight (Latin *pondus*, 'weight') and the basic monetary unit of the UK. The money sense, from Old English, arose because the first pound was literally a pound of silver. The symbol '£' and letters 'lb' are from *libra*, the Latin for 'pound' as well as 'balance' – the star sign is named after a small constellation said to represent the pair of scales which is the symbol of justice.

Quid Slang for a sovereign (or a pound). It may ultimately come from Latin *quid*, 'what', in the sense of 'what one owns' or the 'wherewithal'.

Rhino Slang for money, and a term in use in the 17th century. Its origin is uncertain but one possible suggestion is that it derives from an Eastern belief that the powdered horn of the rhinoceros increased sexual potency and therefore commanded a high price. Or it may come from the Greek *rhi-s, rhinos*, 'nose', as a reference to someone 'paying through the nose'.

Go scot-free, To To be let off payment; to escape payment or punishment. 'Scot' here is is a tax or reckoning, from the Old Norse *skot*, 'a contribution', corresponding to Old English *sceot*.

Spondulicks A slang term for money, dating from the mid-19th century. Its origins are uncertain: one suggestion is Greek *spondulikos*, an adjective derived from *spondulox*, the name of a type of shell used as an early form of money.

Sterling A term applied to British money and also to gold and silver plate denoting that they are of standard value or purity. Hence applied figuratively to anything of sound intrinsic worth, as: 'a man of sterling qualities'. The word is probably from late Old English *steorling*, an unrecorded word for a coin with a star, from the fact that some of the early Norman pennies had a small star on them.

Tanner Slang for a sixpence, originally a silver coin, first minted in 1551.

Up the spout At the pawnbroker's, or more usually now 'down the drain', gone, lost, ruined. The allusion is to the 'spout' up which brokers sent the articles that had been pawned. When redeemed they returned down the spout, i.e. from the storeroom to the shop. The phrase is also used in slang to mean 'pregnant'. The reference here may be to a loaded rifle with a round in its breech ready to fire.

MIDAS TOUCH

Midas touch Midas was a legendary king of Phrygia who requested of the gods that everything that he touched might be turned to gold. His request was granted, but as his food became gold the moment he touched it, he prayed to the gods to take their favour back. To have the 'Midas Touch' is to have the ability to make money out of everything one undertakes.

THE RULING CLASSES

'On one's high horse', 'bigwig', 'nob', 'surly' . . . The ruling classes have rarely enjoyed in language the prestige they have in life. But English has always been egalitarian, and the words and expressions its speakers have created amply reflect its democratic approach.

As drunk as a lord The nobility of bygone days could afford to indulge in excessive drinking if they were so inclined. In the 18th and 19th centuries gross intoxication was common, and many men of fashion prided themselves on the number of bottles of wine they could consume at a sitting.

As rich as Croesus Croesus, the last king of Lydia (560–546 BC), was so rich and powerful that his name became proverbial for wealth.

Bigwig An important person. The term alludes to the large wigs that in the 17th and 18th centuries encumbered the head and shoulders of the aristocracy of England and France. They are still worn by the Lord Chancellor, judges, and (until 2000) the Speaker of the House of Commons. Bishops continued to wear them in the House of Lords until 1880.

Blue blood High or noble birth or descent. The expression translates Spanish *sangre azul*. The inference is probably that 'true' nobles had no Moorish descent in their bloodline, and would show their blue veins visible through their pale skin as evidence.

Cavalier A cavalier, strictly speaking, was a horseman, who took his name from the Italian *cavaliere*, and ultimately from Latin *caballus*, 'horse'. From here grew the sense of a knight or gentleman. As names for supporters of each side of the English Civil War, Roundhead and Cavalier are first recorded in the early 1640s. The former was an insult towards the Puritans who followed Oliver Cromwell and favoured a close-cut hairstyle, while the latter, aimed at supporters of Charles I, implied a swaggering blustering fellow or flamboyant swashbuckler. While each insult was later embraced by those they were used against, the meanings of the modern adjectives 'puritanical' and 'cavalier' are rooted in this conflict.

Court (Old French, from Latin *cohors*, *cohortis*, 'yard', 'company of soldiers') The yard was the central point of a farm and of the buildings that grew up round it. Hence it became the central point of any building or group of buildings, such as a town, a fort and, eventually, a royal palace, with the word at every stage also serving for the people who lived and worked in or round it.

Court cards The king, queen, knave (jack), and ace in a pack of cards. 'Court' is an alteration of 'coat' because, apart from the ace, the cards represent a clothed or coated figure. Court cards are not so called because the king, queen, and knave belonged to a court.

Courtesy Civility, politeness. It was at court that those in attendance practised the refinements of the age. The word originally meant the manners 'of the court'.

Freelance A self-employed person who is not employed continuously by a particular organization but is hired for individual assignments. The word was probably coined by Sir Walter Scott and first appears in his *Ivanhoe* (1820) as a term for a knight who had no allegiance to any single cause and so was 'free' to use his 'lance' for whomever he wished.

Gingerly Cautiously, with hesitating, mincing, or faltering steps. The word dates back to at least the 16th century and has nothing to do with ginger. It is from the Old French *gensor*, 'dainty', and ultimately from the Latin *genitus* (well-born). The suggestion is that the nobility walk very gracefully.

On one's high horse To behave in an arrogant or pompous manner. The image is of a member of the nobility looking down on others from their expensive stallion.

King The male ruler of an independent state, especially one who inherits the position by right of birth. The word is a relative of 'kin', as the first English kings were the chiefs of various tribes – or 'kins' – of Angles and Saxons, who established their own small states.

Knight (Old English *cniht*, 'servant') The word was originally used for a boy or servant; it then came to denote a man of gentle birth who, after serving at court or in the retinue of some lord as a page and esquire, was admitted with appropriate ceremonies to an honourable degree of military rank and given the right to bear arms. The word is from the Germanic *Knecht*, 'boy'; the hard 'k' remained for a while in English until it felt too unfamiliar and fell silent.

Lady The literal meaning of the word is 'bread kneader', from Old English *hlǣfdīge* (*hlāf*, 'bread', and *dīge*, 'kneader', related to modern 'dough'). 'Lady' originally referred to the female head of the family or the mistress of the household.

Levee (French *lever*, 'to rise') A morning assembly or reception. In Britain the word is particularly associated with the royal levees formerly held at St James's Palace, official occasions when the sovereign received men only, most usually in the afternoon. Before the French Revolution it was customary for the French monarch to receive visitors (court physicians, nobles, messengers, and the like) at the time of his *levée*, i.e. just after rising from bed.

Lord A nobleman, a peer of the realm, and formerly (and in some connections still) a ruler, a master, the holder of a manor. The word is descended from Old English *hlāford*, 'bread keeper', i.e. the head of the household.

Mausoleum The name was originally that of the tomb of Mausolus, king of Caria, to whom his wife Artemisia erected a splendid monument at Halicarnassus (353 BC). Parts of the sepulchre, one of the Seven Wonders of the World, are now in the British Museum. The name is now applied to any magnificent tomb, usually with a sepulchral chamber.

Mikado (Japanese *mī*, 'honourable', and *kado*, 'door', 'gate') The title used by foreigners for the emperor of Japan.

Nobby Smart, elegant, or neat. The word is from 'nob', a slang term for one of the upper classes, a contraction of 'noble' or 'nobility'. Hence the nickname Nobby for someone called Clark, a clerk being originally a learned or literate person, as the nobility (mostly) were.

Pharaoh A word from Egyptian meaning 'great house', applied to the kings of ancient Egypt in much the same way as the 'Holy See' came to be used for the pope, or the 'Sublime Porte' for the government of the Ottoman Empire.

Plantagenet A name commonly given since the mid-17th century to the royal line and to the Lancastrian and Yorkist kings from Henry II to Richard III. These were the descendants of Geoffrey, count of Anjou, and Matilda, daughter of Henry I. It may have arisen from Geoffrey of Anjou's habit of wearing a sprig of broom (*plante genêt*) in his cap, or from the fact that he planted broom to improve his hunting covers.

Poet laureate A court official, now appointed by the prime minister, who has no specific duties but who traditionally composes odes in celebration of royal birthdays and national occasions. The laurel crown was anciently a mark of distinction and honour.

Queen A female sovereign or a king's wife. The word comes from Old English *cwēn*, 'woman', 'wife' (which also gives *quean*, formerly used of an impudent woman), from an Indo-European base element that gave Greek *gunē* (English *gyno-*), Russian *zhena*, Irish *bean*, and so on, all meaning 'woman'.

Rajah (Hindi, 'king', from Sanskrit, and cognate with Latin *rex*) The title of an Indian king or prince, given later to tribal chiefs and comparatively minor rulers of various states. 'Maharajah' means 'great rajah'.

Surly Bad-tempered and irritable. The original meaning was 'lordly' or 'haughty', and was spelled 'sirly', because these were qualities associated with 'sirs' or those in power.

Throw down the gauntlet, To To challenge. In medieval times, when one knight challenged another, the custom was for the challenger to throw his gauntlet, or glove, on the ground, and if the challenge was accepted, the person to whom it was thrown picked it up.

Toff An alteration of 'tuft', referring to the gold tassels decorating the caps once worn by titled undergraduates at Oxford and Cambridge.

Tory In the reign of Charles II (1660–85), the name came to be used as an abusive term for the supporters of the Crown and its prerogatives at the time of the struggle over the Exclusion Bills. From Irish *tóraighe*, meaning 'pursuer' or 'outlaw'. The name was applied in the 17th century to Irish Roman Catholic outlaws and bandits who harassed the English in Ireland.

Tycoon A title of the Shogun, also applied to an industrial or business magnate. The word derives from Japanese *taikun*, 'great lord'.

Unready, The Ethelred II, king of England (968, r.978–1016), called the 'redeless', in which 'rede' means 'counsel'. In other words, Ethelred the Unready was ill-advised rather than unprepared.

Walls have ears Things uttered in secret get rumoured abroad; there are listeners everywhere, and you'd better be careful. Certain rooms in the Louvre were said to be so constructed in the time of Catherine de Medici (1519–89) that what was said in one room could be heard distinctly in another. It was by this contrivance that the suspicious queen became acquainted with state secrets and plots. The tubes of communication were called the *auriculaires*.

Whipping boy A boy educated with a prince and whipped when the latter was thought to deserve punishment for some misdemeanour.

POLITICS

The first to be labelled 'ambitious' were Roman political hopefuls, who would walk (or in Latin, *ambire*) around the city pressing the hands of potential voters. The implications of hidden motives have barely left politics since. In fact, it is hard to find any compliments for a politician in the pages of the dictionary. If you're looking for a choice insult, then politics is where it's at. Ultimately, though, its vocabulary reflects the choices of the people – which is apt, for at the heart of the very word 'politics' is the Greek *politēs*, 'citizen'.

Covfefe

Bafflegab Befuddling or obfuscatory language, especially in the field of politics. The term was coined around 1952 by Milton Smith, the assistant general counsel of the US Chamber of Commerce. He declared, 'I decided we needed a new and catchy word to describe the utter incomprehensibility, ambiguity, verbosity and complexity of government regulations.'

Bob's your uncle There you are; it's that simple. The phrase is commonly said to have been inspired by A.J. Balfour's promotion by his uncle Robert Arthur Talbot Gascoyne-Cecil, 3rd Marquess of Salisbury, the Tory prime minister, to the post of chief secretary for Ireland, despite his scant political experience. The suggestion of nepotism was difficult to ignore. However, colourfully circumstantial as this tale is, the chronology suggests that the expression instead played on a 17th-century slang phrase, 'all's bob', meaning everything is all right.

Bunkum Empty talk; nonsense. The word arose in the US in the 1820s, when Felix Walker, Congressional representative for the district of Buncombe, North Carolina, made a long, dull, and irrelevant speech, in a debate other members of the House of Representatives were eager to conclude. In spite of their protests, Walker replied that he was speaking not to the House, but 'for Buncombe'.

Covfefe On 31 May 2017, Donald Trump, former President of the United States, tweeted, 'Despite the constant negative press covfefe'. This tweet was later deleted, but not before it had gone viral. Sean Spicer, the White House Press Secretary at the time, said, 'The president and a small group of people know exactly what he meant.' Later in 2017, the Democrat representative Mike Quigley introduced the Communications Over Various Feeds Electronically for Engagement Act (COVFEFE Act), a bill to amend the Presidential Record Act to cover social media, requiring tweets and other social media posts by the President of the United States to be preserved under law.

Hear, hear! An exclamation approving what a speaker says. Originally disapproval was marked by humming. Those supporting the speaker protested by saying 'Hear him, hear him!', which eventually became 'Hear, hear!'

Lobby A vestibule or corridor, from Medieval Latin *lobia*, 'lodge', 'portico'. In the House of Commons, the Lobby is the large hall to which the public are admitted, especially for interviews with members. Division lobbies are the corridors to which Members retire to vote, and 'to lobby' is to solicit the vote of a Member or to seek to influence Members. A 'lobbyist' is someone who does this.

Mugwump An Algonquian word meaning literally 'great chief'. It came to be used for someone who sat on the fence rather than took sides, and eventually for those politicians whose party vote could not be relied on. In 2017 Boris Johnson, the foreign secretary in the UK government, controversially referred to Jeremy Corbyn, leader of the Labour Party and Leader of the Opposition, as a 'mutton-headed old mugwump'. Tom Watson, the deputy leader of the Labour Party, responded by saying that Johnson was a 'caggy-handed, cheese-headed fopdoodle with a talent for slummocking about'.

Omnishambles A state of total confusion, especially within politics. The word, coined by writer Tony Roche, was first used in an episode of the BBC political satire *The Thick of It*, broadcast in 2009. In 2012 the then leader of the Labour Party, Ed Miliband, used the word in a speech to the House of Commons during Prime Minister's Questions, in criticism of the government's budget. The word is generally seen as the more modern version of 'clusterfuck'.

Truthiness The belief that, regardless of facts, a statement is true because a person wishes or feels it to be true. This sense of the word was coined by the television comedian Stephen Colbert in 2005 to describe the appeal to emotion used in contemporary political discourse. Thanks to former President Donald Trump, it is now more usually known as 'fake news'.

Snollygosters

Diplomat Literally, a person provided with a diploma or letter authorizing them to represent their government abroad. Latin *diploma* literally means 'letter folded double', i.e. in such a way that its contents are kept secret.

Guy An effigy of a man stuffed with combustibles in mockery of Guy Fawkes, carried round and burned on a bonfire on 5 November, in memory of the Gunpowder Plot. In the US, the term was later applied more generically to a person.

Snollygoster A US colloquialism for an unscrupulously ambitious person, especially in the field of politics. Dating from the mid-19th century, it may be the same word as Snallygaster, the name of a mythical monster supposedly living in Maryland, which comes from Pennsylvania German *schnelle geeschter*, 'quick spirits'.

Suffrage A person's vote, approval, or consent, or right to vote, especially at parliamentary and municipal elections. The word is from Latin *suffragium*, 'voting tablet'.

Suffragette A term coined with derisive intent by Charles Hands in the *Daily Mail* in 1906. It referred to women who agitated for the right to vote, notably members of the Women's Social and Political Union (a group separate from, and more militant than, the National Union of Women's Suffrage Societies). The word was later reclaimed, and is now used without negative connotations.

Silhouette A profile drawing of a person giving the outline only, with the whole area within the outline in black; hence a shadow and, figuratively, a slight literary sketch of a person or other subject. The word is derived from the name of the French minister of finance Étienne de Silhouette (1709–67), noted for his stinginess in public expenditure. His name was applied to things made cheaply, and the first silhouettes were cut out from scraps of paper, rather than being drawn.

Three-Line Whip

Ballot This method of voting was common in ancient Greece and Rome. From the Italian *ballotta*, meaning 'little ball'. The name comes from the use of small balls placed into an urn for casting votes. To 'blackball' someone harks back to the same system.

Barricade To block or bar a street, building, or the like against attack. The term arose in France in 1588, when Henri of Guise returned to Paris in defiance of Henry III. The king called out the Swiss Guard, and the Parisians tore up the pavements, threw chains across the streets, and piled up barrels (French *barriques*) filled with earth and stones, from behind which they shot down the opposition.

Boycott A refusal to have any dealings with a person or group of people, as a means of protest or coercion. The term dates from 1880, when such methods were used by the Irish Land League against Captain C.C. Boycott (1832–97), a land agent in County Mayo, as a means of coercing him to reduce rents.

Budget The present use of 'budget' for the annual estimate of revenue and expenditure and statement on financial policy made by the Chancellor of the Exchequer stems from the custom of bringing the relevant papers to the House in a leather bag and laying them on the table. The word is from the French *bougette*, 'little bag'. The modern equivalent of the bag is the battered red despatch box which the Chancellor traditionally holds up outside the door of 11 Downing Street, before departing to the House of Commons to make their budget statement.

Cabal A council of intriguers. One of the most memorable cabals was that established under Charles II of England (1630–85), involving a group of ministers whose initials – Clifford, Ashley, Buckingham, Arlington, Lauderdale – formed the name. But this was not the first recorded use of the word, which came into English via the French *cabale* in reference to the Cabbala, the ancient Jewish tradition of mystical interpretation of the Bible.

Canvass, To To solicit votes, as before an election. The word perhaps derives from an obsolete sense of 'canvas', which was to toss someone in a canvas sheet, and so developed the meaning of treating someone roughly or to harass them, including as a way of soliciting votes.

Capitol, The The meeting-place of the US Congress in Washington, DC. It opened for the first Congress in 1800 and took its name from the temple in ancient Rome, which was itself so called from the Capitoline Hill on which it stood.

Caucus A US word, first recorded as having been used in Boston about 1750. In the US it means a closed meeting of some division of a political or legislative body for the purpose of agreeing upon a united course of action in the main assembly. In England it is applied critically to an inner group that seeks to manipulate affairs behind the backs of its party. The word is probably of Algonquian origin and related to *caucauasu*, 'adviser'.

Cross-benches Seats set at right angles to the rest of the seats in the House of Commons and the House of Lords, on which independent members sit. Hence a cross-bencher is an independent not allied to any particular party.

Fasces (Latin, 'bundles') A bundle of rods tied round with a red strap from which an axe projected. In ancient Rome *fasces* were assigned to the higher magistrates as symbols of authority, representing power over life and limb. In modern times the fasces became the emblem of the Italian Fascists who took their name from it.

Filibuster, To To obstruct legislation by means of delaying tactics. The first filibusters were 18th-century pirates of the Caribbean. It began with the Dutch *vrijbuiter*, from *vrij*, 'free', and *buit*, 'booty', from which we also get 'freebooter'. In the 19th century, the Spanish *filibustero* was used for American adventurers who stirred up revolution in Central and South America, which set it on its path to the modern meaning of behaviour in congressional debates that is intended to sabotage proceedings.

Gerrymander To redraw the boundaries of electoral districts in such a way as to give one political party undue advantage over others. The word is derived from Elbridge Gerry (1744–1814), governor of Massachusetts, who did this in 1812 in order to preserve control for his party. An artist, looking at a map of the new distribution, converted the outline of one district in Essex County to the likeness of a salamander and showed it to Benjamin Russell, editor of the Boston *Sentinel*. 'Better say a gerrymander,' said Russell, and the name caught on.

Hustings A word originating from Old Norse *hústhing*, from *hús*, 'house', and *thing*, 'assembly'. Hence the assembly of a king, earl, or chief, and its subsequent application to open-air meetings connected with parliamentary elections.

Inaugurate, To To install into office with appropriate ceremony; to open formally. The word is from Latin *inaugurare*, which originally meant to study the flight patterns of birds as omens for the future. If the auspices were good (the Roman interpreter of these omens was an *auspex*) then things 'augured well'.

Moot (Old English *gemōt* 'meeting') In Anglo-Saxon times the assembly of freemen. The main moots served as units of local government. In a few towns, such as Aldeburgh in Suffolk, the town hall is still called the Moot Hall. In legal circles the name is given to the students' debates on supposed cases which formerly took place in the halls of the Inns of Court. Here, an issue subject to debate was known as a 'moot point' (nowadays often corrupted to 'mute point').

Ostracism Blackballing or boycotting; otherwise, the exclusion of a person from society. From the Greek *ostrakon*, meaning 'potsherd' or broken piece of pottery. The word arose from the ancient Greek custom of banishing, by a popular vote, anyone whose power was a danger to the state, the citizens writing on a shard of pottery the name of the one whose banishment was deemed desirable.

Parliament From the French *parler*, meaning 'to speak'.

Poll A word of Germanic origin meaning the 'head'; hence, the number of persons in a crowd ascertained by counting heads, and so the counting of voters at an election, reflected in such phrases as 'to go to the polls', to stand for election, and 'poll tax', one levied on everybody.

Protocol In diplomacy the original draft of a diplomatic document such as a dispatch or treaty. The word also denotes the code of correct procedure, etiquette, and ceremonial to be observed in official international exchanges. The word comes from Greek *prōtos*, 'first', and *kolla*, 'glue', this being a sheet glued to the front of a manuscript, or the case containing it, giving certain descriptive particulars.

Shoo-in One who is certain to win, especially in a political election. The image, which originated in US horse-racing in the 1930s, is of a competitor in a rigged race who merely needs to be encouraged across the finishing line with a shout of 'Shoo!' in order to win. The phrase, despite the frequent misspelling 'shoe-in', has nothing to do with shoes.

Thing The Old Norse word for the assembly of the people, otherwise a parliament. It is etymologically the same word as English 'thing' (an object), the original meaning of which was 'a discussion' (from *thingian*, 'to discuss'), hence 'a cause' or 'an object'. The Icelandic parliament, the oldest in the world, is called the *Althing* ('whole assembly').

Whip In British parliamentary usage MPs appointed by a party whose duty it is to see that the members of their party vote at important divisions and to discipline them if they do not attend or vote against the party. The name derives from the whipper-in at a fox hunt.

Three-line whip In politics a written notice, underlined three times to denote urgency, requiring party members to attend a parliamentary vote. As its name suggests, the notice is issued by the party whip. A one-line whip means that the matter in question is not contentious, while a two-line whip means that the government expects opposition and that most backbenchers are expected to vote.

Whistle-stop tour In the USA a brief campaign, usually political, conducted by travelling the country visiting the smaller communities, often talking from the rear platform of a train. A 'whistle stop' is a small town on a railroad where the train only stops on a given signal.

Who goes home? When the House of Commons adjourns at night, the doorkeeper asks this question of the members. In bygone days, when danger lurked in the unlit streets from cut-throats and thieves, the cry was raised to enable them to depart in groups and to escort the Speaker to their residence.

NONSENSE

Sometimes, no matter what we do, it is all 'sound and fury, signifying nonsense' – if so, English also provides us with a good few synonyms to describe what happens when things just don't add up.

All my eye and Betty Martin All nonsense or rubbish. A curious expression, which has attracted a popular suggestion that it was a British soldiers' or sailors' rendering of Latin *O mihi, beate Martine*, a prayer to St Martin. Rather likelier is that Betty Martin was some unidentified 18th-century London character whose favourite expression was 'All my eye', meaning 'hogwash'.

Cobblers A slang word for nonsense or rubbish. It is a short-ened form of 'cobblers' awls', Cockney rhyming slang for 'balls', i.e. testicles, in which an 'awl' is a shoemaker's tool for piercing holes in leather.

Codswallop Nonsense. In 1875 Hiram Codd patented a bottle with a marble stopper which would keep soft drinks fresh.

'Wallop' is an old British dialect term for weak beer. Thus 'Codd's wallop' is said to have become a disparaging term among beer drinkers for mineral waters and soft drinks.

Floccinaucinihilipilification The action or practice of estimating something as worthless. First recorded in 1741, this 29-letter verbal whopper was concocted out of four Latin words, *flocci*, *nauci*, *nihili*, and *pili*, all meaning 'at a small price' or 'at nothing'. Anyone familiar with *The Eton Latin Grammar* would have encountered them and been in on the joke.

Gubbins An object of little or no value, or odds and ends generally; otherwise a stupid person. The name was once applied, pejoratively, to the 'wild and savage' inhabitants of the region around Brent Tor, on the edge of Dartmoor. According to one 17th-century account, they 'lived in cots (rather holes than houses) . . . having all in common, multiplying without marriage into many hundreds . . . Their language is the dross of the dregs of the vulgar Devonian.' He explains the name: 'We call the shavings of fish (which are of little worth) *gubbins*.' The word comes from obsolete 'gobbon', itself probably related to 'gobbet'.

Napoo Soldier slang of the First World War for something that is of no use or does not exist. It represents the French phrase *il n'y en a plus* ('there is no more of it').

LAW AND DISORDER

English has never been a respecter of the law. For a start, it has never itself been subject to it, for it has always evolved democratically rather than at the judgement of a single authority. As for the legal system that governs us, Charles Dickens famously satirized its ploddingness in his novel *Bleak House*: 'Keep out of Chancery. It's being ground to bits in a slow mill; it's being roasted at a slow fire; it's being stung to death by single bees; it's being drowned by drops; it's going mad by grains.'

Its language, too, has long been considered at best stodgy, and at worst incomprehensible, despite great strides in recent years in dropping Latin in favour of plain English. Nonetheless, the weighty matter of legal judgement lies behind many everyday words, including 'cancel' – a nod to the crossbars, or *cancelli*, with which legal documents were voided – and 'chancellor', one who was once separated from the public by physical crossbars.

The focus of law, meanwhile – wrongdoing – has been the subject of dictionaries since the beginning, and its hold over our imaginations is evidenced in the hundreds of expressions we have at our disposal that once had criminal – and often criminally dark – beginnings.

Cat-o'-nine-tails A whip with nine lashes used for punishing offenders, in short known as the 'cat'. It was at one time used for flogging in the armed services and was not formally abolished as a civil punishment for crimes of violence until 1948. Popular superstition says that there were nine tails because flogging by 'a trinity of trinities' would be both more efficient and more efficacious.

Clink A slang word for a prison, derived from the Clink in Southwark, a jail destroyed in the Gordon Riots of 1780. The prison itself may have been so called because its gates clinked shut on the prisoner.

Cop, To To catch, lay hold of, or capture. To get copped is to get caught, especially by the police, hence the words 'cop' and 'copper' for a policeman. The word is probably ultimately connected to the Latin *capere*, 'to take'.

Derrick A contrivance or form of crane used for hoisting heavy objects, so called from Derrick, the surname of a Tyburn hangman of the early 17th century. The name was first applied to the gibbet and, from its similarity, to the crane.

Diddle, To A colloquial verb meaning 'to cheat or swindle'. It appears to have originated in Jeremy Diddler, the name of a character in the farce *Raising the Wind* (1803) by the Irish-born English dramatist James Kenney. Diddler constantly borrows small sums of money and 'forgets' to pay them back. The verb was already well established by the 1810s.

Do porridge, To A slang expression for serving time in prison. It probably alludes punningly to 'stir', an earlier slang name for a prison, perhaps with implied reference to prison fare.

Double-cross, To Properly, to cheat or cross each of two parties, to betray both sides, but now commonly used to mean to betray just one person or side. 'To double' has long been used to mean 'to make evasive turns or shifts', as though one is doubling back on a route. By extension, it came to mean to behave deceitfully. 'Double agent' and 'double dealing' both stem from this idea. 'Double-cross' was greatly popularized by a military counter-espionage unit established by MI5 in 1941, known as the Twenty Committee. The name linked the double crosses of the Roman numerals XX, twenty, with the unit's intention of double-crossing the enemy by coercing German spies to become double agents.

Draconian Of laws or punishment, very severe. Draco was an Athenian of the 7th century BC who drew up a code of laws noted for their severity. As nearly every violation of his laws was a capital offence, Demades, the orator, said that Draco's code was written in blood.

Emancipate To set free; properly 'to send from one's hand' (Latin *e manu capere*). One of the Roman ways of freeing a slave was to take him by the hand before the chief magistrate and say, 'I wish this man to be free.'

Hijacker A term of US origin, first used to denote a bandit who preys on bootleggers and other criminals. The name is popularly said to derive from the gunman's command to his victim, 'Stick 'em up high, Jack', meaning that the arms were to be raised well above the head. Another possibility is that it comes from 'high jack', a slang term for zinc ore in use in the zinc and tin mines of Webb City, Missouri, at the end of the

19th century; this ore was particularly valuable, and miners often tried to steal it. Today's use focuses on the unlawful seizure of a vehicle or goods, or metaphorically to take something over and use it for a different purpose.

Hoodlum A street hooligan. The word originated in San Francisco in the early 1870s and rapidly spread throughout the USA. Its origin is uncertain, but it may well come from German dialect *Huddellump*, 'ragamuffin'. Other theories include a backward spelling of the name 'Muldoon' (once a leading gangster), producing 'noodlum' which was transformed by a printer's error into 'hoodlum'.

Hue and cry An early system for apprehending suspected criminals. Neighbours were expected to join in a hue and cry and to pursue a suspect to the bounds of the manor. It became the old common law process of pursuing 'with horn and with voice'. 'Hue' is from Old French *huer*, to 'shout'.

Hullaballoo A scene or occasion of confused uproar. The word first appeared in the mid-18th century, probably as a reduplicated version of the cry 'Hulloo!', although it has also been suggested that it came from the French hunting call *Bas le loup!*, 'Bring down the wolf!'

Ignoramus The grand jury used to write 'ignoramus' on the back of indictments 'not found' or not to be sent to court. This was often construed as an indication of the stupidity of the jury, hence its present meaning. The word is actually from legal Latin, where it means 'we take no notice of it'.

In camera (Latin, 'in the chamber') In judicial proceedings, the hearing of a case either in the judge's private room or in a court from which the public has been excluded.

In flagrante delicto (Latin, 'with the crime still blazing'). Red-handed; caught in the act.

Kangaroo court A term applied to an irregular court or tribunal which is conducted in disregard of proper legal procedure, as, for example, a mock court held among prisoners in a jail. 'To kangaroo' means to convict a person on false evidence. The term, which probably arose from some resemblance of the 'jumps' of the kangaroo to the progress of 'justice' in such courts, was common in the USA during the 19th century.

Put the kibosh on, To To put a stop to; to prevent from continuing. One of the earliest records of the word's use is by Charles Dickens in a sketch from 1836. A popular suggestion links it with the Irish *caidhp bhais*, literally 'cap of death', worn by a judge when pronouncing a death sentence, or as a covering pulled over the face of a corpse when a coffin was closed. Certainly early uses suggest the 'kibosh' was a physical object, especially one used for striking, and it may alternatively derive from the Arabic *kirbās* (also *kurbāš*), a kind of whip used for judicial punishment.

Newgate prison The first Newgate prison existed in the reign of King John in the 13th century. Many notorious criminals and state prisoners were confined there, as well as debtors. Condemned criminals were executed in the street outside, 'condemned sermons' being preached the preceding Sunday, to which the public were formerly admitted. The name came to be associated with various styles and fashions. A 'Newgate fringe' was thus hair worn under the chin, so called because it took the position of the rope around the neck of a man about to be hanged.

Ombudsman Originating in Scandinavian countries, an official appointed by the legislature whose duty it is to protect the rights of the citizen against infringement by the government. The word is Swedish for 'commissioner'.

Omertà The code of silence which members of the Mafia observe in relation to their colleagues' nefarious activities. This Italian word is probably a dialectal variant of Italian *umiltà*, 'humility', but an alternative suggestion is that it came from Old Spanish *hombredad*, 'manliness'.

Read the riot act, To The original Riot Act was that of 1715, which stated that when 12 or more people were committing a riot it was the duty of the magistrates to command them to disperse, and that anyone who continued to riot for one hour afterwards was guilty of a felony. Figuratively to read the riot act is to try to curb noise, commotion, and misbehaviour of children and others by a vigorous and forceful telling off.

Red tape Official formality, or rigid adherence to rules and regulations, carried to excess; so called because lawyers and government officials tie their papers together with red tape.

Round robin, A A petition or protest signed in a circular form, so that no name heads the list. The device is French, and according to some authorities the term is an alteration of *rond* ('round') and *ruban* ('ribbon'), and was originally used by sailors. In its written form, a round robin is now often simply a circular letter sent by one person to many, rather than by many to one.

Run amok or **amuck, To** To indulge in physical violence while in a state of frenzy. 'Amuck' or 'amok' is from the Malay word *amoq*, 'furious assault'.

Sabotage Wilful and malicious destruction of machinery or plant by strikers, rebels, fifth columnists, and the like. The term came into use after the great French railway strike in 1912. The word is traditionally said to have referred to the action of the strikers, who threw 'sabots', or wooden clogs, into the machinery to damage it, but the idea may simply be the noise made by the wooden shoes in walking, evoking a clumsy or bungling action.

Scream blue murder To scream or shout loudly; to yell at the top of one's voice, especially from terror. The expression seems to pun on the French exclamation *morbleu*, which is actually a form of *mort Dieu*, 'God's death'.

Sell down the river, To To deceive; to betray. The allusion is to the days when the US owners sold domestic slaves to plantation owners lower down the Mississippi, where harsher conditions often prevailed.

Sent up the river, To be In US colloquial usage, to be sent to prison, from the fact that Sing Sing, one of the most widely known prisons, is at Ossining, up the Hudson River from New York.

Shop someone, To To betray them or inform on them. Originally, it meant to shut someone up in prison. 'To grass on someone', with a similar meaning, is from the Cockney rhyming slang 'grasshopper/shopper'.

Give someone short shrift, To To treat them peremptorily and unsympathetically. Short shrift was the few minutes in which a criminal about to be executed was allowed to make his confession, or to 'shrive' his sins. Shrove Tuesday, the day before Ash Wednesday, encourages Christians to repent their sins before the start of Lent.

Stockholm syndrome A term dating from the 1970s for the observed tendency of hostages to try to cooperate with their captors. The phenomenon takes its name from a robbery of the Sveriges Kreditbank in Stockholm in 1973, remarkable for the bonds formed between hostages and captors.

Whipping post A post set up for public punishment by whipping. Many parishes had such a post to which offenders, particularly women, were manacled for this purpose. The name of York's Whip-ma-Whop-ma-Gate may commemorate the whipping post and pillory that stood at the end of this street.

Woke Alert to injustice in society, especially racism. The term is a contraction of 'stay woke', and thought to have been first used in this context by the soul singer Erykah Badu. The once-positive term has since been harnessed as an insult against those considered overly liberal in their attitudes.

WORK

For those of us who find work a little irksome, there is perhaps some consolation in knowing that the Greek for work, *ergon*, also gave us 'energy' and 'orgy'. And if you feel up to either of these, then you may well be 'panurgic', ready for anything.

Boondoggle In North American usage, a verb meaning 'to do useless or futile work'. The word is of uncertain origin. According to one account it was invented in the 1930s by a US scoutmaster, Robert H. Link, for a type of braided lanyard. This took time or trouble to make, hence the word passed to a futile task in general.

Cobbler should stick to their last, A Each person should confine themselves to their own affairs and not meddle in matters they know nothing about. There is the story of a cobbler who detected a fault in a shoe in a painting by the Greek artist Apelles. The artist rectified the fault. The cobbler then ventured to criticize the legs, but Apelles answered, 'Keep to your trade: you understand about shoes, but not about anatomy.' A 'last' is a model of the foot on which boots and shoes are shaped during their making. *See* ULTRACREPIDARIAN.

Ergophobia A fear of working.

Get the sack or **be sacked, To** To be dismissed from employment. The phrase was current in 17th-century France (*on luy a donné son sac*), and the probable explanation of the term is that workmen carried their implements in a bag or sack, and when they were discharged they took up their bags of tools and departed to seek a job elsewhere.

Humdudgeon An imaginary disease, such as might prevent you from working.

Make a cat's paw of someone, To To use them as a tool; to get them to do one's dirty work. The allusion is said to be to the fable of the monkey who wanted to get some roasted chestnuts from the fire, and used the paw of his friend the cat for the purpose.

Pay dirt A mining term for ground that pays for working. Hence 'to hit pay dirt', meaning to attain one's objective.

Sisyphus In Greek legend, Sisyphus was subjected to the punishment of rolling a huge stone up a hill to the top. As it constantly rolled down again just as it reached the summit, his task was everlasting. Hence 'a labour of Sisyphus' or 'Sisyphean toil' is an endless, heartbreaking job.

WATER COOLER MOMENTS

Politicians of ancient Rome knew all about the power of gossip. The orator Cicero scolded the judges of a high-profile trial by asking *vestrae peregrinantur aures?* (are your ears travelling abroad?). Today, ears and mouths, and the gossip they trade in, not only dictate the political landscape, but also sway our opinion on almost everything, even when the 'news' is nothing but cock and bull.

Dish the dirt on, To To spread gossip about someone or something. The allusion is to gold-mining, in which the prospector swirls the dirt about in his pan to separate out the particles of gold. In this case the precious discovery is the juicy gossip.

Furphy In Australian slang, a false or unsubstantiated rumour. The term comes from John Furphy, the name of the manufacturer of the sanitary carts used by Australian forces in the First World War, round which troops used to gather and gossip. A parallel usage in British forces' slang was 'Elsan gen', denoting a rumour ('Elsan' was the name of a make of chemical toilet).

Gossip Trivial or malicious talk, tittle-tattle. In Old English *godsibb* or 'gossip' was the word for a godparent. It meant, literally, 'a person related to God', and came from *god*, 'God', and *sibb*, a 'relative', with *sibb* later appearing in Modern English in the word 'sibling'. 'Gossip' came over time to be applied to a close friend, particularly a female one, who was invited to be present at the birth of a child. At some point that same woman took on the negative aspects of a newsmonger or tattler, indulging in light and trifling chatter.

Rabbit on, To To talk at length; chatter away. 'Rabbit' here is short for 'rabbit and pork', Cockney rhyming slang for 'talk'.

Scuttlebutt Originally, in the early 19th century, a barrel of fresh drinking water on board ship ('scuttle' probably denotes that it had a hole made in it). Such a place of refreshment would have been a natural point for meeting and conversation, the predecessor of today's water cooler, and by the beginning of the 20th century 'scuttlebutt' was being used in US slang for 'gossip' or 'rumour'.

Cock and bull story A highly coloured or unbelievable story. The Cock and Bull inn sign is found in the 17th century and both Cock and Bull as separate signs were always popular. There is a story set in Stony Stratford, Buckinghamshire, that in the coaching days the London coach changed horses at the Bull Inn, and the Birmingham coach at the Cock. From the exchange of jests and stories between the waiting passengers of both coaches the 'Cock and Bull' story is said to have originated. The true source of the expression has been lost, but it was almost certainly a riff on a French expression from the 1600s, *coq-à-l'âne* ('cock to the donkey'), used for an incoherent, rambling story.

CLOTHES

'Clothes make the man' is a proverb recorded since the early 15th century, but the importance of textiles and the wardrobes they create was already evident long before. Any argument we might describe today as 'succinct' has a Roman toga belt to thank, while an 'ultracrepidarian' – one who loves to talk about subjects they know absolutely nothing about – involves the strange story of a Greek painter and a shoe.

Dressed up to the Nines

Another man's shoes 'To stand in another man's shoes' is to occupy the place of another. Among the Vikings, when a man adopted a son, the adoptee put on the shoes of the adopting parent.

Bikini This atoll in the Marshall Islands, the scene of US nuclear weapon testing in 1946 (and 1954), gave its name to a scanty two-piece swimming costume worn by women. The allusion is supposedly to the devastation of the atom-bomb test and the 'explosive' effect caused by a woman wearing such a costume.

Bling A slang term, emerging at the end of the 20th century, for ostentatious and (relatively) cheap jewellery or similarly flashy personal adornment. It may have been inspired by the clinking noise of such jewellery, or by its glitter.

Bowler hat A hard felt hat, said to have been introduced by the 19th-century Norfolk landowner William Coke. Because he found his tall riding hat frequently swept off by overhanging branches, he asked Lock's, the well-known hatters of St James's, to design him a hat with a lower crown. The first 'Coke' is said to have been made from felt supplied by Thomas and William Bowler, and the hat eventually took their name.

Buttonhole, To To detain a person in conversation. The original was 'buttonhold' and it refers to a former habit of holding a person by the button or buttonhole while in conversation. In Italian, an *attaccabottoni* is someone who buttonholes you and proceeds to bore you with endless stories.

Cardigan A knitted jacket or sweater with buttons up the front, named after the 7th Earl of Cardigan (1797–1868), who led the Charge of the Light Brigade. It appears to have been first worn by the British to protect themselves from the bitter cold of the Crimean winter. The Balaclava helmet or cap, a knitted woollen covering for the head and neck, has a similar origin.

Chaperon or **chaperone** A married or mature woman who escorted a young unmarried woman in public places and acted as adviser and protector. The word comes from Old French *chaperon*, 'little hood', the analogy apparently being that the chaperon protected her charge as a hood protects the face.

Cravat The neckscarf takes its name from the neckcloth worn by Croat soldiers serving in the French army in the Thirty Years War (1618–48). The French adopted the style, and from there it spread to England. The word thus came into English, through French, from Serbo-Croat *Hrvat*, 'Croat'.

Domino The word originally applied to a hooded clerical cloak and subsequently to a hooded garment worn at masquerades, then a hood only, and finally a half-mask covering an inch or two above and below the eyes, worn as a disguise. The black ebony pieces used in the game of dominoes may have derived their name from the black domino cloak or the black mask with the eyes showing through as the white pips. The name of the cloak ultimately comes from Latin *dominus*, 'lord', thanks to its original religious associations.

Dressed up to the nines Dressed elaborately or even over-dressed. The origin of the expression remains uncertain. 'Nines' is said by some to be an alteration of *eyne*, the Old English word for 'eyes'. However, the phrase is not recorded before the 18th century. Other authorities claim that 'nine' indicates a high degree of excellence, perfection itself being 'ten'.

Dyed-in-the-wool Wool dyed in its original natural or 'raw' state retains a dye more thoroughly than when it has been treated and made up into a garment. Hence the phrase is used to mean 'through and through', 'genuine', or 'out and out', as: 'a dyed-in-the-wool teetotaller', a firm and definite abstainer.

G-string A minimal item of underwear. Originally spelled 'gee-string', it referred to a loincloth worn by native Americans. The change to 'G-string' may have been influenced by the idea of a violin string tuned to a G, the lowest and thickest of strings.

Glove money A bribe, so called from the ancient custom of a client presenting a pair of gloves to a lawyer who undertook a cause. Mrs Croaker presented Sir Thomas More, the Lord Chancellor, with a pair of gloves lined with forty pounds in 'angels' as a 'token'. Sir Thomas kept the gloves but returned the 'lining'.

Hat tip An acknowledgement of respect, used online to acknowledge that another person or user has brought something to one's attention. The term comes from the practice of raising one's hat in greeting.

Inexpressibles A 19th-century euphemism for trousers, the mention of which was considered rude in polite company. They were also known as 'ineffables', 'inexplicables', 'sit-upons', 'round-me-houses', and 'unmentionables'.

Jodhpurs In the 1860s the maharajah of the Rajputana state of Jodhpur was an extreme devotee of polo, which he played in breeches that were tight-fitting by the ankle and loose-fitting above. British Army officers exported the game and the breeches to England.

Knickerbockers Loose-fitting breeches, gathered in below the knees, formerly worn by boys, cyclists, sportsmen, and others, and by women as an undergarment. They were so named from George Cruikshank's illustrations for Washington Irving's *A History of New York from the Beginning of the World to the End of the Dutch Dynasty* (1809), written under the pseudonym Diedrich Knickerbocker, in which the Dutchmen wore such breeches. Our modern 'knickers' is a short form of this.

Leotard A close-fitting garment worn by acrobats and dancers. It takes its name from the French trapeze artiste Jules Léotard (1839–70), who wore something similar. The costume is first recorded in the USA in the 1920s; similar garments became fashionable in the late 20th century.

Mortarboard A university cap, surmounted by a square 'board' usually covered with black cloth. The word is possibly connected with French *mortier*, the cap worn by the ancient kings of France, and still used officially by the chief justice or president of the court of justice. It is perhaps more likely an allusion to the small square board or hawk on which a bricklayer or plasterer carries their mortar.

Motley Varied, mixed, of things or people, as: 'a motley collection' or 'a motley crew'. The word originally applied to a clown's particoloured costume, or to a clown or jester himself, and it is found in this sense in Shakespeare.

Panache The literal meaning of this French word is a plume of feathers, flying in the wind as from the crest of a helmet. Figuratively, it describes a bold stylishness.

Pantaloons Pants get their name from Pantaloon, a lean and foolish old Venetian of 16th-century Italian comedy, who was dressed in loose trousers and slippers. His name is said to come from San Pantaleone (a patron saint of physicians and very popular in Venice), and he was adopted in later harlequinades and pantomimes as the butt of the clown's jokes.

Pin money A woman's allowance of money for her own personal expenditure. Pins were once very expensive, and in 14th- and 15th-century wills there were often special bequests for the express purpose of buying pins.

Plus fours Loose knickerbockers overlapping the knee and thereby giving added freedom for active outdoor sports. They were particularly popular with golfers in the 1920s. The name derives from the four extra inches (about 10cm) of cloth required below the knee in tailoring.

Pretext A pretence or excuse. The word is from Latin *prae-texta*, a dress embroidered in the front, worn by Roman magistrates, priests, and children of the aristocracy between the age of 13 and 17. Metaphorically, a pretext came to mean an outward display or disguise.

Pyjamas The word has its origins in India, where it originally applied to loose trousers worn by men or women. This was then adopted in the late 19th century as sleepwear. The word is of Urdu origin and literally means 'leg clothing'.

Succinct From the Latin *succinctus*, 'tucked up', referring to the belt that would allow Roman citizens to fold up the billowing folds of their togas so that they didn't sweep the ground. Any succinct argument is one that is pithy or 'tucked in'.

Tawdry An alteration of 'St Audrey'. At the annual fair of St Audrey, in the Isle of Ely, cheap jewellery and showy lace called St Audrey's lace were sold. When said quickly, it sounded like 'tawdry', which was applied to anything gaudy, in bad taste and of little value. The story is that St Audrey, otherwise Etheldreda or Æthelthryth (*c*.630–679), queen of Northumbria and abbess of Ely, died of a throat tumour as a punishment for her fondness in her youth for showy necklaces.

Togs Slang for clothes, hence 'togged out', dressed in one's best clothes, and 'toggery', finery. The word is probably connected with 'toga'. It is also the source of the 'tog' as a unit of thermal resistance used to express the insulating properties of clothes and quilts.

Turncoat A renegade, one who deserts their principles or party. Fable has it that a certain Duke of Saxony, whose domin-ions were bounded in part by France, hit upon the device of a coat that was blue one side and white the other. When he wished to be thought of as backing the French he wore the white outside, switching to the blue when needing to switch his allegiance.

Tuxedo The US name for a dinner jacket, so called because it was first taken to the USA from England by Griswold Lorillard, in 1886, and introduced by him at the Tuxedo Club, Tuxedo, New York.

Whistle Cockney rhyming slang for 'a suit', from 'whistle and flute'.

Y-fronts The proprietary name, registered in 1953, of a make of boys' or men's underpants, with a front opening within an inverted Y-shape. The first trial Y-front was produced in 1934 by Coopers Inc of Kenosha, USA, under the name 'Brief Style 1001', and the style itself was suggested by the pair of swimming trunks worn by a bather on the French Riviera that one of the firm's senior vice presidents had seen in a magazine photograph.

Material Witness

Cotton on, To To catch on, to grasp a line of thought. The allusion is to cotton fibres that catch on clothing.

Denim Twilled cotton material used for overalls and other garments, especially jeans (which are sometimes called denims). Typically dark blue in colour, the fabric was originally chosen for working clothes because it was strong and hard-wearing. The word 'denim' is a contraction of French *serge de Nîmes* ('serge of Nîmes'), from the town in the south of France where it was originally made.

Doily, doyly, or **doyley** A small ornamental mat of lace or lace-like paper, laid on or under cake plates and the like. The Doyleys, from which the material was named, were linen drapers in the Strand, London, from the time of Queen Anne until 1850.

Flannel Evasive or flattering talk; 'soft soap'. Flannel may have acquired this kind of connotation in the same way as 'bombast' and 'fustian'. Unlike these two words, flannel is still more frequently found in its original sense, denoting a woollen cloth used especially to make trousers (known as flannels).

Grogram (French *gros grain*, 'coarse grain') A coarse fabric made of silk and mohair or silk and wool, stiffened with gum. *See* GROG.

Suede Undressed kidskin, so called because the gloves made of this originally came from Sweden (French *gants de Suède*).

Tweed The name of this woollen cloth originated in a mistake. It should have been 'tweel', the Scots form of 'twill', but when the Scottish manufacturer sent a consignment to James Locke of London, in 1826, the name was badly written and misread, and as the cloth was made on the banks of the Tweed, 'tweed' was accordingly adopted. 'Twill' means etymologically 'two-threaded'.

Put a Sock in It

Bootlegger One who traffics illegally in alcoholic liquor. The expression derives from the smuggling of flasks of liquor in boot legs.

Bootstrap A loop at the back of a boot to pull it on. 'To pull oneself up by one's own bootstraps' is to better oneself by one's own efforts. 'Booting up' one's computer is thought to derive from this idea of powering oneself up.

Doc Martens A type of footwear invented in 1945 by Klaus Maertens, a German doctor, who needed a comfortable shoe after a skiing accident. He formed a rubber sole from a tyre and sealed it to an upper, so trapping a cushion of air. The boots were first produced in England under licence in 1960 by R. Griggs & Co, and subsequently became a youth-culture fashion staple and simultaneous anti-fashion statement.

Down at heel Impoverished, as typified by the worn-out condition of one's footwear.

Galosh The word comes from Old French *galoche*, itself from Late Latin *gallicula*, 'Gallic shoe'. It was originally applied to a kind of clog or patten worn as a protection against wet in the days when silk or cloth shoes were worn.

Put a sock in it Be quiet; shut up; make less noise. In the late 19th century and earlier years of the 20th, when gramophones or phonographs amplified the sound through large horns, woollen socks were often stuffed in them to deaden the volume.

Toerag A slang term for a despicable person. The name was originally used for a tramp or beggar, who wrapped pieces of rag around their feet instead of socks.

Toe-cover An inexpensive and useless present.

Ultracrepidarian One who loves to hold forth on matters they know little about. The word is based on the story of the Greek painter Apelles, who overheard a cobbler criticize first the rendering of a sandal in one of his paintings, and then the shape of the subject's leg. *Ne ultra crepidam sutor iudicaret* means 'the cobbler should not judge beyond his shoe'.

Vamp Originally, 'to vamp' meant 'to put new uppers on old boots', and 'vamps' were short hose covering the feet and ankles. 'To vamp up' an old story is to refurbish it, and 'to vamp an accompaniment' to a song is to improvise as one goes along. The 'vamp' used to imply a predatory woman is derived from 'vampire'.

Winkle-pickers Shoes with very elongated and pointed toes, affected by some in the early 1960s. The allusion is to the use of a pin for picking winkles out of their shells.

EGGCORNS

An eggcorn is a linguistic error or slip of the ear in which part of a common expression is replaced by a similar-sounding word that the speaker believes to be not only correct, but logical. The name was the creation of professor of linguistics Geoffrey Pullum in September 2003, using the example of 'eggcorn' being mistakenly used in place of 'acorn': an acorn is a seed, like a grain of corn, and is roughly similar in shape to an egg, so the mistake makes perfect sense. And, much as we like to think that such mishearings are modern evidence of English going to the dogs, etymology proves that we have been producing eggcorns for centuries.

A mute point (moot)

A parting of the waves (ways)

Chuck it up to experience (chalk)

Cognitive dissidence (dissonance)

Curled up in the feeble position (foetal)

Cut to the cheese (chase)

Damp squid, A Said of an enterprise, joke or the like that fails to come off or to satisfy expectations. The original, of course, was a damp 'squib', in which a squib is a firework which, when wet, fails to explode.

Doggy-dog world, A (a dog-eat-dog world)

Forlorn hope The phrase has its origin in Dutch *verloren hoop*, 'lost troop', referring to the vanguard of an attacking army who often fell in battle. The phrase was anglicized to something more familiar.

Give free range (rein)

Give up the goat (ghost)

Goal standard (gold)

Going at it hammer and thongs With great energy, as: 'They were going at it hammer and thongs.' The original is 'hammer and tongs', an allusion to a blacksmith energetically at work, hammering the metal that he holds with the tongs.

In lame man's terms (layman's)

Internally grateful (eternally)

Like a bowl in a china shop (bull)

Mind-bottling (boggling)

Post-dramatic stress disorder (post-traumatic)

Putting the cat before the horse (cart)

Spreading like wildflowers (wildfire)

The chickens are coming home to roast (roost)

Urge on the side of caution (err)

FOOD AND DRINK

'Delectable', 'scrumptious', and 'toothsome': such is the dictionary when it comes to food. Then again, let's not forget 'baloney', 'crumbs', 'nuts', and 'holy mackerel'. In fact, whatever you want to say, there will usually be a foody metaphor to help you out. And if you're in search of ways to liven up the language of your cuisine, you could do worse than turning to 'bags of mystery' and 'cacklefarts'.

Forks at the Ready

As keen as mustard Very keen and enthusiastic. Mustard gives an 'edge' to the food it accompanies.

As sure as eggs is eggs Very sure; certain in fact. It has been suggested that this is an alteration of the logician's formula 'x is x'.

Baker's dozen, A Thirteen for twelve. In earlier times when a heavy penalty was inflicted for short weight, bakers used to give an extra number of loaves, called the 'inbread', to avoid all risk of incurring a fine. The thirteenth was the 'vantage loaf'.

Barbecue (American Spanish *barbacoa*, 'frame made of sticks') A West Indian term formerly used in the USA for a large gridiron upon which an animal could be roasted whole.

Beanfeast An annual dinner given by an employer to employees, and so called because beans and bacon formed an indispensable feature of the meal. The word is now used for any celebration or party and is often shortened to 'beano'.

Bistro A small restaurant. The word may come from Russian *bystro*, 'quick', 'fast', and date from the Allied occupation of France in 1815, when Russian soldiers would enter a café and demand food and drink with the command 'Bystro, bystro!' Others, however, take the word from French *bistouille*, a local word for a drink of coffee and brandy, itself apparently from *bis*, 'twice', and *touiller*, 'to stir'.

Bovril A concentrated beef extract used as a flavouring, a stock, or a drink. It was the invention in 1887 of John Lawson Johnston and took its name from a combination of Latin *bos*, *bovis*, 'ox', together with 'vril', a mystical source of energy in Edward Bulwer-Lytton's utopian novel *The Coming Race* (1871).

Butter up, To To flatter a person with smooth talk, as one spreads butter on bread to make it palatable. There may also be a nod to an ancient Hindu tradition of throwing balls of ghee butter at statues of deities, in order to ask for favours.

Cereal Any food prepared from grain, especially one eaten at breakfast time. The word is from the Latin *Cerealis*, 'relating to Ceres', the goddess of agriculture.

Chopsticks Two thin sticks of wood or ivory that the Chinese, Japanese, and Koreans use to eat with. The word comes from the Pidgin English 'chop' (quick, as in 'chop chop') and English 'stick', and is a translation of the Chinese *kuàizi*, 'nimble ones'.

Cordon bleu (French, 'blue ribbon') The blue ribbon once signified the highest order of chivalry in the reign of the Bourbon kings, hence in cooking it denotes first-class cooking.

Croque-monsieur (French, literally 'sir-muncher') The French equivalent of a toasted cheese and ham sandwich. When served with a fried egg on top, it is known as a *croque-madame*. It is said to have first appeared in the early 20th century in a café on the Boulevard des Capucines in Paris. The name itself may have arisen as a whimsical take on *croque-mitaine* (literally, 'mitten-muncher'), used of a bogeyman.

Cut the mustard, To To do something well and efficiently, especially when it is suspected that one may lack the ability. The expression derives from 'mustard' as a slang word for a thing that is the best, with 'cutting' used in the same sense as 'he cuts a fine figure'.

Deipnosophist (Greek, from *deipnon*, 'dinner' and *sophistēs*, 'wise man') Someone who relishes and excels at dinner-table conversation.

Dress someone down, To To reprimand or scold them. The expression may derive from butchers' jargon, alluding to the initial cut into a carcass on a beam. A more likely reference is to builders' talk, in which to dress a brick down is to scour its front face to make it seem bright and new.

Fine or **fair words butter no parsnips** Nothing is achieved through flattery or empty promises. The phrase is first recorded in the 17th century and took various forms (such as 'fair words butter no fish') before settling on parsnips.

Full of beans Full of energy and high spirits. Beans have long been popularly regarded as an aphrodisiac.

Haggis A traditional Scottish dish, popular on Burn's Night, made from the heart, lungs, and liver of a sheep or calf, chopped up with suet, oatmeal, onions, and seasonings, and boiled like a big sausage in a sheep's stomach bag. The derivation of the name is uncertain: it may have come from northern Middle English *haggen*, 'to chop'.

High-muck-a-muck or **Lord High-muck-a-muck** An arrogant or conceited person. The expression has become associated with English 'high' and 'muck' but originated as Chinook Jargon *hiyu muckamuck*, 'plenty of food'.

High on the hog In great comfort and wealth, enjoying the best of everything. The phrase, which originated in the USA, appears to refer to the upper portions of a pig as being the best for eating.

Hot dog A cooked sausage, especially a frankfurter, served in a roll split lengthways. Sausages had been referred to colloquially in the USA as 'dogs' since the middle of the 19th century, very likely reflecting suspicions about the meat inside them, and there is some circumstantial evidence that the term 'hot dog' may have originated in Yale University slang in the mid-1890s. The following alternative explanation is more colourful but also more dubious. A Bavarian sausage seller, Anton Ludwig Feuchtwanger, began selling hot wieners (a type of sausage) at the World's Columbian Exposition, Chicago, in 1893, giving his customers white gloves to keep them from burning their fingers as they devoured the tasty meat. When the gloves started disappearing as handy souvenirs, Feuchtwanger substituted elongated bread rolls to hold the frankfurters.

Hotchpotch A thick broth containing meat and vegetables and other mixed ingredients; a confused mixture or jumble. It comes from the French *hochepot*, from *hocher*, meaning 'to shake', and *pot*, meaning 'pot'.

Kettle of fish, A An old Scottish expression for a kind of *fête champêtre* or riverside picnic where a newly caught salmon is boiled and eaten. The remnants of the fish in the pan may have led to the phrase 'a pretty kettle of fish', meaning an awkward state of affairs, a mess, or a muddle.

Larder Etymologically, a place for keeping bacon, from Old French *lardier*, from Latin *laridum*, 'bacon fat'. The origin of the word shows that pigs were the chief animals salted and preserved in olden times.

Love apple The tomato, which the Spaniards introduced to Europe from South America. It was said to have aphrodisiac properties, the red skin of the tomato being associated with the colour of passion.

Macaroni A dandy who affects foreign manners and style. The word is derived from the Macaroni Club, instituted in London about 1760 by a set of flashy men who had travelled in Italy and who introduced the newfangled Italian food, *macaroni*.

Mayonnaise A sauce made with pepper, salt, oil, vinegar, the yolk of egg, and so on, beaten up together. When the Duc de Richelieu captured Port Mahon, Minorca, in 1756, he demanded food on landing. In the absence of a prepared meal, his chef took whatever he could find and beat it up together. Hence the original form 'mahonnaise'.

Meat A word that originally meant all food in general, hence a 'sweetmeat' was an item of sweet food, and such sayings as 'one man's meat is another man's poison'.

Mess The usual meaning today is 'a dirty, untidy state of things', 'a muddle', but the word originally signified 'a portion of food' (Latin *missum*, from *mittere*, 'to send'; compare with French *mets*, 'viands', Italian *messa*, 'a course of a meal'). Hence it came to mean 'mixed food, especially for an animal', and so 'a confusion, medley or jumble. Another meaning was 'a small group of persons (usually four) who sat together at banquets and were served from the same dishes'. This gave rise to the army and navy 'mess', the place where meals are served and eaten.

Mustard The condiment is so called because originally 'must', new wine (Latin *mustus*, 'fresh', 'new'), was used in mixing the paste.

Off the cuff Without previous preparation. The phrase may refer to the habit of some after-dinner speakers of making jottings on their stiff shirt cuffs as ideas occurred to them during the meal.

Picnic (French *pique-nique*) A picnic was originally a fashionable social event at which each guest contributed food, but it fairly rapidly became a term for an outdoor meal. The term was probably formed from *piquer*, 'to pick', and *nique*, 'nothing whatsoever'.

Ploughman's lunch A meal of bread and cheese, typically served with pickle and salad and consumed in or outside a pub as a bar snack. The name is said to have arisen as a marketing ploy of the English Country Cheese Council in the early 1970s.

Pot luck To take pot luck is to share a meal of whatever food is available, one that has not been specially prepared for visitors; to take a chance. The expression comes from the days when the family cooking pot, containing a variety of edibles, was kept boiling over the fire. When it was ladled out at mealtimes, what anyone received was 'pot luck'.

Pumpernickel The name of a slightly sour black bread, made of coarse rye flour, eaten in Germany, especially in Westphalia. The word may come from the German *pumpern*, 'to break wind', and *Nickel*, 'goblin', producing something similar to 'Farty Nick' to reflect the bread's gas-creating potential in the human digestive system. *See* NICKEL.

Recipe or **receipt** *Recipe* is Latin for 'take', and is contracted into R when used in doctors' prescriptions. A recipe is now more usually a list of ingredients and instructions for making a food dish.

Sandwich Meat or other filling between two slices of bread, so called from the 4th Earl of Sandwich, John Montagu (1718–92). He was a gambling man, and so resented time spent away from the tables that he had convenience meals prepared for him, which he could eat as he lost money. One of the most successful was a slice of cold roast beef between two pieces of toast, and its successors are to this day called 'sandwiches'.

Satire The term was originally applied to a medley or hotch-potch in verse, and later to compositions in verse or prose in which folly, vice, or individuals are held up to ridicule. It is from Latin *satura*, meaning 'medley', originally *lanx satura*, a dish of varied fruits.

Not a sausage Nothing at all. The expression originally denoted a lack of money, and is said to derive from Cockney rhyming slang, in which 'bangers and mash' (i.e. sausages and mash) represents 'cash'.

Shambles The ultimate source of the word is in Old English *sceamul*, meaning 'stool', 'table', from a word related to Latin *scamnum*, 'bench'. This was adopted for the stall on which meat was sold in a market, and from there it passed, in the plural form, to the term for a slaughterhouse, where the meat was actually prepared. Hence 'shambles' in its colloquial use for any scene of disorder or confusion, as formerly applied to slaughterhouses. The 'meat stall' sense of the word remains in the streets or markets called Shambles in some older towns, as in York.

Slap-bang At once; without hesitation; done with a slap and a bang. The term was formerly applied to a cheap eating house, where one 'slapped' one's money down as the food was 'banged' on the table.

Spam The trade name of a tinned-meat product, first market-ed in the USA by the George A. Hormel Company in 1937. A competition was held for a neat name for the new product and the $100 prize was won by the entry 'Spam', standing for 'spiced ham'. However, years later its low culinary status made it a byword for cheap convenience food, and the product motivated a sketch in the BBC television comedy series *Monty Python's Flying Circus* in which every item on the menu in a desultory café is Spam. It's from here that the term became computer jargon for junk mail received online.

Square meal, A A substantial and satisying one. As with a square deal, square conveys the idea of 'solid' or 'right'. There is no evidence to support the belief that wooden plates aboard Royal Navy ships were once square-shaped to avoid food spillage in stormy weather.

Teach one's grandmother to suck eggs, To To presume to tell somebody how to do something that they already know. Raw eggs were once a popular food enjoyed for their health-giving properties. Older generations clearly needed no instruction about how to consume them.

Tiddy-oggie The local name for the Cornish pasty of meat and potato. 'Tiddy' is the dialect word for potato, while 'oggie' is a pasty. The Cornish miner's lunch usually consisted of a pasty, and its crust was formerly supposed to be sufficiently hard to be dropped down the mine shaft to the man below. When the pasty sellers arrived they would traditionally cry 'Oggie Oggie Oggie!', to which the reply from the miners would be 'Oy! Oy! Oy!'

Walnut The 'foreign nut', called in Middle English *walnote*, from Old English *wealh*, 'foreign', since it came from Persia, as opposed to the native hazelnut.

Welsh rabbit Cheese melted with butter, milk, Worcester sauce, and the like, spread on buttered toast. 'Rabbit' is not an alteration of 'rarebit', but the other way round, the implication being that the Welsh were too poor to afford meat. It thus joins the many other insults unfairly aimed at the Welsh, including a 'Welsh comb', meaning to run one's fingers through one's hair.

Where's the beef? Where is the substance in what you say? The phrase has its origin in a television commercial screened in 1984 by the Wendy International hamburger chain. In this, an outraged old lady, patronizing a non-Wendy establishment that served buns with salad and little else, demanded of the manager, 'Where's the beef?'

Wimpy A proprietary name for a hamburger, as served in a Wimpy restaurant. The name comes from that of J. Wellington

Wimpy, a character who was always portrayed eating a hamburger in Elzie C. Segar's *Popeye* comic strip.

Bags of Mystery

Addled Of an egg, rotten. 'Addle' is used figuratively in 'addle-brained', used of anyone or anything confused or muddled. 'Addle' came from an Old English word meaning 'liquid filth', and specifically 'foul-smelling urine'.

Bags of mystery Victorian slang for sausages, because you never quite know what's in them.

Barmy or **balmy** Mad, crazy. 'Barm' is the froth on fermenting malt liquor. The connection with madness is the idea of 'frothing' over with insanity.

Cacklefart An old dialect term for an egg.

Curate's egg Good in parts. The catchphrase was introduced by *Punch* magazine in the 19th century, in a cartoon showing a timid young curate at his bishop's breakfast table.

I'm afraid you've got a bad egg, Mr Jones.
Oh no, my Lord, I assure you! Parts of it are excellent!
(November 1895)

Come the raw prawn on or **over someone, To** To attempt to deceive them or impose on them. The Australian expression dates from the 1940s and derives from 'raw prawn' as an act of deception. A raw prawn is hard to swallow.

Duff A type of boiled pudding, as: 'plum duff'. The word, a northern English form of 'dough', probably gave the slang sense 'worthless', 'useless', since anything stodgy is dull, heavy, and potentially unproductive.

The Demon Drink

Aqua vitae (Latin, 'water of life') Brandy or distilled spirits. Aquavit, whisky, eau-de-vie, and the Irish usquebaugh (*uisge beatha*) have the same meaning. The name was also used for certain ardent spirits used in alchemy.

Beastly drunk It was an ancient notion that drunken individuals exhibited the vicious qualities of beasts. The 16th-century satirist Thomas Nashe describes seven kinds of drunkards: (1) The *Ape-drunk*, who leaps and sings; (2) The *Lion-drunk*, who is quarrelsome; (3) The *Swine-drunk*, who is sleepy and puking; (4) The *Sheep-drunk*, wise in their own conceit, but unable to speak; (5) The *Martin-drunk*, who drinks themselves sober again; (6) The *Goat-drunk*, who is lascivious; and (7) the *Fox-drunk*, who becomes particularly crafty.

Buck's fizz A cocktail made of champagne and orange juice. It takes its name from its purported place of origin, the Buck's Club, where it is said to have been the invention of the club's first barman. The club opened in 1919 and took its name from its founder, Captain Herbert Buckmaster.

Bucket shop Originally, in the US in the late 19th century, a low-class liquor store selling small quantities of spirits that had been dubiously distilled in buckets. The term then came to be applied to an unofficial or unregistered firm of stock-brokers that engaged in shady dealings with the funds of its clients. It is now mainly used for any small business that is not entirely reliable, but especially one that sells cheap airline tickets.

Cocktail An aperitif, or short drink taken before a meal, normally consisting of spirits, bitters, and fruit juice or other flavourings. The origin of the name is uncertain, but suggestions vary from 'a tail that cocks up' to the name of an Aztec princess, Xochitl, who is supposed to have given a drink to the king with romantic results. It may simply be a drink that makes you feel perky, like a cock's tail, or refer to a traditional embellishment of a cock's feather placed in the drink, the predecessor to the modern paper umbrella. Whatever its origin, the term first emerged in US society in the early 19th century.

Drown the miller, To To put too much water into spirits or tea. The idea is that the supply of water is so great that even the miller, who uses a water wheel, is drowned with it.

Gin A contraction of Dutch *genever*, 'juniper', the berries of which are used to flavour the spirit.

Lampoon A sarcastic or scurrilous personal satire, originally delivered in the form of a drinking song. The word comes from the 17th-century toast *lampons!*, 'let us drink!'.

Lush Beer and other intoxicating drinks. A word of uncertain origin, said by some to be derived from the name of a London brewer called Lushington. Up to about 1895, there was a convivial society of actors called the 'City of Lushington', which met in the Harp Tavern, Russell Street, and claimed to be 150 years old. 'Lush' is also slang for an alcoholic.

Mother's ruin A nickname for gin, of which there were once many, including 'strip-me-naked', 'tittery', 'eyewater', and 'tiger's milk'.

Nuncheon Properly, a drink in the afternoon (from the Middle English *none*, 'noon', and *schench*, 'cup', 'draught'). In extended use it can mean a light refreshment between meals.

One over the eight Slightly drunk. In this expression, the 'eight' is a reference to eight pints of beer, which were traditionally regarded as a reasonable amount for an average person to drink.

Proof spirit A term formerly applied (until 1980) to a standard mixture of alcohol and water used as a basis for customs and excise purposes. In earlier days proof spirit was held to be that which if poured over gunpowder and ignited would eventually ignite the powder. If the spirit was under proof the water remaining would prevent the firing of the powder.

Punch The name of this beverage, which was introduced into England in the early 17th century, derives from Hindi *pānch*, 'five', because it has five principal ingredients (spirit, water, spice, sugar, and fruit juice).

Real McCoy, The The genuine article. Norman Selby, also known as Charles 'Kid' McCoy, was an American boxer who became welterweight champion in 1896 after knocking out Tommy Ryan, his sparring partner, to whom he had previously pretended to be unfit and unprepared. He is said to have resorted often to such feigning of illness, only to appear fighting fit on the day itself, leading commentators to wonder whether this was the real McCoy. The earliest example we have, however, refers not to a McCoy but a Mackay, specifically Messrs G. Mackay & Co, who were popular whisky distillers in Edinburgh. 'A drappie o' the real MacKay' was a slogan advertising the strong stuff in the late 1800s.

Speakeasy A place where alcoholic liquors are sold illegally. A US term, it was widely current in the years of Prohibition (1919–33). 'Easy' here means 'softly', and the name refers either to the fact that such places were spoken about quietly or that people spoke quietly in them, to avoid attracting the attention of police or neighbours.

Supernaculum The very best wine. The word is sham Latin for 'upon the nail', meaning that the wine is so good the drinker leaves only enough in his glass to make a bead on their nail.

Symposium Etymologically, a 'drinking together' (Greek *sun*, 'together', and *pinein*, 'to drink'), hence a convivial meeting for entertainment and intellectual discussion.

Tap the Admiral To suck liquor from a cask by a straw. Some say it was first done by sailors from the rum cask in which the body of Admiral Lord Nelson was brought to England.

Toast The person or thing to which guests are invited to drink in compliment, as well as the drink itself. The reference is to pieces of spiced toast that were once added to tankards or glasses of alcohol. The idea behind a drinking toast is that the person being celebrated improves the flavour of the gathering, just as the toast improves the flavour of the wine.

Toddy Properly the juice obtained by tapping certain palms, fermented so as to become intoxicating. It is also applied to a beverage made of spirits, hot water, and sugar, a kind of punch. The word comes from Hindi *tārī*, 'the juice of the palmyra palm', from *tār*, the name of the tree itself.

Wassail A salutation, especially over a 'wassail bowl', a bowl of spiced ale formerly carried about on New Year's Eve when people went 'a-wassailing' from door to door in their parishes.

The word comes from the Old Norse *ves heill,* 'be in health', related to Old English *wes hāl* in the same sense.

HAIR OF THE DOG

Hair of the dog that bit you, The Another drink in the morning is considered by some to be the best remedy for a hangover. The reference is to the old notion that making a poultice made from the hair of a dog was an antidote to its bite.

Hangover Something remaining from a previous occasion, especially the headache and nausea experienced the 'morning after the night before'. The term is often said to refer to the ropes once provided to drunkards for leaning or sleeping upon in return for a small fee. In the late 19th and early 20th centuries, the Salvation Army operated many homeless shelters, which charged varying amounts for the refuge provided. A 'penny sit-up' provided food and shelter for a penny, but no provision for sleep. For an additional penny, there was the 'two-penny hangover', in which a rope was placed in front of a bench that the customer could lean over. Linguistically, however, such venues were not the inspiration for 'hangover', which from the outset has described something that remains or 'hangs over' as an after-effect.

On the Wagon

Cappuccino From Italian, literally 'Capuchin', because its colour resembles that of the cloak and cowl of a monk from the Franciscan Order of Capuchin.

Chocolate The produce of the cocoa bean (cacao seed) was introduced into England from Central America in the early 16th century as a drink. It was sold in London coffee houses from the middle of the 17th century. The Cocoa Tree Chocolate House, in Pall Mall, London, was one of the best-known coffee houses of the early 18th century. The origin of the word is in Nahuatl *chocolatl*, from *xococ*, 'bitter', and *atl*, 'water'.

Coca-Cola The carbonated drink was the invention in 1886 of John S. Pemberton, a US pharmacist. It is uncertain how he concocted the blend of ingedients that first went into the product, but his book-keeper, Frank Robinson, devised a name that indicated the source of two of the extracts: coca leaves and the cola nut. Coca leaves yield cocaine, a form of which was originally present in Coca-Cola. Hence the curative claims initially made for it, so that people took it for dyspepsia, head-aches, and similar malaises.

Earl Grey A superior type of China tea flavoured and scented with oil of bergamot. The story goes that the recipe for it was given in the 1830s to Charles Grey, 2nd Earl Grey (1764–1845) by a grateful Chinese mandarin whose life had been saved by one of the earl's envoys in China. The blend was then taken up commercially.

Mother, To be To pour the tea, as: 'Shall I be mother?' In Victorian times this became known as 'bitching the pot'.

Teetotal A word expressive of total abstinence from alcoholic liquors. The 'tee-' here was an emphatic iteration of the initial 't' of 'total'.

Tumbler The flat-bottomed stemless glass derives its name from the fact that it was originally made with a rounded bottom, which made it tumble over if placed on a table. This meant that it was intended to be held until it was quickly emptied.

On the wagon Abstaining from alcoholic drink, and a nod to the horse-drawn water wagons that were once a common sight in the US.

Playing with Your Food

Blow a raspberry, To A 20th-century slang expression for showing contempt for someone with a noise through closed lips. 'Raspberry' here is short for 'raspberry tart', Cockney rhyming slang for 'fart'.

Chestnut A stale joke. The term is said to look back to *The Broken Sword*, a forgotten melodrama by William Dimond, first produced at Covent Garden in 1816, in which one of the characters, Captain Xavier, is forever telling the same jokes with variations, one of which concerned his exploits with a cork tree. He is corrected by Pablo, who says, 'A chestnut. I have heard you tell the joke twenty-seven times, and I am sure it was a chestnut.'

Cakewalk A dance based on a march with intricate steps, with its origins in the black communities of the American south. The prize for the best dancer was a cake. Hence the fairground attraction known as the cakewalk, a series of platforms or gangways moved by machinery along which one does one's best to walk. Such competitions also gave us the expression 'takes the cake', meaning to carry off the honours or beat all others in absurdity.

Columbus's egg An easy task once one knows the trick. The story is that Christopher Colombus, in reply to a suggestion that other pioneers might have discovered America had he not done so, is said to have challenged the guests at a banquet in his honour to make an egg stand on end. When none succeeded, he flattened one end of the egg by tapping it against the table and so stood it up, thus indicating that, while others might follow, he had discovered the way.

Eat humble pie, To To be humbled or humiliated. Here 'humble' is a pun on 'umble', the umbles being the heart, liver, and entrails of a hunted deer. When the lord and his family dined off venison at high table, the huntsman and his fellows took lower seats and ate the umbles made into a pie.

Not to care a fig Not to care at all. Here 'fig' is the fig of Spain or 'fico', a traditional gesture of contempt made by placing the thumb between the first and second fingers.

Take the biscuit, To To beat everything for effrontery or outrageousness. Biscuits and cakes containing special spices were once given as rewards in a variety of competitions.

Something Sweet

Apple of one's eye, The The pupil, because it was formerly believed to be a round, solid ball like an apple. The phrase came to apply generally to any very precious or much-loved person or thing.

Apple-pie bed A bed in which the sheets are so folded as a prank that a person cannot lie at full length in it. The phrase is popularly derived from French *nappe pliée*, 'folded cloth'.

As easy as pie Agreeably uncomplicated. The reference is to the ease with which a pie goes down.

Bun Hot cross buns on Good Friday were supposed to be made of the dough kneaded for the Host, and are marked with a cross accordingly. As they are said to keep for 12 months without turning mouldy, some people still hang up one or more in their house as a 'charm against evil'.

Cookie (Dutch *koekje*, from *koek*, 'cake') In American English, the term for what in British English would be referred to as a sweet biscuit. A cookie is also, since the mid-1990s, a computer file that may be sent to an individual computer, without the user's knowledge, by a website. The name is said by some to have been inspired by the tale of Hansel and Gretel, who left trails of crumbs through the dark forest so they could find their way back.

Easter eggs The egg as a symbol of fertility and renewal of life derives from the ancient world, as did the practice of colouring and eating eggs at the spring festival. The custom of eating eggs on Easter Sunday and of making gifts of Easter eggs to children probably derives from the Easter payment of eggs by a serf to his overlord. The idea of the egg as a symbol of new life was adopted to symbolize the Resurrection. Easter eggs are also known as 'pasch eggs' or 'pace eggs', from Old French *pasche*, ultimately from Hebrew *pesakh* (related to 'Passover'). This name came to be used for the hard-boiled, hand-coloured eggs that were rolled down slopes as one of the Easter games, a practice surviving in the yearly egg-rolling held on the lawn of the White House in Washington.

Flapjack Originally, a flat cake of batter cooked on a griddle or in a shallow pan, so called from turning it by tossing it into the air. The word now usually denotes a soft thick biscuit made from rolled oats, butter, and syrup, baked in the oven.

Gooseberry fool A dish essentially made of gooseberries, cream or custard, and sugar, the fruit being crushed through a sieve. Here the word 'fool' probably comes from its standard meaning, with a punning allusion to 'trifle'.

Jammy dodger A type of small biscuit, with a jam filling between two biscuit layers. 'Dodger' was originally a US term for a hard-baked corncake but in the early 20th century came to be used for other kinds of bread and cake. The origin is probably in a dialect sense of 'dodge' meaning 'piece', 'lump'.

Junket The dish of flavoured milk set to a curd developed from a type of custard that was served in a rush basket. Hence the origin of the word in Old French *jonc*, 'rush' or 'reed'. The original cream dish was often eaten at feasts, and this gave 'junket' as a word for a feast or, nowadays, a series of promotional gatherings.

Knickerbocker glory A rich confection consisting of ice cream, jelly, cream, and fruit served in a tall glass, probably named after the Knickerbocker Hotel in Manhattan. Knickerbocker itself was originally used as a term for a New Yorker thanks to a character in Washington Irving's *A History of New York* (1809).

Madeleine A small sponge cake, often baked in the shape of a shell. The name is said to commemorate its concoction by a French cook called Madeleine Paulmier in the 18th or 19th century. It was the taste of a madeleine that inspired the narrator of Marcel Proust's *Remembrance of Things Past* (1913–26) to recall the incidents of his childhood. As a result of this famous passage, the madeleine is now regarded as a symbol for any object that unexpectedly triggers the recall of forgotten things.

Marzipan From the port of Martaban on the coast of south-east Myanmar, once famous for its exports of glazed jars containing preserves and sweet foods. The form 'marchpane' was more usual until the late 19th century, when 'marzipan' (influenced by German *Marzipan*) became more popular.

Melba Melba toast consists of narrow slices of thin toast. Peach or pêche Melba is a confection of peach on vanilla ice cream, covered with raspberry purée. These take their name from Dame Nellie Melba (1861–1931), the Australian soprano. The peach dish was created and named for her in London in 1894 by the French chef Auguste Escoffier following his receipt from the singer of two stalls for *Lohengrin*. The peach and ice cream represents the purity and sweetness of her voice, as well as her own 'peaches and cream' complexion, while the raspberry stands for her 'colour'.

Muffins and **crumpets** 'Muffin' is perhaps from Low German *muffen*, 'cakes'. 'Crumpet', the unsweetened soft cake, is a word of uncertain origin. It may be related to Old English *crump*, 'crooked', the original crumpets having perhaps been more akin to pancakes or girdle cakes, with edges that curled up on contact with heat.

Proof of the pudding is in the eating, The An old proverb meaning that performance is the true test, not appearances or promises, just as the best test of a pudding is to eat it, not just to look at it. The modern contracted version is 'the proof is in the pudding', even though it makes little sense.

Quality Street A confectionery assortment introduced in 1936 by John Mackintosh & Sons Ltd. The name was adopted from the title of J.M. Barrie's play *Quality Street* (1902), set in *c*.1805, and the product's identity was based on the play's main characters, a soldier and his young lady. Early advertisements depicted the couple, renamed 'Miss Sweetly' and 'Major Quality', dressed in period costume, with Miss Sweetly opening a tin of the assortment to show to the Major.

Spotted dick A steamed or boiled suet pudding containing dried fruit. 'Dick' here probably represents a dialect term for 'pudding'. The dried fruit gives it a speckled appearance.

Sundae A dish of ice cream with added ingredients, which first became popular at the turn of the 20th century. It is thought to be a respelling of 'Sunday', when such ice creams might be enjoyed – the altered version being perhaps made out of respect for Sunday churchgoers.

Turkish delight A confection of flavoured gelatin cubes coated in powdered sugar. It is of Turkish origin but in Turkish itself is known as *rahat lokum*, from Arabic *rahat al-hulqum*, literally 'ease of the throat'.

PUB SIGNS

Prominent signs displayed to identify their premises were made compulsory for public-house landlords in the late 14th century. These were often symbolic, taking the form of painted images or assembled objects rather than lettering. Much of Britain's history may be gleaned from their study, as well as folklore, heraldry, and social customs. Many are a compliment to the lord of the manor or a noble family, such as the Warwick Arms and the Bear and Ragged Staff. Others pay tribute to distinguished warriors or their battles. Simon the Tanner, the Good Samaritan, the Gospel Oak, and the Angel have a biblical flavour, while myth and legend are represented by the Apollo, the Phoenix, the Man in the Moon, and the Moonrakers. Some signs indicate sporting associations, such as the Cricketers, the Bat and Ball, and the Angler's Rest, or else trade associations, such as Coopers', Bricklayers', Plumbers', Carpenters', or Masons' Arms. The following are but a few of the hundreds of pub names to be found across Britain.

Bag o' Nails, The From a tradesman's sign, that of an ironmonger; said by some 19th-century writers to be an alteration of 'Bacchanals', a word meaning drunken revelry, once enjoyed in honour of the god Bacchus.

Bush, The As a precursor to the modern pub sign, the Saxon brewer would place a green bush outside their house to show that their ale was ready for drinking.

Case is Altered, The This may derive simply from the fact that the circumstances of a particular inn have altered substantially, but there are several other suggested origins of the sign. One is that it is an alteration of *Casa Alta* (Spanish 'High House'), which was said to be adopted as a name for an inn when soldiers of the 57th Foot returned after the Peninsular War.

Cat and Fiddle, The There are several fanciful derivations for this sign, such as a supposed alteration of French *Catherine la Fidèle*, Catherine the Faithful, alluding to the wife of Peter the Great, but it probably comes from the nursery rhyme:

Hey diddle diddle
The cat and the fiddle.

There is a possible reference to the once popular game of tipcat, with the fiddle representing the dancing that would attract customers to the inn.

Chequers, The This sign has been found on houses in Pompeii, where it may have referred to some game like draughts being played on the premises. Later, in the Middle Ages, some innkeepers were also money-changers and used an 'exchequer board' – a chequered board or tablecloth – as a sign of their calling.

Cross Keys, The The symbol of St Peter, traditionally portrayed as the gatekeeper to Heaven.

Dove, The The traditional Christian sign of peace was commonly used as the sign of a monastic guesthouse.

Eagle and Child, The The crest of the Stanley family and Earls of Derby. The legend is that Sir Thomas Latham, an ancestor of the house, arranged for his illegitimate son to be placed under the foot of a tree in which an eagle had built its nest. When out walking with his wife, they 'accidentally' found the child, which he persuaded her to adopt as their heir. Later he changed his mind and left most of his wealth to his daughter, and the family altered the eagle crest to that of an eagle preying upon a child. The Eagle and Child pub in St Giles', Oxford, popularly known as the 'Bird and Baby', was a frequent meeting place of the Inklings, a group of writers that included J.R.R. Tolkien and C.S. Lewis.

Golden Cross, The A common heraldic symbol.

Golden Lion, The The badge of Henry I and the Percy family of Northumberland.

Hearts of Oak, The A tribute to the British naval tradition.

Man with a Load of Mischief, The A sign in Oxford Street, London, nearly opposite Hanway Yard, said to have been painted by Hogarth, showing a man carrying a woman with a glass of gin in her hand, a magpie, and a monkey.

Nag's Head, The Probably indicating that this small riding horse was available for hire at the inn.

Pig and Whistle, The Said by some to be an alteration of 'pig and wassail', 'pig' being an abbreviation of 'piggin', an earthen vessel used for drinking.

Ram and Teazle, The In compliment to the Clothworkers' Company. The ram symbolizes wool, and the teazle is used for raising the nap of woollen cloth.

Red Lion, The The Scottish lion rampant; also the badge of John of Gaunt, Duke of Lancaster. The most common pub name and sign in Britain.

Rising Sun, The A badge of Edward III.

Rose and Crown, The A sign of loyalty to the monarch and to England.

Royal Oak, The A reference to Charles II, who hid in an oak tree after his defeat at the Battle of Worcester in 1651.

Saracen's Head, The A reference to the grisly souvenirs kept by some Crusaders. The Turk's Head has similar origins.

Star and Garter, The The insignia of the Most Noble Order of the Garter, an order of chivalry founded by Edward III of England in 1348 and the most senior order of knighthood in the British honours system.

Swan with Two Necks, The Said to be an alteration of the 'two nicks' with which the Vintners' Company mark the beaks of their swans.

Tabard, The The original Tabard Inn in Southwark, London, was famous for accommodating people who made the pilgrimage to the shrine of Thomas à Becket in Canterbury Cathedral. In

Chaucer's 14th-century literary work *The Canterbury Tales*, the inn is where the pilgrims gather before setting off.

Three Horseshoes, The The arms of the Worshipful Company of Farriers.

Three Tuns, The A reference to the arms of both the Worshipful Company of Vintners and the Worshipful Company of Brewers.

Wheatsheaf, The Found in many coats of arms, including that of the Brewers' Company.

White Hart, The A white hart with a golden chain was the badge of Richard II (r.1377–99), which was worn by his adherents.

White Horse, The A widespread heraldic symbol, occurring in many coats of arms, including those of many London guilds; it was also the symbol of the kings of Wessex.

LANGUAGE

'The limits of my language,' the philosopher Ludwig Wittgenstein famously wrote, 'are the limits of my world.' Vocabulary and understanding go hand in hand. But what about the building blocks of language? It may be useful to know that when you declare something to be 'fan-bloody-tastic', you are employing a device known as 'tmesis'. If, on the other hand, you are momentarily seduced by the idea of 'burning that bridge when I get to it', or indeed describe someone as a 'minefield of information', then knowing that you have just slipped a 'malaphor' into the conversation is surely a bonus.

Malaphor A recent coinage to describe a blend of a metaphor and a malapropism, when two idioms are accidentally combined. 'I'll burn that bridge when I get to it' is one example, as is 'It's not rocket surgery'.

Mansplaining A word used of men to describe the act of explaining something to a woman in a condescending or patronizing manner, often when the woman knows more about the subject than the man in question. The phenomenon is described in Rebecca Solnit's essay 'Men Explain Things to Me', in which she tells of a man at a party who says he has heard that she is a writer. She starts to talk about her book on Eadweard Muybridge and is cut off by the man asking her whether she has 'heard about the very important Muybridge book that came out this year'. This was in fact Solnit's own book.

Metaphor (Greek, 'transference') A figure of speech in which a name or descriptive term is applied to an object or action to which it is not literally applicable, as: 'The yacht spread her wings to the breeze.'

Metonymy (Greek, 'change of name') The use of the name of one thing for another related to it, as 'the bench' for the magistrates or judges sitting in court, 'a silk' for a King's or Queen's Counsel, or 'the bottle' for alcohol.

Mondegreen A misheard song lyric, first mentioned in an article by Sylvia Wright in *Harper's Magazine* from 1954, who wrote of her own misinterpretation of a phrase in a 17th-century Scottish ballad called 'The Bonnie Earl of Murray'. Here, instead of 'They hae slain the Earl o' Moray / And laid him on the green', Wright understood it to be 'They hae slain the Earl o' Moray / And Lady Mondegreen'.

Nickname Originally 'an eke-name', 'eke' being an adverb meaning 'also'. In a process known as 'false division', the 'n' of the 'an' migrated to 'eke'. Many other words were formed this way: a newt was originally 'an ewt', an adder was 'a nadder', an apron 'a napron', and an umpire 'a noumpere'.

Oxymoron A rhetorical figure in which effect is produced by the juxtaposition of contradictory terms, such as 'Make haste slowly', 'bittersweet', or 'cruel kindness'. The word is the Greek for 'pointedly foolish', or 'sharply blunt', making the term itself an oxymoron.

Palindrome (Greek *palindromos*, 'running back again') A word or line that reads backwards and forwards alike, such as 'Madam' or 'Was it a cat I saw?' They have also been called Sotadics, from their reputed inventor, Sotades, a scurrilous Greek poet of the 3rd century BC. Napoleon Bonaparte reputedly said, 'Able was I ere I saw Elba', while Adam's supposed self-introduction to Eve was 'Madam, I'm Adam.'

Strong verb In grammar, a verb that changes its vowel on altering its tense, e.g. 'bind' and 'bound', 'speak' and 'spoke'. The opposite is a weak verb, which simply adds a syllable or letter, e.g. 'love' and 'loved', 'text' and 'texted'. US English still favours a strong verb – 'sneak' and 'snuck', 'dive' and 'dove' – whilst British English now prefers to add the weak ending of *-ed* to any new verb.

Tmesis (Greek, 'cutting') The grammatical term for the separation of the parts of a compound word by inserting other words between them. Swear words lend themselves particularly to tmesis, as in 'abso-fucking-lutely'.

Vicious circle A term from logic to describe an argument in which the premise is used to prove a conclusion, which is then used to prove the premise. In general use, a vicious circle is a chain of circumstances, in which the solving of a problem creates a new problem which makes the original problem more difficult to solve. While 'vicious circle' is the original expression, the synonymous 'vicious cycle' emerged just a few decades later, in the mid-19th century.

LITERATURE

New words make up only about one per cent of all new coinages – the vast majority of those that take our fancy are older ones that have been repurposed to meet a new need. Of that one per cent, many are born in literature. From Lewis Carroll's 'chortle' to J.R.R. Tolkien's 'hobbit' and J.M. Barrie's 'Wendy', they are often joyful additions to our language. As for the pages they have populated over the centuries, their physical beginnings in our landscape – whether it's the bark of the beech tree that gave us 'book', or the rolls of papyrus that gave us both 'volume' and 'paper' – remind us how literature and civilization are one and the same.

Making One's Mark

Blurb A publisher's promotional description on the dust jacket or cover of a book. The word is said to have originated from the name 'Miss Blinda Blurb', coined in 1907 by the US humorist Gelett Burgess for the figure of a pulchritudinous young lady on a comic book jacket.

Foolscap Properly the jester's cap and bells or the conical paper hat of a dunce. The former standard size of printing paper measuring 13½ × 17in. (343 × 432mm) and of writing paper measuring 13¼ × 16½in. (337 × 419mm) took their name from an ancient watermark showing a fool's head and cap.

John Hancock US slang for one's own signature, derived from the fact that John Hancock (1737–93), the first of the signatories to the Declaration of Independence (1776), had an especially large and clear signature.

Library Before the invention of paper, the thin inner bark of certain trees was used for writing on. The Latin word for this was *liber*, which later also came to mean 'book'. Hence 'library', a place for books, and 'librarian', a keeper of books.

Lower case The printer's name for the small letters of a font of type, as opposed to the capitals. In a typesetter's 'case' these were originally on a lower level than the others. The large letters of a font of type were taken from the 'upper case'.

Make one's mark, To To distinguish oneself; to achieve note. It is an ancient practice for persons who cannot write to 'make their mark'. In old documents, the mark was the sign of the cross, which was followed by the name of the person concerned.

Paper So called from papyrus, the giant water reed from which the Egyptians manufactured a material for writing on.

Pencil The word was originally used for a painter's brush and is still in use for very fine paintbrushes. It comes from Latin *penicillum*, 'paintbrush', a diminutive of *peniculus*, 'brush', itself a diminutive of *penis*, 'tail'. (Hence the words 'penis', and also 'penicillin', from the tufted appearance of the sporangia of the *Penicillium* fungus from which the antibiotic is obtained.)

Raking the Muck

Bumf Short for 'bumfodder' and originally military slang for toilet paper. It was later applied to anything considered worthless and throwaway.

Flimsy An old journalists' term for newspaper copy, arising from the thin paper (often used with a sheet of carbon paper to take a copy) on which reporters and others wrote up their matter for the press. The white £5 Bank of England note, which ceased to be legal tender in March 1961, was known as a flimsy.

Gazette A newspaper. A word of Italian origin derived from the government newspaper issued in Venice from about 1536. It was named after its price, one gazet, a small copper coin whose own name may have come from *gazza*, 'magpie'.

Muckraking The searching out and revealing of scandal. The term was coined by President Theodore Roosevelt in 1906 to describe journalism that exposed corruption and exploitation. He likened its practitioners to the anonymous 'man with the muck-rake' in Part II of John Bunyan's *Pilgrim's Progress* (1684) who 'could look no way but downwards' and so missed the sky above.

Pamphlet A small written work of comparatively few sheets, often controversial and of only temporary interest. The word comes from the name of a 12th-century amatory Latin poem, *Pamphilus seu de Amore* ('Pamphilus ['All-Loving'], or On Love'). The story was such a success that it was reprinted in small booklets that were disseminated far and wide, known as 'pamphilets' or 'little Pamphiluses'. As the popularity of the story faded away, the word became attached to the style of booklet.

Literally Speaking

Cliché In his foreword to an edition of *Brewer's Phrase and Fable*, Terry Pratchett aired the notion that 'the first phrase formally identified as a cliché was the phrase "described as a respectable married woman", used so often in Victorian police court reports that printers left it set up in type'. Winston Churchill is said to have responded to a long-winded report by Anthony Eden with the words 'As far as I can see you have used every cliché except "God is Love" and "Please adjust your dress before leaving".' The word derives from the past participle of the French verb *clicher*, meaning 'to stereotype' (i.e. to print from a plate). *Clicher* is said to represent the sound of a die striking molten metal. The figurative sense of a worn-out expression dates from the late 19th century.

Eucatastrophe A word coined by J.R.R. Tolkien to describe the opposite of a catastrophe; a happy ending.

Faute de mieux (French) For want of anything better.

'*Faute de* what?'
   '*Mieux*, m'lord. A French expression. We should say "for want of anything better".'
   'What asses these Frenchmen are. Why can't they talk English?'

P.G. WODEHOUSE: Ring for Jeeves (1953)

Namby-pamby Wishy-washy, insipid, or weakly sentimental, said especially of novelists and poets. It was the nickname of Ambrose Philips (1674–1749), bestowed on him by the drama-tist Henry Carey (*c.*1687–1743) for his verses addressed to babies, and was adopted by Alexander Pope.

Neither rhyme nor reason Fit neither for amusement nor instruction. An author took his book to Sir Thomas More, chancellor of Henry VIII, and asked his opinion. Sir Thomas told the author to turn it into rhyme. He did so and submitted it again to the Lord Chancellor. 'Ay! ay!' said the witty satirist, 'that will do, that will do. 'Tis rhyme now, but before it was neither rhyme nor reason.'

Speaking from Literature

As mad as a hatter A phrase popularized by Lewis Carroll in *Alice in Wonderland* (1865). Mercurous nitrate was used in the making of felt hats, and its effects can cause kidney and brain damage, as well as personality changes. It has also been suggested that the original 'mad hatter' was Robert Crab, a 17th-century eccentric living at Chesham, who gave all his goods to the poor and lived on dock leaves and grass. Carroll himself is said to have based his character on one Theophilus Carter, a furniture dealer, who was known locally as 'the Mad Hatter', partly because he wore a top hat and partly because of his eccentric notions. An example of the latter was his invention of an 'alarm clock bed' that woke the sleeper by tipping him onto the floor. (Hence perhaps the Mad Hatter's obsession with time and his keenness to stir the sleepy dormouse.)

Box and Cox By turns, turn and turn about, or alternately. The phrase derives from a farce from 1847 written by J.M. Morton, in which Mrs Bouncer, a deceitful lodging-house landlady, lets the same room to two men, Box and Cox. Unknown to each other, they occupy it alternately, one being out at work all day, the other all night.

Braggadocio A blustering braggart, a boaster. The word comes from Braggadocchio, a boastful character in Edmund Spenser's *The Faerie Queene* (1590, 1596). His own name is probably a combination of 'braggart' and the Italian suffix *-occhio*, meaning overall 'big boaster'.

Catch-22 A 'no-win' situation: whichever alternative you choose, you will lose or be in trouble. *Catch-22* is the title of a novel by Joseph Heller, published in 1961. The story centres on Captain Yossarian of the 256th United States (Army) bombing squadron in the Second World War, whose main aim is to avoid being killed.

> There was only one catch and that was Catch-22, which specified that a concern for one's own safety in the face of dangers that were real and immediate was the process of a rational mind. Orr was crazy and could be grounded. All he had to do was to ask; and as soon as he did, he would no longer be crazy and would have to fly more missions.

Do not go gentle into that good night The title, first line, and refrain of a 1951 poem by Welsh poet Dylan Thomas (1914–53). One of his most popular and frequently quoted works, the poem was written for Thomas's dying octogenarian father, a once robust military man whom his son had watched growing blind and frail with old age. In its six stanzas, Thomas urges his father not to surrender meekly to his imminent death, but to be the fierce man he had previously been and to fight against it, and says that wise, good, wild, and grave men refuse to accept death. The poem's other famous refrain is 'Rage, rage against the dying of the light.'

Doghouse, The To be 'in the doghouse' is to be in disgrace, as a dog is confined to his kennel. The phrase is traditionally applied to a husband who has been misbehaving or has displeased his wife and is thus in disgrace or trouble. In J.M. Barrie's *Peter Pan* (1904), Mr Darling lived in the dog kennel until his children returned, as a penance for his treatment of the nursemaid Nana.

Dog in the night-time, A An unconscious conniver; an unwitting party to a crime. The reference is to the dog in Sir Arthur Conan Doyle's story *Silver Blaze* (1892), which did not bark in the night because it knew the man who took the horse from the stables. The exchange between Sherlock Holmes and Inspector Gregory is famous:

'Is there any point to which you would wish to draw my attention?'
'To the curious incident of the dog in the night-time.'
'The dog did nothing in the night-time.'
'That was the curious incident,' remarked Sherlock Holmes.

Mark Haddon adopted the phrase for the title of his novel *The Curious Incident of the Dog in the Night-Time* (2003).

Double whammy A twofold blow ('wham') or setback. The term originated with Al Capp's comic strip *Li'l Abner*, in which the character Evil-Eye Fleegle explains it:

Evil-Eye Fleegle is th' name, an' th' '*whammy*' is my game. Mudder Nature endowed me wit' eyes which can putrefy citizens t' th' spot! . . . There is th' '*single whammy*'! *That,* friend, is th' full, *pure power* o' *one* o' my evil eyes! It's *dynamite,* friend, an' I do not t'row it around lightly! . . . And, lastly – th' '*double whammy*' – namely, th' *full power* o' *both eyes* – which I hopes I never *hafta* use.

Frighten the horses, To To alarm people. The words are attributed to Mrs Patrick Campbell (1865–1940) in Daphne Fielding's *The Duchess of Jermyn Street* (1964): 'It doesn't matter what you do in the bedroom as long as you don't do it in the street and frighten the horses.'

Goody Two-shoes This nursery tale first appeared in 1765 under the full title *The History of Little Goody Two-Shoes; Otherwise called Mrs. Margery Two-Shoes, with The Means by which she acquired her Learning and Wisdom, and in consequence thereof her Estate.* Its virtuous heroine owned only one shoe and when given a pair she was so pleased that she showed them to everyone, saying, 'Two shoes!'

Hobbit One of an imaginary race of benevolent, half-size people, the creation of Professor J.R.R. Tolkien. Sturdy and determined, they resemble human beings except in having hairy feet. They are featured in two of Tolkien's works, *The Hobbit* (1937) and *The Lord of the Rings* (1954–55). The name was their own for themselves, and according to them meant 'hole-dweller'. They are also known as 'halflings'.

Humbug Deceptive or false talk or behaviour; a fraud or sham; an impostor. The word originally meant a trick or hoax. A humbug is also a striped boiled sweet flavoured with peppermint. The source of the word is uncertain. It may be connected in some way with 'hum' and 'bug' (the insect). The word was immortalized by the character of Ebenezer Scrooge in Charles Dickens's *A Christmas Carol* (1843).

'Bah,' said Scrooge. 'Humbug!'

In a nutshell The historian Pliny the Elder recorded a copy of Homer's epic poem *The Iliad* written in so small a hand that the whole work could fit inside a walnut shell.

Jam tomorrow A pleasant thing that is frequently promised but that never appears. The phrase is from Lewis Carroll's *Through the Looking-Glass* (1871), in which the White Queen wants Alice to be her maid and offers her twopence a week and jam every other day. However, she can never actually have it, for: 'The rule is, jam to-morrow and jam yesterday – but never jam *to-day*.'

Legend in one's lifetime A person so famous that they are the subject of popular repeated stories in their lifetime. The expression derives from Lytton Strachey's *Eminent Victorians* (1918), in which he applied it to Florence Nightingale: 'She was a legend in her lifetime, and she knew it.' Veteran journalists of a certain type are sometimes punningly known as 'a legend in their own lunchtime'.

Mad, bad, and dangerous to know Lady Caroline Lamb's much-quoted description of Lord Byron, written in her journal after their meeting at a ball in March 1812.

Moby-Dick The great white whale that is the 'hero' of Herman Melville's novel named after him (1851). He is pursued by Captain Ahab, whose one aim is to kill him. In the end both whale and man are destroyed. Moby-Dick is regarded as representing the elusive reality of life, which in the end brings only death. The whale and his name were apparently based on a real whale, Mocha Dick, which caused loss of life to whalers and damage to whaling ships in the 1830s and 1840s.

Pandemonium A wild, unrestrained uproar, a tumultuous assembly. From Greek, meaning 'all the demons'. The word was first used by the writer John Milton as the name of the principal city in Hell.

Pecksniff A hypocrite, who speaks pompously about morality but does the most heartless things 'as a duty to society' and forgives wrongdoing in nobody but himself. The allusion is to the arch-hypocrite of this name in Dickens's *Martin Chuzzlewit* (1843–44).

Pinocchio The mischievous hero of the puppet story *Le Avventure di Pinocchio* (1883) by Carlo Lorenzini. His name means 'pine seed', since he 'grew' from a piece of pine wood.

Plod In British slang, a policeman. The usage dates from at least the 1970s, and was inspired by the policeman called 'PC Plod' in the Noddy books of Enid Blyton (1897–1968).

Podsnap A pompous, self-satisfied man in Dickens's *Our Mutual Friend* (1864–65), the archetype of someone who is overburdened with stiff-starched etiquette and self-importance. Hence, 'Podsnappery' for arch pomposity.

Ragamuffin A ragged and unkempt person, especially a child. The word comes from the name of Ragamoffyn, a demon in the great poem *Piers Plowman* (c.1367–70), itself probably based on 'rag'.

Roman holiday An allusion to Byron's *Childe Harold's Pilgrimage* (1818), in which the poet describes the death of a gladiator in the arena: 'Butcher'd to make a Roman holiday'. The expression is now current to describe enjoyment derived from the discomfiture of others.

Room 101 In George Orwell's *Nineteen Eighty-Four* (1949), a room in which people are tortured with what they fear most (in the case of the novel's main protagonist, Winston Smith, rats).

Serendipity A happy coinage by Horace Walpole to denote the faculty of making lucky and unexpected 'finds' by accident. In a letter to Sir Horace Mann (28 January 1754) he says that he formed it on the title of a fairy story, *The Three Princes of Serendip*, because the princes

> were always making discoveries, by accidents and sagacity, of things they were not in quest of.

Serendip is an ancient name of modern Sri Lanka, and is an alteration of Sanskrit *Sinhaladvipa*, 'Sinhalese island'.

Shaggy dog story A supposedly funny story told laboriously and at great length with an unexpected twist at the end. It is usually more amusing to the teller than the hearer and is so called from the shaggy dog that featured in many stories of this genre in the 1940s. The following classic shaggy dog story is recounted by Eric Partridge:

> Travelling by train to London from one of its outer dormitories, a businessman got into a compartment and was amazed to see a middle-aged passenger playing chess with a handsome Newfoundland. The players moved the pieces swiftly and surely. Just before the train pulled in at the London terminus, the game ended, with the dog victorious. 'That's an extraordinary dog, beating you like that – and obviously you're pretty good yourself.' – 'Oh, I don't think he's so hot; I beat him in the two games before that.'
>
> ERIC PARTRIDGE: *A Charm of Words*,
> 'The Shaggy Dog' (1960)

Shape of things to come, The The way the future will develop. The phrase derives from the title of a 1933 novel by H.G. Wells which chillingly predicted war in 1939 followed by plague, rebellion, the first rocketship to the moon, and the establishment of a world government in 2059.

Toby jug A small jug in the form of a squat old man in 18th-century dress, wearing a three-cornered hat, one corner of which forms the lip. The name comes from a poem (1761) about one 'Toby Philpot'.

Voldemort An evil wizard who is the chief antagonist of the young hero in the Harry Potter sequence of novels. His name, which is so terrible that none dare utter it, translates from the French as 'flight of death' or 'theft of death'.

Not waving but drowning A phrase describing a situation in which a gesture may be misinterpreted. It derives from a poem of this name by Stevie Smith (1901–71), written in 1953 when its author was suffering from clinical depression.

> Nobody heard him, the dead man,
> But still he lay moaning:
> I was much further out than you thought
> And not waving but drowning.

Wendy A girl's name, supposedly invented by James Barrie for his play *Peter Pan*. The poet and playwright W.E. Henley (1849–1903) was a friend of Barrie and used to address him as 'Friend'. Henley's young daughter, Margaret, copied this but pronounced the word 'Fwend' and duplicated it childishly as 'Fwendy-Wendy'. The latter half of this gave the name of Wendy Darling in the play. It also led to 'Wendy house', a toy house large enough for children to play in.

Wreck of the Hesperus, The An episode made famous by H.W. Longfellow's ballad of 1840. The *Hesperus* was wrecked on Norman's Woe, near Gloucester, Massachusetts, in 1839.

Anyone looking particularly dishevelled is said in British dialect to 'look like the wreck of Hesperus'.

Yahoo Jonathan Swift's name, in *Gulliver's Travels* (1726), for brutes with human forms and vicious propensities. Swift may have based the word on a blend of the two exclamations of disgust, 'yah!' and 'ugh!'

SHAKESPEAREAN MATTERS

Few scholars today would argue that Shakespeare invented all 1,580 of the words and phrases for which he is credited as first user in the *Oxford English Dictionary*. But those he didn't himself coin or repurpose – he was the master of creating new word combinations – he certainly popularized. It is thanks to him and his actors that a myriad words entered the English stage and, most emphatically of all, have never left them. Among them is the word 'laughable' – so natural to our tongues now, but derided as an invention by Shakespeare's critics: it should be 'laugh-at-able', they cried. Clearly they wouldn't be laughing now.

All Greek to me Quite unintelligible; a foreign language. Shakespeare's Casca says, 'For mine own part, it was Greek to me' (*Julius Caesar*, I, ii (1599)).

All that glitters is not gold Do not be deceived by appearances. A saying most familiar from Shakespeare: 'All that glisters is not gold; Often have you heard that told' (*Merchant of Venice*, II, vii (1596)). As he implies, the proverb dates from earlier times, and was familiar to Chaucer.

Bark or **bay at the moon, To** To agitate uselessly, especially those in high places, as a dog attempts to frighten the moon by baying at it. There is a superstition that when a dog does this it portends death or ill-luck.

> I had rather be a dog, and bay the moon,
> Than such a Roman.
>
> *Julius Caesar*, IV, iii (1599)

Bowdlerize, To To expurgate. In 1818 the editor Thomas Bowdler (1754–1825) published a ten-volume edition of Shakespeare's works 'in which nothing is added to the original text; but those words are omitted which cannot with propriety be read aloud in a family'. He thus cut Juliet's speech of longing for Romeo from 30 lines to 15, and in King Lear's speech of madness, beginning 'Ay, every inch a king', he cut 22 lines to 7.

Break a leg! A traditional wish of good luck in the theatre. The expression is often said to relate to the assassination of Abraham Lincoln in his private box at Ford's Theatre, Washington, DC, on 14 April 1865. The murderer, John Wilkes Booth, a Shakespearean actor of some repute, made good his escape after firing the shot by leaping down on to the stage, breaking his leg. 'Break a leg' supposedly arose subsequently as an example of black humour. However, there is no record of the phrase before the 1950s, and it seems more likely to be simply an example of the convolutions through which superstitious theatrical folk will go to avoid tempting fate (in this case, by apparently wishing someone the reverse of good luck). It may have been a partial translation of *Hals- und Beinbruch*, 'neck and leg break', which serves the same purpose in German.

Bully A person who harms, hurts, or threatens weaker people. The original meaning of the noun was 'sweetheart', as in:

> I kiss his dirty shoe, and from my heart-string
> I love the lovely bully.
>
> *Henry V*, IV, i (1598)

Its origin is probably in Middle Dutch *boele*, 'lover'. The sense development seems to have gone from lover, to fine fellow, to blusterer, and on to the modern meaning.

Cat has nine lives, A Cats have traditionally been regarded as more adept at survival than many animals, owing perhaps to their natural wariness and their ability to land safely on their feet after falling.

> TYBALT: What wouldst thou have with me?
> MERCUTIO: Good king of cats, nothing but one of
> your nine lives.
>
> *Romeo and Juliet*, III, i (1595)

Devil rides on a fiddlestick, The Much fuss over nothing. Shakespeare among others uses the phrase 'Fiddlesticks!' as an exclamation meaning 'nonsense', 'rubbish'. When the prince and his companions are at the Boar's Head, first Bardolph rushes in to warn them that the sheriff's officers are at hand, then the hostess enters to warn her guests. But the prince says:

> Heigh, heigh! the devil rides upon a fiddlestick: what's the matter?
>
> *Henry IV*, Pt I, II, iv (1597)

Down in the dumps Out of spirits, depressed.

> Why, how now, daughter Katharine! in your dumps?
>> *The Taming of the Shrew*, II, i (1591)

The source of 'dumps' in this sense is uncertain (Middle Dutch *domp* 'haze', 'mist' has been suggested), but from the mid-16th century it was also used, in the singular, for a mournful song or tune, or for a dance performed to such a tune.

Eavesdropper Someone who secretly listens to other people's conversation.

> Under our tents I'll play the eavesdropper,
> To hear if any mean to shrink from me.
>> *Richard III*, V, iii (1592)

The 'eavesdrop' or 'eavesdrip' was the space of ground around the house that received the water dripping from the eaves. An eavesdropper was a person who took up a position in the eaves-drip to overhear what was said in the house or that of a neighbour.

Elf-locks Tangled hair. It used to be said that one of the favourite amusements of elves overnight was to tie people's hair in knots. When Edgar impersonates a madman in Shakespeare's *King Lear* (II, iii (1605)) he says that he will 'elf all my hair in knots'.

Flibbertigibbet One of the five fiends that possessed 'poor Tom' in *King Lear* (IV, i (1605)). Shakespeare got the name from Samuel Harsnet's *Declaration of Egregious Popish Impostures* (1603), which tells of 40 fiends cast out, among which was Fliberdigibbet, a name that had been previously used for a mischievous gossip. Its origin is in a meaningless representation of chattering.

Green-eyed monster, The So Shakespeare called jealousy:

> IAGO: O! beware, my lord, of jealousy;
> It is the green-ey'd monster which doth mock
> The meat it feeds on.
>
> *Othello*, III, iii (1604)

A greenish complexion was formerly held to be indicative of jealousy, and as all the green-eyed cat family 'mock the meat they feed on', so jealousy mocks its victim by loving and loathing it at the same time.

Knock, knock! An invitation to respond to a riddle punning on a personal name. In Shakespeare's *Macbeth*, a drunken porter, rudely awakened, fancies himself to be the porter of the gates of hell, and delivers a long, humorous speech that follows the familiar pattern of the modern knock-knock joke:

> (*Knock.*)
> Knock, knock, knock! Who's there, i'th' name of Beelzebub? Here's a farmer that hanged himself on th'expectation of plenty. Come in time! Have napkins enough about you; here you'll sweat for 't.
>
> *Macbeth*, II, iii (1606)

Milk of human kindness, The Sympathy; compassion.

> LADY MACBETH: Yet do I fear thy nature;
> It is too full o' the milk of human kindness
> To catch the nearest way.
>
> *Macbeth*, I, v (1606)

Pricking of one's thumbs, The In popular superstition, a portent of evil. The Second Witch in Shakespeare's *Macbeth* (IV, i (1606)) says:

> By the pricking of my thumbs
> Something wicked this way comes.

Macbeth then enters.

Salad days Days of youthful inexperience, when people are very green or naive.

> My salad days,
> When I was green in judgement, cold in blood,
> To say as I said then!
> > *Antony and Cleopatra*, I, v (1606)

Scepter'd isle, This England. The expression comes from the first line of an extended paean to his country delivered by John of Gaunt:

> This royal throne of kings, this scepter'd isle,
> This earth of majesty, this seat of Mars,
> This other Eden, demi-paradise.
> > *Richard II*, II, 1 (1595)

It has since taken on a life of its own as a patriotically poetic way of referring to England (usually not to Britain, which would be more geographically accurate).

Seven ages of man, The According to Jaques in Shakespeare's *As You Like It* (II, vii (1599)), the seven ages of man are: (1) the infant, (2) the schoolboy, (3) the lover, (4) the soldier, (5) the justice, (6) the pantaloon, and (7) second childhood.

Something is rotten in the state of Denmark There is something wrong, although it is hard to say precisely what. The quotation, from Shakespeare's *Hamlet*, I, iv (1600), is often used facetiously.

There's the rub That's the difficulty; that's the snag. The phrase comes from Hamlet's 'To be or not to be' speech, with the rub itself alluding to anything that checks or hinders the smooth passage of the ball in a game of bowls.

> To sleep: perchance to dream: ay, there's the rub;
> For in that sleep of death what dreams may come
> When we have shuffled off this mortal coil.
>
> *Hamlet*, III, i (1600)

Thereby hangs a tale There is an interesting or intriguing story behind that.

> And so, from hour to hour we ripe and ripe,
> And then from hour to hour we rot and rot,
> And thereby hangs a tale.
>
> *As You Like It*, II, vii (1599)

Tide The word is used figuratively of a tendency, a current or flow of events, as in 'a tide of feeling', and in Shakespeare's

> There is a tide in the affairs of men,
> Which, taken at the flood, leads on to fortune.
>
> *Julius Caesar*, IV, iii (1599)

Tide here comes from Old English *tīd*, meaning 'time', 'season', 'tide'. The word is cognate with 'time' and with modern German *Zeit*, 'time'.

World is your oyster, The The world is the place from which you can extract success and profit, as a pearl can be extracted from an oyster.

> FALSTAFF: I will not lend thee a penny.
> PISTOL: Why, then the world's mine oyster,
> Which I with sword will open.
> > *The Merry Wives of Windsor*, II, ii (1597)

The character Arthur Daley, in the television series *Minder* (1979–94), transmogrified the saying into the malapropism 'The world is your lobster.'

THAT'S ENTERTAINMENT

The vocabulary of entertainment is some of the oldest in the business. Designed to instruct as much as amuse, the tragedies and comedies of ancient Greece gave us such fundamental words as 'person', a sibling of the 'persona' we portray to others and derived from a word meaning 'mask'. The language of the carnies and circus workers, centuries old, speaks of a life on the margins, while comedians (and I've worked with a few) straddle the line between the private and the public, the permitted and the shocking. It's a strange world, in which the guffaws and the boffolas hide a few tales of gallows and demons.

Make 'Em Laugh

As daft as a brush Completely crazy; quite mad. The expression is said to have been adapted from the northern phrase 'as soft as a brush' by the comedian Ken Platt when entertaining troops during the Second World War.

Boffola A little 'boff' – in other words, a hearty laugh.

Corpsing Laughing uncontrollably on stage or camera. The idea is of an actor playing a dead body on stage, only to be overcome by giggles.

Cushty A term of approval borrowed from the Romani *kushti*, 'good', and probably influenced by the adjective 'cushy'.

Gadgie A man, derived from the Romani word *gadjo*, meaning a non-Roma and often an outsider at the circus.

Malaprop, Mrs Malapropisms frequently flourish where the uninitiated attempt technical or professional language. Philip Norman, writing in *The Times* (4 May 1985), reported a miners' leader who denounced his bosses as 'totally incontinent', and a parishioner who complained to her vicar about the church's poor 'agnostics'. Medical terms are particularly prone to malapropism, genuine examples including 'teutonic' ulcers, 'malingering' tumours, 'hysterical rectums', and 'Cistercian' deliveries. The phrase is from the French *mal à propos*, 'not to the purpose'. Mrs Malaprop is the character in Richard Brinsley Sheridan's *The Rivals* (1775), noted for her misuse of words.

Muppet Any of a range of puppets that appeared on the television comedy series *The Muppet Show* from 1976 to 1981. They were the creation of the US puppeteer Jim Henson (1936–90) and originally appeared on the US children's programme *Sesame Street*, first screened in 1969. The name 'Muppet' seems to be a blend of 'marionette' and 'puppet', although Henson himself said it was 'simply a word that sounded good to him'.

Pantomime From the Greek *pantomimos*, 'imitator of all'. In Latin *pantomimus* was used for an actor using mime. This later developed into a comic dramatization, particularly when it featured the stock characters of Clown, Pantaloon, Harlequin, and Columbine in the Italian *commedia dell'arte*. The modern panto, based on fairy tales such as Cinderella and involving music, topical jokes, and slapstick comedy, developed in the 18th century, with a new set of characters.

Scaramouch The English form of Italian *Scaramuccia* (through French *Scaramouche*), a stock character in old Italian farce, introduced into England soon after 1670. He was a cowardly and foolish boaster of his own prowess, who was constantly being cudgelled by Harlequin. The clever impersonation of the part by Tiberio Fiurelli, who brought his company of Italian players to London in 1673, greatly popularized the term in England during the last quarter of the 17th century, when it was used to describe a rascal. A relative of the English 'skirmish', the name became familiar to modern ears through Queen's 'Bohemian Rhapsody':

> I see a little silhouetto of a man,
> Scaramouch, Scaramouch, will you do the Fandango!

Slapstick Literally two or more laths bound together at one end with which Harlequins, clowns, and other performers strike one another with a resounding slap or crack. The word is now more often applied to any broad comedy with knockabout action and horseplay.

Spieler A voluble talker at a carnival or funfair who sells the show to prospective visitors, often with the traditional cry of 'Roll up! Roll up!'

Top banana The top comedian in a show, or the top person or leader generally. The expression originated from an old skit involving the sharing of a banana.

Wag As used of a humorous person, one given to jest. The word may well be a darkly humorous shortening of *waghalter*, a rascal or someone full of mischief, one who 'wags' or shakes the 'halter' of the gallows.

Zany The buffoon who mimicked the clown in the Italian theatre as part of *commedia dell'arte*, hence someone considered a little eccentric. The name comes from Italian *zanni*, 'buffoon', a familiar form of Giovanni (i.e. John).

Meanwhile, Back at the Ranch . . .

Blow the gaff, To To let out a secret, to inform against a companion. In carnival slang, a gaff is a concealed device that makes it impossible for the customer to win. To blow the gaff is thus to reveal the device's hidden mechanism, as if exposing a conjuror's trick.

Charlatan A person who claims knowledge or skill that they do not possess. The term was particularly applied to mounte-banks: vendors of quack remedies, who covered their ignorance with high-sounding blather. The word is from the Italian *ciarlare*, meaning 'to prattle'.

Claptrap In the 18th century 'claptrap' was something contrived to bring applause: in other words, a trap to make people clap. The word moved on to mean empty talk or waffle.

Close, but no cigar An expression of commiseration or 'nice try'. The allusion is to the Highball, a fairground try-your-strength machine with a pivot that the contestant hit with a hammer in the hope of sending a projectile up high enough to ring a bell. Those who succeeded were awarded a cigar by the proprietor.

Gaffer (alteration of 'godfather') An old country fellow, or more specifically the boss, overseer, or foreman. In the world of cinema and television, the gaffer is the senior electrician.

MacGuffin A device (e.g. a piece of stolen jewellery) in a film or other fiction that is included merely to initiate or facilitate the plot and has no other significance within the story. The term was particularly associated with the director Alfred Hitchcock (1899–1980), and seems to have been first used by him in a lecture delivered at Columbia University, New York, in 1939. Where he got it from remains unclear; he himself was wont to 'explain' it as the name of a Scotsman who appeared in a story about two men on a train, but it could simply be that he coined it from 'guff', a word meaning 'wordy nonsense, piffle'.

Meanwhile, back at the ranch A phrase originally used in old westerns as a segue from one scene to another. It appeared as a stock caption in silent films and was spoken by the narrator in films and television shows of the 1940s and 1950s, such as *Bonanza*.

Mug up, To To study hard for a specific purpose, e.g. to pass an examination. This old university phrase may come from the theatre, where an actor, while making up their face or 'mug', would hurriedly scan their lines.

Oscar A gold-plated figurine awarded annually by the American Academy of Motion Picture Arts and Sciences for the best film acting, writing, production, and so on of the year. There are two claims for the origin of this name. One is that in 1931 the future executive secretary of the Academy, Mrs Margaret Herrick, joined as librarian, and on seeing the then-nameless gold statue for the first time exclaimed, 'It reminds me of my Uncle Oscar.' The other claim is that it derives indirectly from

Oscar Wilde (1854–1900). When on a lecture tour of the USA he was asked if he had won the Newdigate Prize for Poetry, and he replied, 'Yes, but while many people have won the Newdigate, it is seldom that the Newdigate gets an Oscar.'

Paparazzi The Italian term for press photographers who pester celebrities is not related to any form of the word 'paper'. It comes from the name of a photographer in Federico Fellini's film *La Dolce Vita* (1960), a cynical presentation of modern Roman high life.

Upstage As a technical theatrical direction this means 'at the back of the stage', which in many theatres slopes down slightly to the footlights. Colloquially, the term 'upstage' means aloof; putting on airs of consequence or superiority. An actor upstage of another has the advantage, the latter having to act with his back to the audience.

Ventriloquism The trick of producing vocal sounds so that they appear to come, not from the person producing them, but from somewhere else. The art is so called from Latin *venter*, 'belly', and *loqui*, 'to speak' (speaking from the belly), from the Roman belief that the voice of the ventriloquist proceeded from his stomach as a result of demonic possession.

MUSIC

Victor Hugo believed that 'music expresses that which cannot be put into words and that which cannot remain silent'. In Old English, a delight in music was known as a 'glee-dream'. In Arabic, the emotional impact of music is known as 'tarab'. And the pang we so often feel when we hear a particular song? That's a 'stound'. Music is as much the food of language as it is of love.

As fit as a fiddle In a very healthy condition; in excellent physical form. The allusion is probably to a street fiddler, who sways and swings about as he saws away energetically with his bow. The alliteration helps too.

Bells and whistles Additional features or trimmings. The inspiration is old fairground organs with their assortment of bells and whistles. From here we also have the expression 'pull out all the stops'.

Cant The specialized vocabulary of a particular group of people, such as thieves, lawyers, or journalists. The word probably derives from Latin *cantare*, 'to sing', and thus originally applied, in a disparaging sense, to the chanting in medieval religious services. The term later came to be applied to the perceived whining speech of beggars, who were known as the 'canting crew'.

Carol The first printed collection of Christmas carols came from the press of Wynkyn de Worde in 1521. It included the Boar's Head Carol, which is still sung at Queen's College, Oxford. The word is from the Old French *carole*, perhaps from Latin *choraula*, 'flute player', but influenced by Latin *corona*, 'garland', 'circle'. The earliest use of the word in English was for a round dance, then later it came to denote a light and joyous hymn, especially one associated with the Nativity.

Carry a torch for someone, To To suffer unrequited love for them, the torch being the torch of love. A torch singer is one who sings of such love.

Cool The earliest record of the slang use of 'cool' in the sense of 'stylish' or 'admirable' is from Eton College, where a 'cool fish' was a cocky, self-possessed schoolboy. This meaning is a development of the older meaning of dispassionate, cold-blooded, calm, and self-contained. The positive senses of 'cool' were greatly popularized by the jazz movement of the 1940s, and especially Charlie Parker's 1947 record *Cool Blues*, where the idea is of music that is relaxed and the converse of 'hot'.

Doh ray me Doh is the first or tonic note of the solfeggio system of music, otherwise known as solmization. The commonest European system, still in use, originally named the notes *ut, re, mi, fa, sol, la*, using syllables from a Latin hymn for St John the Baptist's Day, in which each phrase begins on the next note in the scale: ***Ut*** *queant laxis* ***re****sonare fibris* ***Mi****ra gestorum* ***fa****muli tuorum,* ***So****lve polluti* ***la****bili reatum, Sancte*

Iohannes. A seventh note *si* was added later (from the initials of Sancte Iohannes). Today's systems tend to use the sequence that was arbitrarily adapted in the 19th century: *doh, ray, me, fah, soh, la, ti*.

Gamut In medieval music, 'gamma ut' was the name of the lowest note in the scale, but the term also came to be applied to the full potential range of notes from a human voice or an instrument. Metaphorically, 'to run the gamut' is to perform the complete range of something.

Grandfather clock The traditional name for the formerly common weight-and-pendulum eight-day clock in a tall wooden case. It derives from the popular song 'My Grandfather's Clock' by Henry Clay Work (1832–84). The clock that inspired Work's song now stands in the George Hotel, Piercebridge, County Durham.

In the groove In the right mood; doing something successfully, fashionable. Hence the dated slang word 'groovy' for something fashionable or exciting. The allusion is to the accurate reproduction of music by a needle in the groove of a gramophone record.

Highfalutin' Pompous or pretentious. 'Falutin'' may derive from 'fluting', denoting something strident and high-pitched.

Honky-tonk A disreputable nightclub or low roadhouse; a place of cheap entertainment. A honky-tonk piano is one from which the felts of the hammers have been removed, thus making the instrument more percussive and giving its notes a tinny quality. Such pianos are often used for playing ragtime and popular melodies.

Jitterbug Originally a swing-music enthusiast in the late 1930s, with the name probably coming from Cab Calloway's song 'Jitter Bug' (1934), in which a 'jitter bug' was a person who drank regularly and so 'has the jitters ev'ry morning'. The name passed to a person who danced the jitterbug, a fast, twirling, whirling US dance to a jazz accompaniment, popular in the 1940s. Hence also more generally, a nervous person, one who 'has the jitters'.

Karaoke A popular feature of the British pub and club from the early 1980s, in the form of a pre-recorded track of popular music without the vocal part, enabling a person to sing along with it. The system derives from Japan and the word means literally 'empty orchestra'; the *-oke* comes from a Japanese version of English 'orchestra'.

Live the life of Riley, To To live luxuriously. Riley, or Reilly, is said to be a character in a 19th-century comic song. One possible candidate is Pat Rooney's 'Are You the O'Reilly?', originally 'Is That Mr Reilly?' (1883), which describes what the hero would do if he 'struck it rich'.

Mascot A person or thing that is supposed to bring good luck. The word is French slang (perhaps connected with Provençal *masco*, 'sorcerer'), and was popularized in England by Edmond Audran's opera *La Mascotte* (1880).

Music From Greek *mousikē tekhnē*, meaning 'art of the muses'.

Old grey whistle test, The In Tin Pan Alley, writers would play their compositions to the 'old greys', the elderly door-keepers and other employees in the offices of the music publishers. If the 'old greys' were still whistling the tunes after a week or so, then they were likely to be worth publishing. The phrase was adopted for the title of a weekly television pop music programme first shown in 1971.

Pie in the sky The good time or good things promised that will never come. The phrase comes from a song from 1911 called 'The Preacher and the Slave' by the activist and song-writer Joe Hill. His lyrics are a parody of the Salvation Army hymn 'In the Sweet By-and-By'.

> You will eat, bye and bye,
> In the glorious land above the sky;
> Work and pray, live on hay,
> You'll get pie in the sky when you die.

Pop goes the weasel

> Up and down the City Road,
> In and out the Eagle.
> That's the way the money goes,
> Pop goes the weasel.

The rhyme refers to the Eagle Tavern in London's City Road. Any serious amount of drinking there might mean the customer has to 'pop', or pawn, their 'weasel', which was rhyming slang for a coat ('weasel and stoat').

Second fiddle In musical terms, the second violin in a string quartet or one of the second violins in an orchestra. Figuratively, to play second fiddle is to adopt a subordinate status to someone else.

Going for a song For sale very cheaply. The allusion is prob-ably to the trifling cost of the old ballad sheets or to the small change given to itinerant songsters outside inns and public houses.

Stound A pang of emotion that evokes a strong memory when you smell a familiar scent or hear a certain piece of music.

Tarab Arab culture has given voice to the emotional transformation induced by music with a word that has no equivalent in Western languages. 'Tarab' expresses an intense spiritual response to music, one that is felt particularly in a live performance and is shared by both audience and musician – a collective summoning of memories.

Tin Pan Alley The district of New York City, originally in the area of Broadway and 14th Street, where popular music is published. London's Denmark Street, off Charing Cross Road, was so called as the centre of the popular music industry. The name probably derives from the 19th-century jazz musician's nickname 'tin pan' for a cheap tinny piano.

When the fat lady sings When everything is finally over. The full expression runs: 'The opera's never over till the fat lady sings.' The reference is to the final act of the opera, in which the heroine often appears. Opera singers are stereotypically endowed with figures as full as their voices.

RELIGION AND SPIRITUALITY

The word 'religion' is relatively recent, having entered English in the 13th century via French. Its roots, however, lie in the Latin *religare*, 'to restrain' or 'to tie back'. The idea, perhaps, is that religion both bonds you to a god and ties you to consequent obligations. Much of our history has been inspired by religion – for good and bad – and the same very much goes for language, too.

Writing on the Wall

Adam's ale Water, first man's only drink, sometimes called Adam's wine in Scotland.

Apocrypha From Late Latin *apocrypha scripta*, meaning 'hidden writings', from Greek *apokruptein*, meaning 'to hide away'. In ancient Christian usage the word originally meant a text read in private, rather than in public church settings. It later came to apply to any text that was 'withheld from general circulation' (for various reasons) and therefore regarded as of doubtful origin, false or spurious.

By the skin of one's teeth Only just, by a mere hair's breadth. The phrase is biblical: 'My bone cleaveth to my skin, and to my flesh, and I am escaped with the skin of my teeth' (Job 19:20).

Jeroboam Wine bottle sizes are often expressed through biblical names, with the exception of 'magnum' (two bottles, from the Latin for 'great') and 'Sovereign' (35 bottles, based on Latin *super*, 'above'). The most commonly found large-format wine bottles include, in order of increasing size: magnum, double-magnum/jeroboam, rehoboam (no longer produced), methuselah, salmanazar, balthazar, nebuchadnezzar, melchior, solomon, and sovereign.

Land of Nod, The This was the desolate land to which Cain was exiled after he had slain Abel (Genesis 4:16). Jonathan Swift, in *A Complete Collection of Genteel and Ingenious Conversation* (1738), said that he was 'going into the land of Nod', meaning that he was going to sleep; it has retained this meaning ever since.

Manna The miraculous food provided for the children of Israel on their journey from Egypt to the Holy Land. The word is popularly said to be derived from Aramaic *man-hu* ('what is this?'), but it is probably Hebrew *mān*, the term for the honey-like secretion of a plant bug that congeals in the evening but melts in the sun.

Moses basket A portable cot for babies in the form of a basket with handles. The name alludes to the 'ark of bulrushes' in which the baby Moses was left by the Nile.

Prodigal The word ultimately goes back to Latin *prodigere*, meaning 'to squander', literally 'to drive forth', from *pro*, 'forth', and *agere*, 'to drive'. The notion in Roman times was that persons who had spent all their patrimony were 'driven forth' to be sold as slaves to their creditors. The biblical story of the Prodigal Son involves the younger of two sons who wastes his share of his father's inheritance on riotous living. On his return in poverty, his father kills the fatted calf in celebration. When the elder son, who had stayed at home and worked faithfully, protests, the father replies that we should always celebrate when one that was dead returns to life.

Raise Cain, To To cause a commotion or make a noisy disturbance. 'Cain' here is either used as an alternative to 'the Devil', or is a direct allusion to Cain's violent anger, which drove him to kill his brother.

Seraphim The highest of the nine choirs of angels, so named from the seraphim of Isaiah 6:2. The word is perhaps the same as *saraf*, 'serpent', from *saraf*, 'it burned', possibly alluding to the 'fiery serpents' that 'bit the people' in Numbers 21:6. The connection with burning suggested to early Christian interpreters that the seraphim were specially distinguished by their fiery zeal and love.

Shibboleth A test word, a catchword or principle to which members of a group adhere long after its original significance has faded, and so a term for a worn-out or discredited doctrine. *Shibboleth* (meaning 'flood', 'stream') was the word the Ephraimites could not pronounce when they were challenged at a ford on the Jordan by their pursuers, Jephthah and the Gileadites. The Ephraimites could only say *Sibboleth*, thus revealing themselves to the enemy.

Under the sun Anywhere in the world. 'There is nothing new under the sun' is a saying commonly used to mean that whatever may seem new or original will probably already have occurred or been found elsewhere. It is first mentioned in a 14th-century translation of the Bible.

Ur A city of ancient Sumer, in southern Mesopotamia, on the River Euphrates. It flourished around 3000 BC. Its site, lost for many centuries, was rediscovered in 1854. As the original home of Abraham, it is commonly referred to in the Bible as 'Ur of the Chaldees' (Chaldea was a country in that region), and that name has come to be used to typify a place of almost prehistoric antiquity.

Writing on the wall, The Said of something foreshadowing trouble or disaster. The reference is to Daniel 5:5–31, when a mysterious hand appeared writing on the wall while Belshazzar was feasting. Daniel interpreted the words ('*mene, mene, tekel, upharsin*', 'numbered, numbered, weighed, divided') as portending his downfall and that of his kingdom. Belshazzar was slain that night.

Ram's Horn

Jubilee In Jewish history the year of jubilee was every fiftieth year, which was held sacred in commemoration of the deliverance from Egypt. In this year the fields were allowed to lie fallow, land that had passed out of the possession of those to whom it originally belonged was restored to them, and all who had been obliged to let themselves out for hire were released from bondage. The jubilee was proclaimed with trumpets made from ram's horns. The word actually comes from Hebrew *yōḇēl* 'ram's-horn trumpet', but was influenced by Latin *jubilare*, 'to shout for joy'.

'Jubilee' subsequently came to apply to any 50th anniversary, especially one marked with great celebration, and by the end of the 19th century it was being extended to other notable anniversaries.

Kosher A Yiddish word (from Hebrew) denoting that which is 'right', 'fit', or 'proper'. It is applied usually to food.

Menorah (Hebrew) A many-branched sacred candlestick used in Jewish worship. The word derives from an ancient root meaning 'to give light'.

Messiah The title of the expected leader of Jews who shall deliver the nation from its enemies and reign in permanent triumph and peace. Equivalent to the Greek word Christ, it is applied by Christians to Jesus. The word comes from the Hebrew *māshīach*, 'anointed one'.

Sabbatical year One year in seven, when the land, according to Mosaic law, was to lie fallow. The term is used in universities and the academic world generally for a specified period of freedom from duties, during which time a professor or lecturer is released to study or travel. It is a relative of the word Sabbath.

Scapegoat Part of the ancient ritual among the Hebrews on the Day of Atonement involved two goats being brought to the altar of the Tabernacle, where the high priest would cast lots. One goat was sacrificed while the other had the sins of the people laid upon it. The scapegoat, or 'escape-goat', was taken to the wilderness and allowed to escape.

Shofar (Hebrew) A trumpet still used in modern synagogues. It is made of the horn of a ram or any ceremonially clean animal, and takes its name from the Hebrew *shōphār*, 'ram's horn'.

The Mountain and Mohammed

If the mountain will not come to Mohammed When Mohammed was asked for miraculous proofs of his teaching he ordered Mount Safa to come to him, and as it did not move, he said, 'God is merciful. If it had obeyed my words, it would have fallen on us to our destruction. I will therefore go to the mountain and thank God that He has had mercy on a stiff-necked generation.' The phrase, sometimes in the form 'if the mountain will not come to Mohammed, Mohammed must go to the mountain', is now used of someone who is unable to get their own way and who is therefore obliged to bow to the inevitable.

Koran or **Al Koran** The sacred book of Muslims, containing the religious teaching of the Prophet Mohammed with instructions on morality and Islamic institutions. The Koran (more correctly *Qur'an*), which contains 114 chapters or suras, is said to have been communicated to Mohammed at Mecca and Medina by an angel, to the sound of bells. Its name comes from the Arabic *qurān*, 'reading'.

Mufti An Arabic word meaning 'an official', 'an expounder of the Koran and Muslim law'. The word passed into English to denote civil, as distinct from military or official, costume. The modern meaning dates from the early 19th century, and probably arose from the resemblance that the flowered dressing gown and tasselled smoking cap worn by off-duty officers bore to the costume of an Eastern Mufti. The word itself comes from Arabic *muftī*, from *aftā*, 'to give a (legal) decision'.

Holy Smoke

Adore Means 'to carry to one's mouth', 'to kiss' (Latin *ad-os*, *ad-orare*). The Romans performed adoration by placing their right hand on their mouth and bowing. The Greeks paid adoration to kings by putting the royal robe to their lips. The Jews kissed in homage. Today, we continue to do homage to the monarchy by kissing the hand of the sovereign.

Agnostic An atheist denies the existence of God. An agnostic says that it is impossible to know whether God exists or not. The word comes from the Greek *a-*, meaning 'not', and *gnostic*, meaning 'knowing'.

Cardinal In Rome, a cardinal church was a parish church, as distinct from an oratory attached to it, and the word was next applied to the senior priest of such a church. From the mid-8th century the word denoted urban as distinct from rural clergy, and subsequently the clergy of a diocesan town and its cathedral. The word is from the Latin *cardo*, *cardinis*, meaning 'hinge'. The literal sense has been taken up figuratively in English and other languages to mean 'that on which something turns like a hinge', and so 'principal' or 'chief'.

Cardinal sin Any of the seven deadly sins and, by extension, a serious error of judgement.

Cardinal virtues The most important moral qualities, traditionally the four virtues of justice, prudence, temperance, and fortitude, on which all other virtues hang or depend.

Chapel The word originally denoted a chest containing holy relics, which was so called from the *capella* (Latin, 'little cloak') of St Martin, preserved as a sacred relic. According to medieval accounts about his life, Martin was a Roman soldier who converted to Christianity after an encounter with a half-naked beggar. Martin cut his cloak in half in order to share it with the beggar, who in the night appeared to him in a vision and revealed himself as Christ. The shrine in which the half cloak was kept was called the *chapele*, and its keeper the *chapelain*, the forerunners to 'chapel' and 'chaplain'. Music performed without instrumental accompaniment, 'in the chapel style', is known as a cappella.

Christingle A lighted candle that symbolizes Christ as the light of the world, traditionally held by children around Advent. It is an alteration of German *Christkindl*, 'little Christ child'.

Conclave (Latin *conclave*, 'place that can be locked up', from *con-*, 'with', and *clavis*, 'key') Literally, a room or set of rooms that can be opened by only one key. The word is applied to small cells erected for the cardinals who meet, after the death of a pope, to elect a successor. Hence, by extension, the word came to denote the assembly of cardinals themselves and so, in general, any private assembly for discussion.

Devil dodger A colloquial name for a preacher. It may also refer to a churchgoer, specifically (according to *The Chambers Dictionary*) 'someone who attends churches of various kinds, to be on the safe side'.

Devil take the hindmost, The A phrase from late medieval magic, now denoting selfish competition. The Devil was said to have had a school at Toledo (or Salamanca) where the students, after making certain progress in their mystic studies, were obliged to run through an underground hall. The last man was seized by the Devil and became his imp.

Enthusiasm The word represents Greek *enthousiasmos*, literally 'possessed by a god', from *en-*, 'in', and *theos*, 'god'. 'Inspiration' is very similar, from Latin *inspirare*, literally 'to breathe in' (the godlike essence). In the 17th and 18th centuries the word 'enthusiasm' was applied disparagingly to overly emotional dedication.

Feng shui In Chinese thought, a system of good and evil influences in the natural surroundings, now taken into account by some in the West when designing buildings or simply when deciding where to sit. The words represent Chinese *feng*, 'wind', and *shui*, 'water'. For the Chinese, *feng shui* is both an art and a science, the former as a means of counteracting evil influences by good ones, the latter determining the desirability of space from the configuration of natural objects such as rivers, trees, and hills.

Karma (Sanskrit, 'action', 'effect') In Buddhist philosophy, the name given to the results of action, especially the cumulative results of a person's deeds in one stage of their existence as controlling their destiny in the next.

Maudlin Mawkishly sentimental. 'Maudlin drunk' is sentimentally drunk and inclined to tears. The word is derived from the repentant tears of Mary Magdalene, who is often portrayed in the Bible with eyes swollen after weeping.

Paternoster (Latin, 'Our Father') The Lord's Prayer, from the first two words in the Latin version. Every eleventh bead of a rosary is so called, because at that bead the Lord's Prayer is repeated. The name is also given to a certain kind of fishing tackle, in which hooks and weights to suit them are fixed alternately on the line in rosary fashion.

Patter The running talk of conjurors, comedians, and market traders, etc. The word is based on 'paternoster', the Lord's Prayer in Latin. When saying Mass, the priest often recited the prayer in a low, rapid, mechanical way until he came to the words 'and lead us not into temptation', which he spoke clearly and deliberately.

Pope The word represents Old English *papa*, from ecclesiastical Latin, and Greek *pappas*, a child's word for father. The smoke that emerges from the chimney of the Sistine Chapel during a papal election is known as the *fumata*. Black smoke indicates there is no clear majority; white smoke is issued when a final choice has been made.

Precarious A word applied to what depends on prayers or requests. A precarious tenure is one that depends solely on the will of the owner to accept a request, hence the general use of the word to mean uncertain or not to be depended on. The word comes from the Latin *precarius*, meaning 'obtained by begging'.

Rosary (Latin *rosarium*, 'rose garden', 'garland') The bead-roll used by Roman Catholics for keeping count of the recitation of certain prayers, also the prayers themselves. The sense of 'series of prayers' is recorded from the 1540s, from French *rosaire*, a figurative use of the French word meaning 'rose garden', on the notion of a 'garden' of prayers.

Slough of Despond A period of, or fit of, great depression. In John Bunyan's *Pilgrim's Progress* (1678), it is a deep bog, which Christian has to cross in order to get to the Wicket Gate.

Talent An ability, aptitude, or 'gift' for something or other. The word was originally the name of a weight and piece of money used by the Babylonians, Assyrians, Romans, and

Greeks. The use of talent to mean 'natural aptitude or skill' comes from the biblical Parable of the Talents in the Gospel of Matthew. In this story a master gives one, two, and ten talents of silver to each of three servants. Two of them use their talents well and double the value of what they have been given, but the third buries his coin and fails to benefit from it.

Wake A watch or vigil. The name was originally applied to the all-night watch kept in church before certain holy days, and to the festival kept at the annual commemoration of the dedication of a church. Over time, the festive element took over and the name came to be associated with annual fairs and revelries held at such times. Today the term more usually denotes the watching of the body of the deceased before the funeral, and the feasting that follows.

Weathercock By a papal enactment made in the middle of the 9th century, the figure of a cock was set up on every church steeple as the emblem of St Peter – an allusion to his denial of Christ three times before the cock crowed twice. On the second crowing of the cock the warning of Jesus flashed across his memory, and the repentant apostle 'went out and wept bitterly'. A person who is always changing his mind is, figuratively, a weathercock.

Zen A Japanese school of Buddhism that believes that the ultimate truth is greater than words and is therefore not to be wholly found in the sacred writings, but must be sought through 'inner light' and self-mastery. It originated in the 6th century in China. Its name means 'meditation'.

MYTHS AND FABLES

Etymology is all about unravelling the past. Its stories run through our language just like the ball of thread that led the Greek hero Theseus back out of the 'Labyrinth' to escape the monstrous Minotaur. That thread was called a 'clew', and is the ancestor of our modern 'clue'.

Ancient (and urban) myths are the inspiration for words and expressions as diverse as 'sirens' and 'cloud-cuckoo-land', 'echoes' and 'syringes'. And if you have ever 'blown hot and cold', 'had sour grapes', or sought out 'the naked truth', you have the most fabled fabulist of all to thank: Aesop.

Cloud-Cuckoo-Land The *Nephelokokkugia* in the play *The Birds* by Aristophanes (*c*.450–*c*.385 BC), an imaginary city built in the air by the birds to separate the gods from humans. Hence the use of the name for any fantastic or impractical scheme.

Echo In Greek mythology, Echo was a nymph who was in love with Narcissus, but when her love was not returned, she pined away until only her voice remained.

Elysium In Greek mythology, the abode of the blessed. Hence the Elysian Fields, the paradise or 'happy land' in Greek poetry, whose name translates Greek *Ēlusion pedion*, 'plain of the blessed'. The Champs-Élysées ('Elysian Fields') is an imposing central thoroughfare in Paris.

Gordian knot A great difficulty. Gordius, a peasant, being chosen king of Phrygia, dedicated his wagon to Jupiter, and fastened the yoke to a beam with a rope of bark so ingeniously that no one could untie the knot. Alexander the Great was told that whoever undid it 'would reign over the whole East'. 'Well then,' said the conqueror, 'it is thus I perform the task,' and, so saying, he cut the knot in two with his sword. 'To cut the Gordian knot' is thus to get out of a difficult position with one decisive stroke, or to resolve a situation by force or by evasive action.

Labyrinth A structure with complicated passages through which it is baffling to find one's way. The original labyrinth was a maze constructed by Daedalus to imprison the Minotaur; the only means of finding a way out was by following a ball of thread.

Lethargy In Greek mythology, Lethe was one of the rivers of Hades, which the souls of all the dead are obliged to taste so they may forget everything said and done when alive. *Lēthē* means 'oblivion', and 'lethargic' came to mean sluggish and apathetic.

Meander To wind, to saunter about at random, so called from the Maeander, now the Menderes, a winding river that leads to the Aegean Sea. The term is also applied to an ornamental pattern of winding lines, used as a border on pottery, wall decorations, and the like.

Mentor A guide, a wise and faithful counsellor, so called from Mentor, the adviser to the son of Odysseus, Telemachus, when he was searching for his father.

Narcissistic Having an excessive interest in oneself. In Greek mythology, Narcissus was a beautiful youth who saw his reflection in a fountain and thought it a nymph. He repeatedly strained to reach it, but all his attempts resulted in failure, so that he pined away.

Pander To pander to one's vices is to act as an agent to them, and such an agent is termed a pander, from Pandarus, the go-between in the story of Troilus and Cressida.

Pandora In Greek legend Pandora was the first mortal female. Her name means 'All-Gifted' because each of the gods gave her some power or attribute, such as beauty, grace, and intelligence, which were to bring about the ruin of man.

Pandora's box A present that seems valuable but that in reality is a curse. Pandora was sent by Zeus as a gift to Epimetheus, who married her, against the advice of his brother Prometheus. She brought with her a large jar or vase (Pandora's box), which she opened and all the evils flew forth, and they have ever since continued to afflict the world. Hope alone remained in the box.

Sword of Damocles, The Impending danger or disaster. Damocles, a flatterer of Dionysius of Syracuse (4th century BC), was invited by Dionysius to try out the role of a sovereign. Accepting, Damocles was presented with a sumptuous banquet, but over his head a sword was suspended by a hair. Damocles was afraid to stir and sat through the feast in utter torment. Finally, he begged Dionysius to remove him from a situation which exposed his life to such dangers. It is this story that also gave us the saying 'hanging by a thread'.

Tantalize In Greek mythology, Tantalus was a Lydian king, highly honoured and prosperous, but, because he offended the gods, he was plunged up to the chin in a river of Hades, a tree hung with clusters of fruit being just above his head. Because every time he tried to drink the waters receded from him, and because the fruit was just out of reach, he suffered agony from thirst, hunger, and unfulfilled anticipation. It is from here that English took the word 'tantalize', to excite a hope and disappoint it, as well as 'tantalus', a lock-up spirit chest in which the bottles are visible but unobtainable without the key.

Blowing Hot and Cold: Fables

Add insult to injury, To To wound by word or deed someone who has already suffered an act of violence or injustice. The expression is one of many credited to the Greek storyteller Aesop. In this story, a bald man, in attempting to kill a fly that had bitten him on the head, missed and dealt himself a sharp smack. Whereupon the fly said, 'You wished to kill me for a mere touch. What will you do to yourself since you have added insult to injury?'

Bell the cat, To To undertake a dangerous mission. The allusion is to the fable of the cunning old mouse who suggested that they should hang a bell on the cat's neck to give notice to all mice of her approach. 'Excellent,' said a wise young mouse, 'but *who* will bell the cat?'

Blow hot and cold, To To be inconsistent; to vacillate. The allusion is to the fable of a traveller who was entertained by a satyr, a woodland god. The traveller blew on his cold fingers to warm them and afterwards on his hot soup in order to cool it. The indignant satyr turned him out of doors, because he was unable to fathom someone who blew both hot and cold with the same breath.

Cry wolf, To To give a false alarm. The allusion is to the fable of the shepherd boy who so often called 'Wolf!' merely to make fun of the neighbours that when, at last, the wolf came no one would believe him. This fable appears in almost every nation of the world.

Lion's share, The The larger part, all or nearly all. In Aesop's *Fables*, several beasts joined the lion in a hunt, but when the spoil was divided the lion claimed one quarter as his own prerogative, another for his superior courage, a third for his dam and cubs, 'and as for the fourth, let who will dispute it with me'. Intimidated by his fierce frown, the other beasts silently withdrew.

Naked truth, The The plain, unvarnished truth; truth without trimmings. An ancient fable relates how Truth and Falsehood went bathing. Falsehood came first out of the water, and dressed herself in Truth's garments. Truth, unwilling to take those of Falsehood, went naked.

Sour grapes Something disparaged because it is beyond one's reach. The allusion is to Aesop's well-known fable of the fox who tried in vain to get at some grapes, but when he found they were beyond his reach went away saying, 'I see they are sour.'

GODS, HEROES,
AND MONSTERS

The names of gods, and the areas and objects associated with them, have inspired an often surprising lexicon, ranging from 'juggernauts' to 'panic'.

Avatar (Sanskrit *avatāra*, 'descent') In Hindu mythology, the advent to earth of a deity in a visible form. In computing, particularly in social media, gaming, or virtual-reality settings, an avatar is a graphical representation of a user.

Champ de Mars The prominent park in Paris, by the Seine, was laid out in 1765 as a parade ground for the nearby École Militaire; hence its name, referring to Mars the Roman god of war. The name was adopted from that of the Campus Martius, in Rome, which was the exercise ground for Roman armies between the Capitol and the River Tiber.

God A word common, in slightly varying forms, to all Germanic languages, and whose precise origins are uncertain. It may stem from an ancient root that meant 'to call', but others trace it back to a word meaning to 'pour', perhaps in reference to a drink poured out as an offering to the deity. Although 'god' and 'good' have followed very similar paths in English, they are not related etymologically.

Gods, The The gallery in a theatre or its occupants. Those 'up in the gods' were originally the most critical and vociferous section of the audience. The name alludes to the lofty location.

Hermes The Greek Mercury, whose busts, known as Hermae, were affixed to pillars and set up as boundary markers at street corners. The name has been linked with Greek *hermēneus*, 'interpreter', meaning that Hermes was the interpreter of the gods. Hence 'hermeneutics' as the science of interpretation, especially of the Scriptures.

Hypnos (Greek *hupnos*, 'sleep') In Greek mythology, the god of sleep, hence the name's inspiration for 'hypnosis', a technique that induces a different state of consciousness.

Janus The ancient Roman deity who kept the gate of heaven and is, therefore, the guardian of gates and doors. He was represented with two faces, one in front and one behind, and the doors of his temple in Rome were thrown open in times of war and closed in times of peace. Janus inspired both 'janitor', a caretaker or doorkeeper, and 'January', a month that stands as a gateway between the old year and the new.

Jove Another name for Jupiter, hence the exclamation 'by Jove'.

Juggernaut A Hindu god, whose name originates with the Sanskrit *Jagannātha*, 'lord of the world'. The name is a title of Vishnu, chief of the Hindu gods, represented by an idol of Krishna (an avatar of Vishnu) in a temple at Puri in Orissa. The chief festival involves Jagganath, measuring 35ft (10.7m) square and 45ft (13.7m) high, being pulled in a heavy chariot across the sand to another temple. The ritual inspired the use of 'juggernaut' to describe a large, heavy, and often unstoppable vehicle or force.

Mars The Roman god of war. The planet of this name was so called because of its reddish tinge.

Morpheus Ovid's name for the son of Sleep, and god of dreams, from Greek *morphē*, 'form', because he gives form to the contents of our dreams. Hence the name of the drug, 'morphine'.

Muses In Greek mythology, the nine daughters of Zeus and Mnemosyne. They were originally goddesses of memory only, but later identified with individual arts and sciences. Their names are Calliope, Clio, Euterpe, Thalia, Melpomene, Terpsichore, Erato, Polyhymnia, and Urania.

Museum Literally, a home or seat of the Muses. The first building to have this name was the university erected at Alexandria by Ptolemy Soter about 300 BC.

Nectar In classical mythology, the drink of the gods. Like their food ambrosia, it was said to confer immortality, hence the name of the nectarine, so called because it is as 'sweet as nectar'.

Nemesis (Greek, 'righteous indignation', from *nemein*, 'to give what is due') The Greek goddess of retribution or vengeance, who rewarded virtue and punished the wicked and all kinds of immoral behaviour. As such, she was the personification of divine retribution, and so her name is used for retributive justice generally.

Nike (Greek, 'victory') The Greek winged goddess of victory Nike is now most famously a make of training shoes, which first went on sale in 1972. The name is appropriate, as the goddess is standardly depicted on vases of the classical period as striding or running.

Pan In Greek mythology, the god of pastures, forests, flocks, and herds, and also the universal deity. He is traditionally represented with the upper part of a man and the body and legs of a goat, and with little goat horns on his head. The medieval image of the Devil was based on him. His name comes from the Greek, meaning 'all', 'everything'.

Panic The god Pan inspired 'panic' because the sounds heard by night in the mountains and valleys, causing sudden and unwarranted fear, were attributed to him. He was said to make men, cattle, and other creatures bolt in 'Panic' terror.

Wheel of fortune, The Fortuna, the goddess, is represented on ancient monuments with a wheel in her hand, symbolic of her inconstancy.

Zephyr In Greek mythology, Zephyros was the god of the west wind, one of the four seasonal Anemoi (Wind-Gods). Zephyros was a rival of the god Apollo for the love of Hyacinth. One day he spied the pair playing a game of quoits in a meadow, and in a jealous rage blew the disc off course with a gust of wind, causing it to strike the boy in the head, killing him instantly.

THE FATES

Atropos (Greek, 'not turning', 'unchangeable') In Greek mythology, the eldest of the three Fates, and the one who severs the thread of life.

Clotho (Greek *klōthein*, 'to draw thread', 'to spin') The Fate who presides over birth and draws from her spindle the thread of life.

Lachesis The Fate who spins life's thread and determines its length. Her name represents Greek *lakhesis*, 'destiny'.

Heroes and Villains

Amazon A member of a legendary race of female warriors believed by the ancient Greeks to live in Scythia, now near the Black Sea in Russia. The name was popularly thought to have been derived from Greek *a-*, 'not', and *mazos*, 'breast', as they were said to cut off their right breast to improve their use of a bow. More plausible is an ancient word meaning 'fighting together'. The word is now used of any tall, strong, or athletic woman.

Hector A Trojan warrior in Homer's *Iliad*. After holding out for ten years, he was slain by Achilles, who lashed him to his chariot and dragged the dead body in triumph around the walls of Troy. In 17th-century stage representations of him, he was played as a blustering bully. Hence 'to hector' means 'to browbeat' or 'to bluster'.

Herculean strength (Greek *Hēra*, 'Hera', and *kleos*, 'glory') In Greek mythology, Heracles (Hercules to the Romans) is a hero of superhuman physical strength. In a fit of madness inflicted on him by the goddess Juno, he slayed his wife and children, and as penance was ordered to serve the king Eurystheus for 12 years. The latter imposed 12 tasks of great difficulty and danger on him. After these labours and many other adventures, he was rewarded with immortality.

Hermaphrodite A person or animal with both male and female sexual characteristics, or in botany a flower with both male and female reproductive organs. The word is derived from Hermaphroditus, son of Hermes and Aphrodite. The nymph Salmacis became so enamoured of him that she prayed that they might be so closely united that 'the twain might become one flesh'. Her prayer was heard and the nymph and the boy became one body.

Stentorian Having a loud voice. Stentor was a Greek herald in the Trojan War. In Homer's *Iliad*, his voice was as loud as that of 50 men combined.

Valkyries (Old Norse *valr*, 'the slain', and *kyrja* '*chooser*') The 'choosers of the slain', as handmaidens of Odin, who, mounted on swift horses and holding drawn swords, rushed into the thick of battle and selected those destined to die.

. . . And Monsters

Gargantuan Of enormous size. Gargantua was a legendary giant, famous for his enormous appetite. In a satire by Rabelais of the same name (1535), he swallows six pilgrims, complete with their staves, in a salad. He became proverbial as a voracious and insatiable guzzler.

Rumpelstiltskin A small and vindictive elf of German folklore. A miller's daughter was commanded by a king to spin straw into gold, and the elf did this for her, on condition that she would give him her first child. The maiden married the king, and grieved so bitterly when the child was born that the dwarf promised to relent if within three days she could find out his name. Two days were spent in vain guesses, but on the third day one of the queen's servants heard a strange voice singing:

> Little dreams my dainty dame
> Rumpelstiltskin is my name.

The child was saved, and the dwarf killed himself with rage. The name literally means 'wrinkled foreskin'.

Selkie (From Scottish English *sealgh*, 'seal') In the folklore of the Orkney and Shetland islands, a seal-like sea creature with the capacity to take human form on land.

Siren (perhaps from Greek *seira*, 'rope', so 'entangler') One of the mythical monsters, half woman and half bird, said by Greek poets to entice seamen by the sweetness of their song to such a degree that the sailors forgot everything and died of hunger. The word thus came to be applied to any dangerous, alluring woman.

In 1819 the word was adopted by the French physicist Charles Cagniard de la Tour (1777–1859) as the name of an acoustical instrument used to produce musical tones and to measure the number of vibrations in a note. It was this that gave the term for the modern mechanical siren.

Sop to Cerberus, A A bribe. 'To give a sop to Cerberus' is to quiet a troublesome customer. Cerberus is Pluto's three-headed dog, stationed at the gates of the infernal regions. When people died, the Greeks and Romans used to put a cake in their hands as a sop to Cerberus to allow them to pass without molestation.

Vampire A fabulous being, supposed to be the ghost of a heretic, criminal, or the like, who returned from the grave in the guise of a monstrous bat to suck the blood of sleeping persons, who would then usually become vampires themselves. The only way to destroy them was to drive a stake through their body. The superstition is essentially Slavonic, from a word related to Russian *upyr*, 'vampire'.

Weird sisters, The A term initially applied, in the Middle Ages (and in accordance with the original meaning of 'weird', which was 'destiny'), to the Fates. Their power over men's destinies was to some extent shared by the three witches in Shakespeare's *Macbeth* (1606), and so they in their turn were dubbed 'the weird sisters'. This application led in the 19th century to the use of 'weird' to mean 'uncanny' or 'spooky'.

Werewolf A 'man-wolf' (Old English *wer*, 'man'), i.e. a man who, according to ancient superstition, was turned, or could at will turn himself, into a wolf.

THE STARS

Have you ever yearned for something in the past that can never be revived? If so, you have 'desiderated', a beautiful word for an emotion of longing and loss, and one that is built upon the idea of wishing upon the stars. Much of our vocabulary rests on the belief that the constellations determine our life and our destiny. We can either count our lucky stars, or anticipate a 'disaster'.

Asterisk An asterisk is a little star, the meaning of its source, Greek *asteriskos*.

Astronaut The Greek *astēr* also gave us 'asteroid', 'astronomy', and 'astronaut'. The beautiful metaphor of the latter is that an astronaut is a 'star sailor'.

Cry for the moon, To To crave for what is unattainable. The allusion is to foolish children who 'cry for the moon to play with'. The French say *Il veut prendre la lune avec les dents* ('He wants to take the moon between his teeth').

Desiderate To yearn for something you once had. It is built upon the Latin *sidus, sider-*, 'star', which also hides behind the word 'consider', as when we might look to the stars for wisdom.

Disaster From the Italian *disastro*, meaning an 'ill-starred event'.

Falling star A meteor. A wish made as a star falls is supposed to come true. Muslims believe them to be firebrands, flung by good angels against evil spirits when they approach too near the gates of heaven.

Galaxy, The (Greek *gala, galaktos*, 'milk') The Milky Way. A long, white, luminous track of stars, which seems to encompass the heavens like a girdle. It is composed of a vast collection of stars so distant that they are indistinguishable as separate stars but appear as a combined light. According to classic fable, it is the path to the palace of Zeus.

Mercury The Roman counterpart of the Greek Hermes, son of Jupiter, to whom he acted as messenger. He was the god of science and commerce, the patron of travellers and also of rogues, vagabonds, and thieves. Hence, the name of the god is used to denote both a messenger and a thief. The alchemists credited the metal mercury with great powers and used it for many purposes, often using the alternative name 'quicksilver'.

Mercurial Light-hearted or volatile. Those of such temperament were said by the astrologers to be born under the planet Mercury.

Over the moon, To be To be highly excited; extremely delighted; in raptures about something. The expression comes from the phrase 'to jump over the moon', in turn from the familiar nursery rhyme about the cow that jumped over the moon, dating from at least the 18th century. In sport, it is a routine phrase in post-match interviews.

Planets The celestial bodies that revolve round the sun in elliptical orbits, so called from Greek *planētēs*, 'wanderer', because to the ancients they appeared to wander about among the stars instead of having fixed places.

Pluto In Greek mythology, one of the titles of Hades, the ruler of the underworld, the kingdom of the dead. His Greek name *Ploutōn* meant literally 'wealth-giver', wealth being seen as coming out of the earth. A plutocracy is therefore a government based on wealth not merit.

Saturnine Grave, phlegmatic, gloomy, dull, and glowering, from the belief that such a personality is given to those born under the influence of the leaden planet Saturn.

Talisman A lucky charm or magical figure or word, which is cut on metal or stone under the influence of certain planets. The word is from Arabic *tilsam*, from Medieval Greek *telesma*, 'ritual'. It is one of the few English nouns ending in '-man' that forms its plural with an '-s'.

Venereal Venus is the second planet from the sun in the solar system and the brightest celestial object after the sun and moon. It is named after Venus, the Roman goddess of beauty and sensual love. One legacy in English is the word 'venereal', relating to sexual desire.

Zodiac The imaginary belt or zone of the heavens, extending about eight degrees each side of the ecliptic, which the sun traverses annually. From Greek *zōidiakos*, meaning 'pertaining to animals', from *zōion*, 'animal'.

MAGIC/SUPERSTITION

Any lover of language and its construction will appreciate the fact that 'glamour' and 'grammar' were once one and the same, and both had quite magical beginnings. Lexicographers have long desired to be glamorous – perhaps we might call ourselves 'grammarous' instead? It just goes to show that magic can be found in the most surprising of places.

Magic Words

Abracadabra In modern use, a verbal accompaniment to conjuring tricks, but historically a significant magical word. The word was written on parchment and hung from the neck by a linen thread in the following pattern:

```
A B R A C A D A B R A
A B R A C A D A B R
A B R A C A D A B
A B R A C A D A
A B R A C A D
A B R A C A
A B R A C
A B R A
A B R
A B
A
```

Gimmick The first use of this word in US slang was to describe some device by which a conjuror or fairground showman
worked his trick. In later usage it applied to some distinctive
quirk or trick associated with a film or radio star, then to any
device. The origin of the word is uncertain. It may be an alteration of 'gimcrack' or even a form of 'magic'.

Glamour Although the two words rarely go hand in hand,
'glamour' and 'grammar' are related. 'Glamour', originally a
Scots word meaning 'enchantment or magic', was an altered
form of 'grammar'. Both descend from the Greek *gramma*, 'a
letter of the alphabet, something written down', and in the
Middle Ages 'grammar' described all learning, including the
important study of books on astrology and the occult.
'Glamour' later took on the magical side of things, while
'grammar' embraced the learning and, specifically, the study
of language.

Hocus pocus Words traditionally uttered by conjurors when
performing a trick. Hence the trick itself, also the juggler himself.
The phrase dates from the early 17th century and is the opening
of an absurd string of mock Latin used by the performer: *hax*

pax max Deus adimax. The modern 'hoax' is probably a contraction of 'hocus pocus'.

Prestige A word that has undergone a significant change in meaning. Latin *praestigiae*, from which it is derived, means 'juggling tricks', hence the extension to 'illusion, fascination, charm' and so to the present meaning of 'standing, influence, and reputation'.

Wizard A magician, one adept in the black arts, the male counterpart of a witch. The word is derived from 'wise'.

Superstitions

Get out of bed on the wrong side, To To be in a bad temper from early morning. It was formerly thought to be unlucky to set the left foot on the ground first when getting out of bed. The same superstition applies to putting on the left shoe first. Augustus Caesar was said to be very superstitious in this respect.

Hand of glory, The In folklore, a dead man's hand, preferably one cut from the body of a man who has been hanged, soaked in oil and used by witches for its special magical properties. The poet Robert Graves wrote that 'hand of glory' is a translation of the French *main de gloire*, itself an alteration of *mandragore*, the plant mandragora (mandrake), whose roots had a similar magic value.

Mojo A US term, though probably of West African origin, for a magic charm or talisman. It reached a wider audience via the 1950s blues song 'Got my mojo working, but it just won't work on you'.

Nightmare A very frightening dream. The term originally denoted a sensation in sleep as if something heavy were sitting on one's chest, supposedly caused by a monster that actually did this. It was not infrequently called the 'night hag' or the 'riding of the witch'. The second part of the word is Old English *mare* (Old Norse *mara*), an incubus, and it appears in the French *cauchemar*, 'the fiend that tramples'. It is not related to the word for a female horse, although one of the most famous artistic representations of the experience, Henry Fuseli's painting *The Nightmare* (1781) contains both images. The picture shows a fiend sitting on the chest of a sleeping woman, with a horse's head emerging from the curtains behind the bed. The woman is lying on her back, a position said to be conducive to nightmares.

Oaf A variant of the Old English *ælf* ('elf'). A clumsy fool is so called from the notion that an idiot is a changeling: a child left by the elves or fairies in place of a stolen one.

Raven A bird of ill omen, fabled to forebode death, and to bring disease and ill luck. The ravens in the Tower of London are the last remnant of the former royal menagerie. It is said that their departure would presage the fall of the kingdom, so their wings are kept carefully clipped.

Right foot foremost It is considered unlucky to enter a house, or even a room, on the left foot, and in ancient Rome a boy was stationed at the door of a wealthy man's home to caution visitors not to cross the threshold with the left foot.

Sinister Foreboding ill; ill-omened. From Latin, meaning 'on the left hand'. According to Roman augurs, birds appearing on the left-hand side forebode ill luck, but on the right-hand side, good luck. Plutarch, following Plato and Aristotle, gave the reason that the west (or left side of the augur) was towards the setting or departing sun.

Touch wood, To An old superstition to avert bad luck or misfortune, or to make sure of something good. Traditionally, certain trees, such as the oak, ash, hazel, hawthorn, and willow, held a sacred significance and thus protective powers.

MAKING FRIENDS

Friends and good manners will carry you where money won't go.

MARGARET WALKER, poet and author

Bridle at, To To show anger or indignation at something. The metaphor is from a horse being pulled up suddenly and sharply.

Chum A close friend; a 'mate'. The word began as Oxford University slang and arose as a short form of 'chamber fellow'. Its Cambridge equivalent is 'crony', which has more or less the same meaning but a different origin. It comes from Greek *khronios*, 'of long duration', from *khronos*, 'time'.

Dog in the manger, A A person who prevents another enjoying something but does not enjoy it themselves. The allusion is to the fable of the dog that made his home in a manger. He would not allow the ox to come near the hay, even though he would not eat it himself.

Gentle Originally, belonging to a family of position, well-born, having the manners of genteel persons (hence 'gentleman'); however, this meaning has been eclipsed by the modern sense of tender and mild – qualities expected of a gentleman. The word is from Latin *gentilis*, 'belonging to the same family'.

Genuine From the Latin *genuinus* and an ancient root meaning to 'beget' or 'produce' – with the idea that family creates authenticity. Another possibility is a link with the Latin *genu*, 'knee', with reference to the Roman custom of a father formally acknowledging that a newborn child was his by placing the baby on his knee.

Job's comforter A person who means to sympathize with you in your grief but implies that you brought it on yourself and so adds to your sorrow. The allusion is to the rebukes the biblical Job received from his friends: 'I have heard many such things: miserable comforters are ye all' (Job 16:2).

Mutt and Jeff Originally, a pair of male cartoon characters introduced in the USA in 1907 by Harry C. 'Bud' Fisher (1885–1954), in what has been claimed to be the first daily comic strip. Mutt was tall, lanky, and lugubrious, Jeff smaller, more feisty and bald. Before long, the joint name was being applied to any pair of male associates, one noticeably taller than the other. In British rhyming slang, 'Mutt and Jeff' means 'deaf'.

Solecism A deviation from correct idiom. The word is also applied to any impropriety or breach of good manners. From the Greek *soloikismos*, 'speaking incorrectly', so named from Soloi, an ancient Greek city on Cyprus, said to speak a debased form of Greek.

In someone's black books To be out of favour with someone. A black book was once a record of the names of people liable to censure or punishment. In the 16th century, the term was given to an official report prepared for King Henry VIII, after an investigation into the condition and administration of the monasteries.

Take the mickey out of someone, To To tease them. 'Mickey' probably represents 'Mickey Bliss', Cockney rhyming slang for 'piss', so that the expression is a euphemism for 'to take the piss'. Who Mickey Bliss was, no one is quite sure.

Umbrage, To take (Latin *umbra*, 'shade') Originally to feel overshadowed or slighted and hence to take offence. To 'give umbrage' was the 17th-century equivalent of 'throwing shade'.

EUPHEMISM

Euphemisms are unpleasant truths wearing diplomatic cologne.

QUENTIN CRISP: *Manners from Heaven* (1984)

Gad, By 'Gad' is a minced form of 'God', occurring also in 'Gadzooks' (God's hooks, i.e. the hands of the cross), 'Begad' and 'Egad'. Many such euphemisms, or 'minced oaths', date from the late Middle Ages, when religious blasphemy was far more taboo than any reference to a bodily function. They were followed by other disguised references, such as 'Gadsbudlikins' (God's body), 'strewth' (God's truth), and 'zounds' (God's wounds), as well as euphemisms for Jesus Christ such as 'jeepers creepers' and 'Jiminy Cricket'.

Meiosis A figure of speech in which an impression is deliberately given that a thing is of less size or importance than it actually is. An example is the typical English understatement 'rather good', said of something that is excellent, or 'rather a setback', said of a major disaster. A famous modern meiosis was Harold Macmillan's 'little local difficulty' following the resignation of his entire Treasury team. In biology, the term denotes a type of cell division in which four new cells are created, each containing half the number of chromosomes of the original. Meiosis is essential for sexual reproduction in animals and plants. The word is from the Greek, meaning 'lessening'.

No more, To be To exist no longer; to be dead.

> This parrot is no more. It has ceased to be. It's expired and gone to meet its maker. This is a late parrot.
>
> MONTY PYTHON'S FLYING CIRCUS
>
> (14 December 1969)

Taken for a ride, To be To have one's leg pulled; to be made the butt of a joke. More sinisterly, the expression is also used by gangsters as a euphemism for murder. The victim is induced or forced into a vehicle and murdered in the course of the ride.

Visit the Spice Islands, To One of many euphemisms for going to the toilet, favoured by the Victorians. In the 1800s, those caught short would 'play arse music', 'use the thunder jug', or even 'starch the potatoes'. In the last hundred years, we have turned to 'emptying the anaconda' or 'draining the lizard'.

What the dickens What the Devil. 'Dickens' here is a euphemism for 'Devil', adopted from the surname.

EMOTIONS

For thousands of years, our behaviour has been thought to be governed by six basic emotions: happiness, sadness, disgust, surprise, fear, or anger. Today, it's clear that our emotions are a complicated mix, but equally that it's vital that we have the language to express them.

Age-otori (Japanese) The misery of a bad haircut.

Cacoethes (Greek *kakoēthēs*, 'of an evil disposition') An irresistible or uncontrollable urge, especially to do something unwise.

Esprit de l'escalier (French, 'staircase wit') The rejoinder that comes too late; the witty retort that occurs to one after the moment has passed. The original reference was to the afterthought that occurred to a person when going downstairs from the salon to the street door.

Frobly-mobly The 18th-century equivalent of 'meh'. It was described by the lexicographer Francis Grose, in his glossary of local and provincial words, as meaning 'indifferently well' – neither one thing nor the other.

Halcyon days Times of happiness and prosperity. Halcyon represents Greek *alkuōn*, 'kingfisher', popularly derived from *hals*, 'sea', and *kuōn*, 'conceiving'. It was once believed that the kingfisher incubated its eggs for 14 days on the surface of the sea, during which period, before the winter solstice, the waters were always calm.

As happy as a sandboy Very happy. An old-established expression from the days when sandboys (or men) drove their donkeys through the streets hawking bags of sand, usually obtained from beaches. The sand was used by people for their gardens, by builders, and by publicans for sanding their floors. The happiness of sandboys was due to their habit of indulging in liquor with their takings.

Lose one's rag, To To lose one's temper. The allusion is to the 'red rag', or tongue, which is unbridled when one is in a rage.

Meh An interjection expressing indifference or apathy. It appeared during the 1990s and was popularized by *The Simpsons*.

Melancholy Lowness of spirits, formerly thought to arise from a superfluity of black bile (Greek *melas kholē*), one of the four humours whose balance was essential for physical and mental well-being.

Mulligrubs A fanciful term dating from the late 16th century and denoting both a general feeling of low spirits and also, more specifically, colic or diarrhoea. This brand of melancholy was also known as the 'mubble-fubbles'.

Nepenthe or **Nepenthes** A drug, mentioned in the *Odyssey*, that was fabled to drive away care and make people forget their woes. From Greek *nē*, meaning 'not', and *penthos*, 'grief'.

Psyche From the Greek for 'breath' and hence life, soul, and the human spirit or self. The tale of Cupid and Psyche, from the 2nd century AD, is an allegory of love and the self. Psyche is often represented as a butterfly, a metaphor for the liberation of the soul.

Quick Living, and hence animated or lively. The quick of the nail is the soft, tender flesh below the growing part of a finger-nail or hoof – it is the sense referred to in 'cut to the quick'. Quicksand is sand that shifts its place as if it were alive.

Cocking a Snook

Baffle Originally the punishment or public disgracing of an errant knight, taking the form of hanging him or his effigy by the heels from a tree. The word moved from the meaning of 'disgrace' to 'hoodwink', and on to 'confuse'.

Cock a snook, To To put the thumb to the nose and spread out the fingers: a rude gesture also sometimes known as 'Queen Anne's fan'. 'Snook' may be descended from an old word for a promontory or point of land, which could easily have been transferred metaphorically to the nose. In modern usage 'snoot' (with its implication of snootiness) is often substituted for it.

Cold shoulder, The A show of intentional indifference; a deliberate slight. The expression is often said to relate to medieval times, when a host supposedly offered an unwelcome guest a meal of cold shoulder of mutton, this being the normal fare for the servants of a household. Much more probable is that the cold shoulder is metaphorical, indicating disdain – akin to 'turning one's back' on someone.

Dutch kiss In US slang, a kiss in which the participants grab each other's ears.

Joblijock A domestic disturbance. An old term from Yorkshire for cockerels whose insistent crowing at dawn destroyed the peace of the neighbourhood. More generally, it can be applied to anything or anyone that rudely interrupts.

Mouton enragé (French) An extremely angry person; applies to someone who is usually calm but who suddenly becomes enraged. The literal meaning of the French expression is 'mad sheep'.

Pull someone's leg, To To tease a person; to chaff someone; to make fun of them. The reference is to tripping someone up by kicking their legs from under them or by hooking their legs with a stick or with one's own leg.

WAYS TO SAY YES

Saying yes can be a lot more fun than saying no. Then again, we could probably have avoided many of life's pickles if we hadn't said yes so quickly. Unsurprisingly, the word 'yes' is one of the oldest words in English, although in its earliest forms it was usually only an affirmative to a question framed in the negative – if a question was framed in the positive the answer would have been 'yea'. This distinction, still preserved in other languages such as German and French, became obsolete by the 1600s, and 'yes' has become a linguistic multitasker. Still, if you're looking for some alternative ways to answer in the affirmative, here are a few.

Hunky-dory A US expression of approval, dating from the mid-19th century. Its origin is uncertain, but it is perhaps an elaborated form of 'hunky', derived from Dutch *honk*, 'goal', 'station', 'home', as in tag and other games. If you are 'home', you are in a good or satisfactory position. Another theory links it with slang amongst 19th-century sailors who remembered a street in the Japanese city of Yokahoma named Honcho-Dori, well known for its bars and brothels and other sources of amusement for sailors on shore leave: *honcho dori* translates roughly as 'main street'.

Langue d'oc and **langue d'oïl** (French *langue*, 'tongue') The former is the old Provençal language, spoken south of the River Loire. The latter is Northern French, spoken in the Middle Ages to the north of that river. The languages are so called because 'yes' in Provençal was *oc*, from Latin *hoc*, 'this', and in the northern speech *oïl*, which later became *oui*.

Nice one! An exclamation of commendation of something well done (or often, ironically, of criticism of something badly done). It came to fame in Britain in the early 1970s in the phrase 'Nice one, Cyril!', which was used in a television advertisement for Wonderloaf. This was enthusiastically taken up by football fans as a chant aimed at the Tottenham Hotspur player Cyril Knowles. The Spurs team went on to record, under the name 'Cockerel Chorus', a song based on the phrase:

> Nice one, Cyril,
> Nice one, son!
> Nice one, Cyril,
> Let's have another one.

SPIRO AND CLARKE: 'Nice One, Cyril' (1973)

OK All correct; all right. Its first recorded use occurs in 1839. It originated as an abbreviation of 'Orl Korrect' ('all correct'), a facetious spelling typical of the 1830s, but its use received a considerable boost from 1840 onwards from the slogan 'OK', short for 'Old Kinderhook', used by supporters of the Democratic candidate, Martin Van Buren, who came from Kinderhook in New York State.

Ouija A device employed by spiritualists for receiving spirit messages. It consists of a small piece of wood on wheels, placed on a board marked with the letters of the alphabet and certain commonly used words. When the fingers of the communicators are placed on the Ouija board, it moves from letter to letter and thus spells out sentences. The word is a combination of French *oui* and German *ja*, both meaning 'yes'.

Roger In radio communications, a term meaning 'message received and understood'. It represents a former telephonic name for the letter R, the initial of 'received'.

Tickety-boo In good order; all right. The phrase, now somewhat dated, goes back to at least the 1930s and may be an elaboration of 'that's the ticket', which alludes to a custom among 19th-century charities of issuing tickets to the needy that could be exchanged for soup, clothing, coal, and the like.

Wilco Military jargon for '(I) will comply', denoting acceptance of a message received by radio or telephone. The phrase became familiar from its use by the RAF in the Second World War.

LOVE, SEX, AND MARRIAGE

Love comes in many forms, yet today we have just the single word for it. Sex and romance, on the other hand, have a field day, particularly in dictionaries of slang. 'Firkytoodling', as the Victorians liked to call it (leading perhaps to a bit of 'fandango de pokum'), will never go out of fashion.

Heart on Sleeve

Philtre (Greek *philtron*, from *philos*, 'loving') A draught or charm to incite in another the passion of love. It is a relative of 'philtrum', the vertical dimple between the upper lip and the base of the nose.

Platonic love Spiritual love between persons of opposite sexes; the friendship of man and woman, without any sexual implications. The phrase is founded on a passage towards the end of *The Symposium* (4th century BC) in which the philosopher Plato was extolling the loving interest that Socrates took in young men. This was considered pure and therefore noteworthy in the Greece of the period.

Play gooseberry, To To be an unwanted third person when two lovers are together. The origin of the phrase may derive from the tact of the person occupying the time in picking gooseberries while the others were more romantically occupied.

Wear one's heart on one's sleeve, To To reveal one's secret thoughts or intentions to others; to show one's feelings plainly. The reference is to the knightly custom of tying one's lady's emblem or ribbon to one's sleeve, thus revealing the secret of one's heart.

Wear the willow, To To go into mourning, especially for a sweetheart or bride; to lament a lost lover. The willow, especially the weeping willow, has long been associated with sorrow.

Hanky-Panky

Aphrodisiac A substance, such as oysters, thought to stimulate sexual desire. Aphrodite was the Greek goddess of love, her name coming from the foam (*aphros*) of the sea from which she is said to have been born, as depicted in Botticelli's painting of her Roman counterpart, *The Birth of Venus*.

Dildo An artificial substitute for an erect penis. The word may derive from Italian *diletto*, 'delight', from Latin *diligere*, meaning 'to esteem highly'.

Eunuch A man who serves as a guard in a harem and who to this specific end has been castrated. From Greek *eunoukhos*, meaning 'attendant of the bedchamber', from *eunē*, meaning 'bed', and *ekhein*, meaning 'to keep'.

Fandango de pokum Sex, 19th-century style.

Fanny A slang word either for the female genitals or (in the USA) for the buttocks. The former sense is traced back by some to the name of Fanny Hill, the lusty heroine of John Cleland's *Memoirs of a Woman of Pleasure* (1748–49), her own name (often used as a short title of the book) apparently a pun on the anatomical term *mons veneris* ('mount of Venus'). However, there is a long gap between the publication of this work and the emergence of 'fanny' in this sense in the late 19th century.

Firkytoodling Victorian slang for foreplay.

French letter A euphemism for a condom. The French themselves call a condom a *capote anglaise*, 'English cap'.

G-spot A sensitive area, literal or figurative, that reacts uncontrollably to excitation or stimulation. The origin is in the Gräfenberg spot, an erogenous zone identified by the German-born US gynaecologist Ernst Gräfenberg (1881–1957).

Hanky-panky Suspicious behaviour; covert sexual activity. The phrase was originally used of jugglery or legerdemain, and is an altered form of 'hocus pocus', the fake Latin of the conjuror.

Kamasutra (Sanskrit, literally 'thread of love', from *kāma*, 'love', and *sūtra*, 'thread'). An ancient Hindu text on erotic pleasure and related topics, attributed to the 1st-century AD Indian sage Vatsyayana. It ranges widely over the relationship of the sexes within society, touching on areas as unsensational as the arrangement of furniture (a pot for spitting is recommended, and a lute hanging from a peg made from the tooth of an elephant), but in the West, since the English translation by Sir Richard Burton and F.F. Arbuthnot appeared in 1883, it has been best known for its systematic analysis of sex and its positions.

Kompromat A word used in Russian politics to describe compromising material collected for use in blackmailing, discrediting, or manipulating someone. The compromising material is often sexual in nature.

Masochism The name for the condition in which sexual gratification is derived from humiliation and pain inflicted by another person, so called after Leopold von Sacher-Masoch (1836–95), the Austrian novelist who described this.

Plonker Originally, in mid-19th-century slang, anything large or substantial. By the 1960s the term was being applied to the penis. This usage was widely popularized in the 1980s by the BBC television sitcom *Only Fools and Horses*.

Prick Since at least the 16th century, 'prick' has been used for 'penis'. The metaphor rests on 'prick' as a spine, thorn, or other sharp projection, and comes via another sense, now lost, 'upright tapering spike or pole'. In the 20th century, in common with several other words for the penis, it came to mean 'fool'.

Bringing Home the Bacon

Bachelor (Old French *bacheler*, from Vulgar Latin *baccalaris*, 'farm worker') A man who has not been married. The word was applied in the Middle Ages to knightly hopefuls, while knights of the lowest rank were known as knights bachelor, those too young to display their own banners.

Bring home the bacon, To To bring back the prize; to succeed. The expression may refer to the tradition of the Dunmow flitch, a side of bacon awarded at Great Dunmow in Essex on Whit Monday to any married couple who will swear that they have not quarrelled or repented of their marriage vows for at least a year and a day. The expression 'eating Dunmow bacon' was formerly used of happily married couples, especially those who had lived long together and never quarrelled.

Confetti The practice of throwing confetti over the bridal pair after their wedding is a substitute for the old custom of throwing corn and, later, rice. It derives from an ancient fertility rite, the intent of which was to ensure prosperity and fruitfulness. The word represents Italian *confetti*, 'bonbons', with reference to the little sweets, or imitations of them, thrown at carnivals in Italy.

Honeymoon A holiday spent together by a newly married couple. The word was originally used for the first month of marriage, although 'moon' does not mean 'month' here, as sometimes supposed. The reference is a cynical one, for no sooner is the moon full than it begins to wane. Other languages have a similar term, such as French *lune de miel*, Italian *luna di miele*, and Russian *medovy mesyats*. A German honeymoon is *Flitterwochen*, literally 'fondling weeks'.

Morganatic marriage One between a man of high (usually royal) rank and a woman of lower station, as a result of which she does not acquire the husband's rank and neither she nor any children of the marriage are entitled to inherit the title or possessions. It is often called a 'left-handed marriage' (in German *Ehe zur linken Hand*) because the custom is for the man to pledge his troth with his left hand instead of his right. The term comes from the Medieval Latin phrase *matrimonium* *ad morganaticam*, 'marriage based on the morning-gift', the latter being a token present given by a husband to his wife after consummation and representing his only liability. *Morganatica* is related ultimately to German *Morgen*, 'morning'.

Paraphernalia Originally, this was all that a married woman could legally claim as her own that would not be given as a dowry upon marriage. This included personal articles, clothes, and jewellery. From here it developed to mean articles in general, anything for show or decoration. The word is from the Greek *para*, 'beside', and *phernē*, meaning 'dowry'.

Skimmington It was an old custom in rural England and Scotland to make an example of nagging wives by forming a ludicrous procession through the village to ridicule the offender. A man, mounted on a horse with a distaff in his hand, rode behind the woman with his face to the horse's tail, while the woman beat him about the chops with a ladle. As the procession passed a house where the woman was paramount, the participants gave the threshold a sweep. The event was called 'riding the Skimmington'. The origin of the name is uncertain, but illustrations from the period show the 'offending' woman brandishing a skimming ladle.

FOUR-LETTER WORDS

Observing our shifting squeamishness over time is a useful test of where society sets its boundaries. Our expletives have long drawn strength from two chief taboos: religious profanity and bodily functions. The ten worst words in ancient Latin centred on bodies and sex. Our modern landscape is no different.

Bloody Several derivations are suggested for this expletive, for example that it is an alteration of 'By our Lady', and therefore blasphemous, leading to its being banned for indecency for some time. More likely is that it refers to aristocratic rowdies, or 'bloods' as they were known, of the 17th and 18th centuries, whose night-time revelries led to the expression 'drunk as a blood' and, eventually, 'bloody drunk'.

Cock-up An error; a 'bungle'. The term may derive from printers' jargon for a letter that 'cocks up', or rises above the level of other letters in a line of print.

Crap The real source of 'crap' is uncertain. At first glance, it seems to be a mash-up of various words, including 'scrape' and a French word *crappe* meaning 'dregs' or 'rubbish'. The word's first mention in the *Oxford English Dictionary* is as husks of grain or chaff – the discarded or 'unwanted' bits. Not long after, it was used for the small scraps of pork fat remaining after lard has been rendered off, a sense that still lingers today in some parts of Britain, where 'craps' are essentially pork scratchings. Throughout there runs the thread of something left over, a messy by-product. It was perhaps inevitable then that 'crap' became a synonym for excrement in the middle of the 19th century, when a 'crapping ken' was a blunt term for a toilet. The word has no etymological links with Thomas Crapper, the mass producer of flushing toilets.

Cunt What is today our biggest taboo was fairly innocent when it was first recorded in the 13th century, when it was freely used in anatomy and gynaecological manuals as a straight-forward description of a woman's genitals. At this time, religious profanity was the big taboo, and there was far less squeamish-ness towards the body and its functions. Several street and place names included the word, including Kunteclive in Lancashire (now Cunliffe) and Gropecuntelane in Oxford (now Magpie Lane). On the sidelines, however, its reputation began to sour, and the word became an insult for a 'slut' – or indeed for any woman at all. By the time of the publication of D.H. Lawrence's *Lady Chatterley's Lover*, in 1928, the full descent to what is seen as our most offensive word was complete.

Fico (Italian, 'fig', from Latin *ficus*) A popular term in Shakespeare's England for an obscene gesture of contempt made by thrusting the thumb (representing the penis) between the first and second fingers (suggesting the vagina). 'Figo' is another form.

Four-letter word One of various short swear words relating to sex or excrement. The two words commonly regarded as

357

most taboo are those that came to be widely known in the 1990s as the 'F-word' ('fuck') and the 'C-word' ('cunt'). The otherwise liberally minded *Oxford English Dictionary* did not even admit these two to its pages until it issued the first volume of its supplement (A–G) in 1972.

Fuck 'Fuck' contains four letters in search of an etymology. It is, sadly, easy to dismiss the popular myth that 'fuck' is an acronym, said to have arisen during a time of plague when the population was in perilous decline, prompting the monarch to instruct all fertile couples to go forth and procreate. These couples would hang a sign outside their house to warn against disturbance, because they were engaged in Fornicating Under Command of the King. There is no evidence at all to support this, and a possible, darker, source is the Latin *pugnare*, 'to fight'. Many of the earliest references to 'fuck' involve hitting people rather than having sex. If this is indeed the root of the word, then the meaning was perhaps extended to reflect a misogynistic view of man's power over women.

Naff Lacking taste or style. The first recorded example is from the script of the BBC radio programme *Round the Horne*: 'I couldn't be doing with a garden like this. I mean all them horrible little naff gnomes.' One of the most popular theories about its origin is the suggestion that the word was formed from the initial letters of Normal As Fuck, but it is more likely to come from Polari (a form of theatrical slang used especially within the gay community) and that it comes ultimately from Italian *gnaffa*, 'despicable person'. The expression 'naff off', popularized by the BBC comedy series *Porridge*, is likely to have a different origin and to be a riff on 'eff off', a euphemism for 'fuck off'.

Profane Literally before or outside the temple (Latin *pro fano*). Hence the idea of irreverence, disregard of sacred things, blasphemy, etc. A profanity is generally a swear word.

Shit Despite the euphemism 'Anglo-Saxon word' for our modern swear words, most of them appeared much later. 'Shit' is an exception, originating in the Old English *scitta*, which at the time was no ruder than 'excrement' or 'defecation' would be today. This began to change towards the end of the Middle Ages, when it began to take on extended uses. A poem of 1508 gives us the earliest record of the word's use for an obnoxious individual: 'Thou art a schit but wit'. Today, rather like 'bollocks', 'shit' has seen a reversal of fortune in slang, so that it can denote something excellent too.

WISDOM AND LEARNING

Before the brain stole the limelight, it was the heart that was considered to be the seat of learning and of wisdom. It is why we 'learn something by heart', and why we 'record' (from the Latin *cors*, 'heart') something in our memories. Of course, many of us might opt instead for a spot of 'omphaloskepsis' instead.

Bluestocking A sometimes disparaging nickname for a scholarly or intellectual woman. In 1400 a society of men and women was formed in Venice, distinguished by the colour of their stockings and called *della calza*. The name is derived directly from such a society, founded in about 1750 by Elizabeth Montagu, née Robinson (1720–1800), from the fact that a prominent member wore blue worsted stockings in place of the usual black silk.

Bone up on, To To study intensively; to gain information on. The expression suggests a stiffening of one's knowledge, as a strip of whalebone strengthens a corset, but there may also be an influence from the classical translations published by Henry

Bohn (1796–1884) whose books were in demand among 19th-century students when cramming for an examination.

Cynic The ancient school of Greek philosophers known as the Cynics, made famous by Antisthenes and his pupil Diogenes, who were ostentatiously contemptuous of ease, luxury, and convention. The name is derived either from their dog-like, or dogged, habits or from the fact that Antisthenes held his school in the Gymnasium called Cynosarges ('white dog'), from an incident when a white dog carried away part of a victim that was being offered in sacrifice to Hercules.

Egghead A 'brainy' or intellectual person. The term derives from the supposition that intellectuals are often bald.

Genius In Roman mythology, the genius was the spirit that attended a man from cradle to grave, governing his fortunes and determining his character. The word is from Latin *gignere*, 'to beget', from the notion that birth and life were due to these *dii genitales*. Hence 'genius' is used for an innate talent.

Grey matter A pseudoscientific name for the brain, used generally to mean common sense. The active part of the brain is composed of a greyish tissue, which contains the nerve endings.

Muttonhead A stupid or ignorant person. The 'mutt' that is a dog, especially a mongrel, is an abbreviation of 'muttonhead'.

Omphaloskepsis The technical term for navel-gazing or complacent self-absorption.

Philosopher The sages of Greece used to be called *sophoi* ('wise men'), but Pythagoras thought the word too arrogant, and adopted the word *philosophos* ('lover of wisdom').

361

Pundit In India, a learned man, one versed in Sanskrit, law, religion, and the like. The word is from the Hindi *pandit*. In English, the word came to be used generally for an expert or authority. It is now commonly used – sometimes dismissively – of any supposed expert or opinion-leader called upon by the media to discuss a topic of general interest, e.g. culture, politics, or sport.

Rack one's brains, To To strain them to discover or recollect something; to puzzle about something, as though the mental contortions are like being stretched on a rack.

Record That which is recorded, originally 'got by heart', from Latin *cor, cordis*, 'heart'. Hence the best performance or most striking event of its kind known, especially in such phrases as 'to beat or break the record'; 'to win in record time'.

Use your loaf A slang expression meaning 'use your brains', 'use your head'. 'Loaf (of bread)' is operating here as rhyming slang for 'head'.

Wooden spoon, The A booby prize in the form of a giant wooden spoon awarded to the student who received the lowest exam results in the mathematical tripos at Cambridge. More broadly it means a booby prize generally.

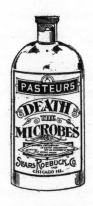

SCIENCE

At the heart of 'science' is the Romans' word for knowledge. Based on the Latin *scire*, 'to know', it originally described any branch of knowledge, including the arts. You can also find it in 'conscience' – one's inner knowledge.

Alchemy (Arabic *al-kīmiyā*, 'the transmutation') The pseudo-scientific predecessor of chemistry sought to find a way of transmuting base metals into gold by means of the philosopher's stone, and of discovering a panacea ('cure-all') and elixir of life.

Geek In *Webster's New International Dictionary of the English Language*, from 1954, a 'geek' is defined as 'a carnival "wild man" whose act usually includes biting off the head of a live chicken or snake'. It is a long journey from a performer at a freak show to today's nerdy expert, but both meanings come from an old dialect word 'geck', meaning 'fool'. The word was resolutely negative for a long while, implying someone so foolish as to undertake extreme or obsessive acts. More positive meanings crept in during the closing decades of the 20th century, and 'geek' is now a badge of pride for someone genuinely and passionately interested in their subject.

Ghost in the machine, The The mind ('ghost') as distinct from the body ('machine'). The expression was coined by the philosopher Gilbert Ryle in *The Concept of Mind* (1949).

Meme A cultural symbol, object, or idea that can be replicated, altered, and passed on in a manner analogous to the transmission of the gene in biology. The term was coined in 1976 by Richard Dawkins, giving a name to an existing anthropological concept. The arrival of the internet gave rise to the 'internet meme', a cultural item in the form of an image, GIF, video, etc. that becomes a viral sensation.

Nerd A term of insult for someone thought odd or unprepossessing in some way, or lacking in social skills; also, someone with an obsessive and meticulous interest in some activity or hobby. The word, which emerged in the USA around 1950, is of uncertain origin. It may have been inspired by the name of a character invented by the US children's author Dr Seuss.

> And then, just to show them, I'll sail to Ka-Troo
> And Bring Back an It-Kutch, a Preep and a Proo,
> A Nerkle, a Nerd, and a Seersucker too!
>
> *If I Ran the Zoo* (1950)

On the side of the angels The phrase with which Disraeli thought he had settled the problems raised by Darwin's theory of the origin of species. It occurred in his speech at the Oxford Diocesan Conference, 25 November 1864:

> The question is this: Is man an ape or an angel? Now I am on the side of the angels.

Quark A type of subatomic particle, thought to be one of the basic constituents of matter. The name was coined by the US physicist Murray Gell-Mann in the 1960s, who initially spelled it 'quork'. He changed the spelling after encountering the line 'Three quarks for Muster Mark' in James Joyce's *Finnegans Wake* (1939). Joyce's word is meant to suggest the cawing sound seagulls make, but the association with three appealed to Gell-Mann, because at the time only three varieties of quark (known as up, down, and strange quarks) were believed to exist.

Robot An automaton with semi-human powers and intelligence. From Czech *robota*, meaning 'forced labour'. The name comes from the mechanical creatures in Karel Čapek's play *R.U.R.* (*Rossum's Universal Robots*), which was successfully produced in London in 1923.

Specie or **species** The word means literally 'that which appears' (Latin *species*, 'appearance'). As things are distinguished by their visible forms, it has come to mean 'kind' or 'class'. As drugs and condiments at one time formed the most important articles of merchandise, they were called 'species', still retained in the French *épices* and English 'spices'.

EUREKA

Eureka (Greek *heurēka*, 'I have found [it]') An exclamation of delight at having made a discovery, originally that of Archimedes, the Syracusan philosopher, when he discovered how to test the purity of Hiero's crown. The story is that Hiero gave some gold to a smith to be made into a crown, but suspecting that the gold had been alloyed with an inferior metal, asked Archimedes to test it. The philosopher did not know how to proceed, but in getting into his bath, which was full, observed that some of the water ran over, and immediately concluded that a body must displace its own bulk of water when immersed. Silver is lighter than gold, therefore a pound weight of silver is bulkier than a pound weight of gold and would consequently displace more water. Thus he found that the crown was deficient in gold.

REAL PEOPLE

Was there ever a real Fanny Adams, Flipping Ada, or Flaming Nora? What about Billy No Mates or Jack the Lad? English celebrates its heroes and villains – some fictional, some all too real – in style.

Dunce A fool or stupid person. The word is taken from John Duns Scotus (*c.*1265–1308), the schoolman so called from his birthplace, Duns in Scotland. John Duns Scotus was a profoundly influential figure whose followers became known as Scotists or Dunsmen. By the 16th century the Scotists' views were seen as outmoded and were ridiculed for their pedantry and fine distinctions. 'Dunsman' or 'Duns' consequently became a byword for a 'hair-splitter' and also one who is slow at learning.

Guillotine An instrument for inflicting capital punishment by decapitation, so named from Joseph-Ignace Guillotin (1738–1814), a French physician, who proposed its adoption to prevent unnecessary pain.

Hobson's choice No choice at all. The saying derives from Thomas or Tobias Hobson (*c.*1544–1631), a Cambridge carrier well known in his day (John Milton commemorated him in two epitaphs), who refused to let out any horse except in its proper turn.

Jack the Lad A notorious thief, the son of a carpenter in Smithfield, London, and brought up in Bishopsgate workhouse, Jack Sheppard (1702–24) was known for his multiple prison escapes, especially when he broke out of 'the Castle' of Newgate via the chimney. Celebrated as a folk hero, he was soon afterwards taken and hanged at Tyburn, allegedly in sight of 200,000 spectators.

Like billy-o Very much; strongly. The word is said to have been derived from the following: (1) Joseph Billio, rector of Wickham Bishops, Essex, ejected for nonconformity and the first Nonconformist minister of Maldon (1696), who was noted for his drive and energy; (2) Nino Biglio, one of Garibaldi's lieutenants, who would dash keenly into battle shouting, 'I am Biglio! Follow me, you rascals, and fight like Biglio!'; (3) *Puffing Billy*, an early steam locomotive, so that 'puffing like Billy-o' and 'running like Billy-o' were common phrases. None of these is particularly likely, and the more prosaic truth may be that 'billy' is simply the pet form of the name William, used here as a substitute for 'the devil' (there is evidence for such a euphemism from earlier centuries).

Mesmerism So called from Franz Anton Mesmer (1734–1815), an Austrian physician who introduced his theory of 'animal magnetism' at Paris in 1778. It was the forerunner of hypnotism. Denounced as a practitioner of magic in his native city of Vienna, he made a name for himself in Paris, attracting the attention and support of Marie Antoinette. For their treatment, patients are said to have joined hands and sat in a circle around a large tub of sulphuric acid, from which several iron bars, touched by Mesmer and therefore apparently imbued with animal magnetism, protruded. The result, it was claimed, were crises of the body that preceded a total cure. It was later recognized that it was the mind of the patient that contributed towards recovery.

Mona Lisa Leonardo da Vinci's famous portrait (1506) is of an otherwise obscure Florentine lady named Lisa Gherardini, wife of the merchant Francesco di Zanobi del Giocondo. Her husband's name gave the painting's alternative Italian title, *La Gioconda*, i.e. wife of (Francesco del) Giocondo. *Mona* means 'Lady'. *La Gioconda* happens to translate as 'the merry one', but this is hardly appropriate for the enigmatically smiling lady.

Occam's razor *Entia non sunt multiplicanda praeter necessitatem* (Latin, 'No more things should be presumed to exist than are absolutely necessary'), a maxim that means that all unnecessary facts or constituents in the subject being analyzed should be eliminated. The expression is named after William of Occam (*c.*1285–1349), an English philosopher and Franciscan friar, who recommended the principle.

Smart Alec or **Aleck** A US term for a bumptious, conceited know-all. The name goes back to at least the 1860s, but the identity of Alec is uncertain. The allusion may be to Aleck Hoag, a notorious pimp, thief, and confidence man in New York in the 1840s, who was dubbed 'smart Alec' by the police because he believed himself to be too smart for his own good.

Sweet Fanny Adams This phrase, meaning 'nothing at all' or 'sweet nothing', is of tragic origin. In 1867 eight-year-old Fanny Adams was raped and murdered in a hop garden at Alton, Hampshire, and her body dismembered. A 21-year-old solicitor's clerk, Frederick Baker, was tried soon after and hanged at Winchester. The Royal Navy, with grim humour, adopted her name as a synonym for tinned mutton, which was first issued at this time. Sweet Fanny Adams became, as a consequence, a phrase for anything worthless and then for 'nothing at all'. The 'F' of the initials is often taken as the 'F-word'.

Tich or **Titch** A diminutive person, from the celebrated short music-hall comedian Harry Relph (1868–1928), known as Little Tich. He was nicknamed 'Tichborne' or 'Tich' in allusion to the Tichborne claimant, the label applied to Arthur Orton, who was the central actor in the most celebrated impersonation case in English legal history.

In March 1853 Roger Charles Tichborne, heir to an ancient Hampshire baronetcy, sailed for Valparaiso, Chile, and after travelling a while in South America embarked on 20 April 1854 in a sailing ship named the *Bella*, bound for Jamaica. The ship went down and nothing more was heard or seen of Roger Tichborne. In October 1865 'R.C. Richborne' turned up at Wagga Wagga, in Australia, and on Christmas Day 1866 he landed in England as a claimant to the Tichborne baronetcy, asserting that he was the lost Roger. Lady Tichborne, the real Roger's mother, professed to recognize him, but the family could not be deceived. The case came into the courts, where the man's claims were proved to be false, and he was identified as Arthur Orton (1834–98), the son of a Wapping butcher. A further trial for perjury, lasting 188 days, ended in his being sentenced to 14 years' penal servitude.

Harry Relph was given the nickname 'Little Tich' not on account of his shortness, but because of his resemblance in babyhood to the tubby Orton. The name came to be applied to anyone of small stature, and by the middle of the 20th century 'titchy' was a general British colloquialism for 'small'.

WARTS AND ALL

Cicero Marcus Tullius Cicero (106–43 BC), the great Roman orator, philosopher, and statesman, formerly known to English students of the classics as Tully. He is said by Plutarch to have been called Cicero – from Latin *cicer*, 'chickpea', 'wart' – because he had 'a flat excrescence on the tip of his nose'. Other sources claim that he inherited the name from his father, who had such a wart.

Warts and all Said of a description, biography, or the like that seeks to give a rounded portrait including the blemishes and defects. Oliver Cromwell, whose face was not without blemishes, when having his portrait painted by Sir Peter Lely, apparently told him to 'Remark all these roughnesses, pimples, warts, and everything as you see me.'

HEALTH

Good health is real wealth, and our preoccupation with it, and attempts to achieve it, are amply reflected in the dictionary. Our methods may (thankfully) have changed, but the importance of medicine has not.

Bad Air

Diarrhoea Also known as 'the runs', which conveys the sufferer's fleetness of foot to the lavatory. 'Diarrhoea' itself comes from the Greek for 'flow through'.

German measles An infectious disease so named as it is milder than 'proper' measles. 'German' here denotes inferiority, as 'Dutch' does in many other English expressions. The modern name for the disease is 'rubella'.

Gout (Old French *goute*, from Latin *gutta*, 'drop') The disease is so called from the belief that it was caused by the dropping of diseased matter from the blood into the joints.

Legionnaires' disease A form of pneumonia first identified in 1976 as being caused by a previously unknown bacillus, *Legionella pneumophila*, which thrives in contaminated air-conditioning units. The name comes from a convention held that year at a Philadelphia hotel by members of the American Legion, an organization of retired US servicemen. A total of 182 Legionnaires contracted the disease, 29 of them fatally.

Malaria. Before the discovery that malaria is transmitted by mosquitoes, the disease was thought to emanate from the unwholesome atmosphere of marshlands. The Italian *mal'aria* is a contraction of *mala aria*, 'bad air'.

Spanish flu A misnomer for the influenza pandemic of 1918, the worst in history, in which some 21 million people died. The outbreak did not begin in Spain but received its name simply because a news agency in Madrid issued the first uncensored wartime report of its existence.

Syphilis The hero of a Latin poem by Girolamo Fracastoro, *Syphilis, sive Morbus Gallicus* ('Syphilis, or the French Disease'), published in 1530. In the poem the shepherd Syphilis (the name comes from the Greek *suphilos*, 'lover of pigs') angers the god Apollo and is struck down by a new and highly infectious disease. The name of the poem's protagonist later became associated with the venereal disease.

All-overish

All-overish Not at one's best; beset with weariness and indifference, as before the onset of an illness.

Crisis The Greek physician Hippocrates stated that all diseases had their periods, when the humours, or vital fluids, of the body ebbed and flowed like the tide of the sea. These tidal days he called 'critical days', and the tide itself a 'crisis', because it was on these days the physician could determine whether the disorder was taking a good or bad turn. In English, this decisive turning point in a disease was the original meaning of the word 'crisis', which comes from the Greek *krinein*, 'to decide'.

Every picture tells a story An evocative truism popularized by the caption for an advertisement of 1904 for Doan's Backache Kidney Pills, showing a person bent over with pain. The phrase may have been current before this but has been put to good use ever since.

Fettle In some specialized and dialect senses, the verb means 'to repair, prepare, or put in order'. As a noun it means 'condition or state of health', as: 'in fine fettle'. It comes from Old English *fetel*, 'belt', alluding to the act of girding oneself up.

Humour According to the ancient philosophers, there were four principal humours in the body: phlegm, blood, choler (or yellow bile), and melancholy (or black bile). As any one of these predominated it determined the temper of the mind and body, hence the terms 'phlegmatic', 'sanguine', 'choleric', and 'melancholic'. A just balance made a good humour, and a preponderance of any one of the four an ill or bad humour.

Sneeze St Gregory has been credited with originating the custom of saying 'God bless you' after sneezing, introducing it during an outbreak of plague, in which sneezing was a mortal symptom. Aristotle, however, mentions a similar custom among the Greeks, when sneezing was a 'crisis' symptom of the great Athenian plague. The Romans followed the same custom, their usual exclamation being *Absit omen!* ('May evil omen be absent'). The English response 'Bless you!' is on similar lines.

Doctor, Doctor

Barber's pole This pole, painted spirally with two stripes of red and white and displayed outside barbers' shops, derives from the days when barbers also practised bloodletting. The pole represents the staff gripped by the patient, which was painted red since it was usually stained with blood. The white spiral represents the bandage that was twisted round the arm before bloodletting began. The gilt knob at the end of the pole represents the brass basin which caught the blood.

Caesarean section The delivery of a child from the womb through an incision in the abdomen. The operation is said to be so called because Julius Caesar was born via this method, but a more plausible derivation is the Latin *caesus*, '(having been) cut'.

Elixir of life, The The supposed potion of the alchemists that would prolong life indefinitely. It was sometimes imagined as a powder, sometimes as a fluid. The origin of 'elixir' is in Arabic *al iksīr*, 'the elixir', itself probably from Greek *xērion*, the term for a powder used for drying wounds (from *xēros*, 'dry'). The term 'elixir' is now given to any sovereign remedy or panacea, or any special medicinal 'concoction', especially an exotic one.

Leech Formerly, a doctor, literally a person skilled in 'leech-craft'. The word comes from Old English *læce*, from *lacnian*, 'to heal'. The blood-sucking worm, the leech, gets its name from the same source.

Medicine From Latin *ars medicina*, 'art of healing', from *medicus*, 'doctor'. The alchemists applied the word 'medicine' to the philosopher's stone and the elixir of life.

Mickey Finn A draught or powder slipped into liquor to render the drinker unconscious. The term is said to come from a notorious figure in 19th-century Chicago, who ran the Lone Star and Palm Saloons there between around 1896 and 1906 and frequently dispensed knockout drops.

Placebo An innocuous medicine designed to humour a patient, and which may have a beneficial psychological and physical effect. It is the Latin for 'I shall please', 'I shall be acceptable'.

Quack or **quack doctor** Once called a 'quacksalver' (Dutch *zalver*, a 'person who cures by using ointments', from *zalven*, 'to rub with ointment'), an itinerant drug vendor at fairs who 'quacked' (hawked) his wares to the credulous rustics.

Surfeit water An old name for a 'water' used to cure 'surfeits', i.e. the effects of gluttony. Hannah Glasse's 18th-century recipe requires 4 gallons (18 litres) of brandy and 27 other ingredients, mostly herbs. This surfeit water was drunk from special tapering fluted glasses, and the standard dose of this highly alcoholic pick-me-up was two spoonfuls.

Treacle The word, which etymologically means 'an antidote against the bite of wild beasts', is from Greek *thēriakē*, ultimately from *thēr*, 'wild beast'. The ancients gave the name to several sorts of antidotes, but it was applied chiefly to Venice treacle (*theriaca androchi*), a compound of some 64 drugs in a sugary syrup.

Vitamin The word as proposed in 1912 by the US biochemist Casimir Funk was originally 'vitamine', from Latin *vita*, 'life', and English 'amine', the latter referring to the amino acid that the substance was believed to contain. When it was found this was not the case, the term was modified to its present spelling in 1920.

Pipe Dreams

Fag A colloquial word for a cigarette, possibly connected with 'flag' in the sense of 'droop', alluding to a cigarette dangling from the lips.

Heroin The so-called recreational drug was introduced in the 1890s by Friedrich Bayer & Co in Germany as a substitute for morphine. The sense of euphoria it induces suggests that its name may derive from Greek *hērōs*, 'hero'.

Hype Originally, a slang abbreviation of 'hypodermic', meaning a hypodermic needle or an injection from it. 'To be hyped up' is hence to be self-injected with a drug or to be artificially excited or stimulated. From this, the meaning extended to a deception or racket, and to misleading, inflated, or highly exaggerated advertising publicity.

Nicotine So named from *Nicotiana*, the Latin name of the tobacco plant, given to it in honour of Jean Nicot (*c.*1530–1600), French ambassador to Portugal, who introduced tobacco into France about 1560.

Pipe dream An impossible, imaginary and fanciful hope or plan indulged in at one's ease when smoking a pipe. The expression originated with opium smoking.

Syringe Syrinx was a nymph of Greek legend who, when pursued by Pan, took refuge in the River Ladon and prayed to be changed into a reed. Her prayer was granted, and Pan made his pipes from the reed. Hence her name is given to the pan pipes or reed mouth organ, and also to the vocal organ of birds. A syringe, based on the same word, is a pipe or channel for medicines.

Up to snuff In good condition; in good health. An allusion to the tobacco preparation which makes one perky and lively.

ORPHANED NEGATIVES

An orphaned negative is a word whose positive 'parent' once existed but is no longer in use. The following lost positives can all be found in historical dictionaries, but have inexplicably faded from view.

Capacitated Capable of doing something.

Consolate Consoled or comforted.

Couth Polite and well-mannered.

Defatigable Easily tired.

Ept Suitable and fitting.

Feckful Strong and vigorous ('feck' here is a shortening of 'effect').

Gormful Full of care and attention. 'Gorm' is a word based on Old Norse, meaning to 'take heed'.

Gruntled Contented (the creation of this sense was by P.G. Wodehouse).

Kempt Tidy and presentable.

Peccable Liable to sin.

Pecunious Handy with money.

Persona grata An acceptable or welcome person.

Ruly Following the rules.

Ruthful Compassionate.

Whelmed Not quite an orphaned negative, as 'whelmed' means 'capsized'. The 'over' was added for effect.

Wieldy Good at handling things.

DEATH

A preoccupation with death in periods such as the Middle Ages led to graphic portrayals of dying and even the printing of manuals educating readers on how to die in a graceful and proper manner. Nursery rhymes created at this time are packed full of black allusions to dying: The Death and Burial of Poor Cock Robin ('Who caught his blood? / I, said the fish, / With my little dish, / I caught his blood'), and, most famously, Ring-a-Ring o' Roses ('A-tishoo, A-tishoo, / We all fall down'), said to refer to the consequences of the Black Plague. Today, while we have greater transparency in matters of sex, the taboo of death and dying seems to have taken a stronger hold of our sensitivities (and, often, of our humour).

As dead as a doornail A doornail is either one of the heavy-headed nails with which large outer doors used to be studded, or the knob on which the knocker strikes. As this is frequently knocked on the head, it cannot be supposed to have much life left in it. But since other roughly contemporary expressions include 'as deaf as a doornail' and 'as dumb as a doornail', alliteration probably played as great a role in its origin as anything. Other well-known similes include 'as dead as the nail in a coffin' and Chaucer's 'as dead as stone'.

Bonfire Originally a 'bone fire', that is, a fire made of bones, especially a ceremonial one in Midsummer.

Capital punishment The imposition of the death penalty for crime takes its name from the Latin *caput*, 'head'.

Croak, To In slang this means to die, the term probably coming from the hoarse death rattle or croak of the expiring breath. A quack or charlatan medic was sometimes known as a 'Crocus': someone who made his patients croak.

Give up the ghost, To To die. The idea is that life is independent of the body and is due to the habitation of the ghost or spirit in the material body.

Graveyard shift In the Second World War the name given by shift workers in munitions factories and other workplaces to the shift covering the midnight hours. The allusion is perhaps to the watchmen who at one time patrolled the graves of the wealthy in order to deter grave robbers, but there is no evidence to support the story that coffins were once fitted with bells lest anyone be buried alive. Any watcher on the 'graveyard shift' might hear any ringing, and the victim was said to have been 'saved by the bell' (which actually originated in the sport of boxing).

Kick the bucket, To To die. There are several gruesome suggestions as to the phrase's origin. It may be the reference to the bucket that a person wanting to hang themselves kicks away once the noose is around their neck. Another idea looks back to an old sense of 'bucket' meaning 'a beam', in which case the reference would be to a beam from which a pig, about to be slaughtered, was suspended by its heels.

Lich A corpse (Old English *līc*). A 'lich gate' is the covered entrance to a churchyard, intended to afford shelter to the coffin and mourners while awaiting the clergyman who is to conduct the cortège into church.

Memento mori (Latin, 'remember you must die') An emblem of mortality, such as a skull, that reminds people of the inevitability of death. The purpose of the reminder has been variously interpreted as a warning of the vanity of earthly pleasures or an exhortation to make the most of earthly life. Some still-life paintings, especially those produced by Dutch artists in the 16th and 17th centuries, contain a fading flower or a piece of rotting fruit as a memento mori. Other images include hourglasses, clocks, watches, and burning candles, symbolizing the constant passage of time.

Mummy The word for an embalmed body comes from Persian *mūm*, 'wax', alluding to the custom of anointing the body with wax and preparing it for burial.

Not on your Nellie or **Nelly** Not likely; not on any account; not on your life. Probably from rhyming slang: 'Not on your Nellie Duff', 'Duff' rhyming with 'puff', which is old slang for 'breath' and thus life itself.

Pop one's clogs, To To die. As in 'Pop goes the weasel', 'pop' means pawn, and the underlying image is obviously of making a bit of money on a pair of clogs whose owner will no longer need them.

Sarcophagus A stone coffin. From Greek *sarx*, 'flesh', and *phagein*, 'to eat', so called because it was made of stone that, according to Pliny, consumed the flesh in a few weeks.

To the bitter end Until the present hard time or task is over, or until final defeat or death. In nautical parlance, the bitter end is the end of a rope or chain secured in a vessel's chain locker, or tied to one of the bitts, the strong posts on the deck to which mooring lines are attached. The association with bitter in the sense of 'sharp', 'unpleasant', may have been helped along by the biblical words: 'But her end is bitter as wormwood' (Proverbs 5:4).

FAREWELL

Adieu A farewell based upon the French for 'to God'.

Farewell Since the 14th century, 'farewell' has been an expression of good wishes at the parting of friends, originally addressed to someone setting out on a journey, wishing that they 'fare well' or prosper. It eventually became a standard show of civility at parting. Today, it is mostly restricted to poetic use, and often comes with a tinge of regret.

Goodbye A contraction of 'God be with you', and so similar to the French *Adieu*. 'God' became 'good' under the influence of similar expressions, such as 'Good morning' and 'Good night'.

Toodle-pip Toodle-pip, and its cousin 'toodle-oo', are probably early 20th-century manglings of the French *à tout à l'heure*, 'see you soon'. The 'pip pip' sound also suggests a quick toot on a car horn.

ACKNOWLEDGEMENTS

As always I am hugely appreciative of the wisdom and energy of the team at John Murray. First and foremost, my editor Georgina Laycock (always George to me) led me back to the delights of *Brewer's Dictionary of Phrase and Fable*. It's she I have to thank for many more happy hours riffling through its eccentric but utterly joyful pages. I am once again so grateful to Caroline Westmore for her calm and steady stewardship throughout the book's schedule, and to Charlotte Robathan for gently nudging me towards completion (even when a few shouts were probably more appropriate). I'd also like to thank Sara Marafini in design, Diana Talyanina in production, and Eleanor Bailey in marketing. Tim Waller is the cream of the copy-editing crop, while Alice Herbert continues to be the publicity director every author should aspire to have on their team. Finally, my biggest homage is of course to Ebenezer Cobham Brewer, the master whose skill in bringing familiarity to the unfamiliar continues to amaze.

INDEX

INDEX